At Home and Astray

At Home and Astray

The Domestic Dog in Victorian Britain

PHILIP HOWELL

UNIVERSITY OF VIRGINIA PRESS

Charlottesville and London

For Elizabeth and the Mozzillo family,
and in loving memory of Jade

University of Virginia Press
© 2015 by the Rector and Visitors of the University of Virginia
All rights reserved
Printed in the United States of America on acid-free paper

First published 2015

ISBN 978-0-8139-3686-4 (cloth)
ISBN 978-0-8139-3687-1 (e-book)

9 8 7 6 5 4 3 2 1

Library of Congress Cataloging-in-Publication Data
is available from the Library of Congress

ALL THOSE THAT WANDER

After the ark survived the Flood,
it was taken apart
to be made into cages.

This is the nature of religion.

BESTIARY

I want to tell you I have grown

and become acquainted
with the cages
and am myself, admittedly,

a cage, only it is
  a cage that will let

the creature out.

—Christina Davis, *An Ethic*

Contents

Illustrations

Acknowledgments

I am grateful to the University of Cambridge and to Emmanuel College for allowing me the time and space to finish this long-mooted book, and also to Hilda Kean for providing important impetus and advice, as well as her example of scholarship and engagement. My wonderful editor, Boyd Zenner, has been enthusiastic and supportive throughout this whole process, and I have benefited from the comments from two referees, one of whom, Garry Marvin, waived his anonymity to provide additional feedback—I really appreciate that he "got" this book, in both senses of the word. It has also been a pleasure working with the University of Virginia Press, with Boyd, Ellen Satrom, Angie Hogan, Morgan Myers, and Colleen Romick Clark. I hope that this book does their efforts justice.

I would like to record that my greatest academic debt is to Chris Philo, for helping introduce the "animal turn" in Geography, and convincing me of "animal geography's" intellectual worth and its capacity for generating moral insight. Chris's research, together with that of the geographers Kay Anderson, Jody Emel, Chris Wilbert, and Jennifer Wolch, among others, has been central to my own contributions. More recently, it was a pleasure to have been involved with the work of Pete Atkins and Paul Laxton, whose knowledge of urban and environmental historical geography has been especially helpful. Talking to a number of others within and beyond the ranks of "animal geographers" has also aided me along the way: scholars such as Daniel Allen, Maan Barua, Fabio Coltro, Ben Garlick, Russell Hitchings, James Milne, and Anthony Podberscek. Among my colleagues in the Department of Geography at the University of Cambridge, Bill Adams, Harriet Allen, Alan Baker, Tim Bayliss-Smith, Emma Mawdsley, Steve Trudgill, and Liz Watson have provided similar insight. David Beckingham, Jim Duncan, Nancy Duncan, Steve Legg, Francesca Moore, David Nally, and Catherine Sumnall have been so supportive over so many years that I cannot but thank them separately. I have also benefited from recently running these ideas past John Morrissey. At Emmanuel College, I would also like to thank Corinna Russell, Robert Macfarlane, and Penny Watson. I don't know how many of the above would recognize their contribution, but in different ways they have helped make this book better. The errors and omissions and infelicities that remain are, naturally, all my own work.

I am indebted to the editors and publishers who have allowed me to rework material that has come out previously:

Chapter 2 is a revised version of "Flush and the *Banditti*: Dog-Stealing in Victorian London," in *Animal Spaces, Beastly Places: New Geographies of Human-Animal Relations*, edited by Chris Philo and Chris Wilbert, 35–55, London: Routledge, 2000. Reprinted by permission of the publisher, Taylor & Francis Ltd.

Chapter 5 is an expanded and heavily amended version of "A Place for the Animal Dead: Pets, Pet Cemeteries and Animal Ethics in Late Victorian Britain," *Ethics, Policy and Environment* 5, no. 1 (2002): 5–22. Reprinted by permission of the publisher, Taylor & Francis Ltd: www.tandf.co.uk/journals.

Chapter 6 is based on material first published as "Between the Muzzle and the Leash: Dog-Walking, Discipline, and the Modern City," in *Animal Cities: Beastly Urban Histories*, edited by Peter Atkins, 221–41, Farnham: Ashgate, 2012. Reprinted by permission of the publisher, Ashgate.

I am very grateful to many students over the years who have been interested in this project, and I would like to give a shout-out to Jay Levy, Marigold Norman, Evelyn Owen, and Kate Evans, who were there at the beginning. Thank you all again. And the same too to Julia Shelley for trying to get me into the Battersea archives.

Thank you as always to my mum and dad, and the rest of my family—especially for all the books, Jen. To my other family, Ros Pappenheimer and Andy Zimmermann: it was great to talk with you in the final stages of the writing. Thanks to Christina Davis for letting me use two of her marvelous poems as epigraphs. "All Those That Wander" and "Bestiary" are copyright © 2013 by Christina Davis. Reprinted with the permission of The Permissions Company, Inc., on behalf of Nightboat Books, www.nightboat.org.

Finally, I dedicate this book to my wife and to her family, who have long appreciated the value of dogs as companions. They, and their dogs, have taught me a great deal about love for the world and for all its creatures.

At Home and Astray

A Public Life for a Private Animal

*W*HEN DID Britain become, to use the hackneyed phrase, a "nation of animal lovers"? This may be an impossible question as it stands, for historians of animal welfare have the greatest difficulties in narrating any significant amelioration in the treatment of animals in modern Britain, despite the early emergence of an organized animal protection and welfare movement.[1] We might focus instead on the *profession* of a national attachment to animals. A belief that the British were animal lovers par excellence, always to be found in the vanguard of the "humane" movement, had emerged at least by the early twentieth century, with its assumed superiority over other nations, "races," and cultures.[2] But the "humane" treatment of animals in Britain was typically seen as honored more in the breach than in the observance: the notion of a "nation of animal lovers" seems to have been mobilized largely to discredit complacency and disavow cultural self-congratulation.[3]

What if we focus, more specifically, on Britain as a "nation of *dog* lovers"? The apparently improved welfare of pet dogs presents us perhaps with a more plausible proposition. In 1910 the British dog fancier Robert Leighton asserted that "our national love of dogs" could be observed in the fact that "more dogs are kept in this country than ever there formerly were, and they are more skilfully bred, more tenderly treated, and cared for with a more solicitous pride than was the case a generation ago. There are fewer mongrels in our midst, and the family dog has become a respectable member of society."[4] Yet, even if we set aside the focus on the breed dog rather than the characteristically unloved cur, the striking fact is that Leighton's assertion, for all its confidence, is an isolated one.

1

There are surprisingly few references to any pronounced or providential British affection for dogs, and I find none earlier than the end of the nineteenth century.[5] Furthermore, the skeptical strain is again not hard to find, one commentator observing in 1948, "It is, in fact, not far from the truth to say that we are a nation of dog-owners, and not, as we like to make out, a nation of dog lovers."[6] Little wonder that the historians Neil Pemberton and Michael Worboys have recently judged that tracing the emergence of Britain as "a nation of dog lovers" is an impossible task.[7]

We are better off arguing that, at least before the end of the nineteenth century, while there were individual dog owners and dog lovers, a dog breeding "fancy," and even an emerging dog lobby, there was no settled conviction that the dog was fully accepted, even in the leading nation for animal advocacy. The dog was a companion, but neither a comrade nor a citizen, not even (yet) a "respectable member of society," as Leighton put it. It is a moot point whether the dog has *ever* achieved this status, in Britain or any other country, but while the Victorians may plausibly have invented the modern dog, the struggle over the dog's *place* was never decisively settled in these years. Even as late as the early twentieth century, the dog lobby pictured itself in opposition to a large proportion of the national community that had no affection for dogs, regarding the animal with grudging tolerance at best, and disdain and hostility at worst.[8] The Victorian age, accordingly, was even less convincingly a canophile culture. William Gladstone, as chancellor of the exchequer, acknowledged this irreconcilable situation in a parliamentary debate over the dog tax, here complete with backbench responses: "Mankind might almost be divided into two classes—the dog-lovers and the dog-haters. (A laugh.) There was no medium. Every man either keeps a dog or hates it. (A laugh.)"[9]

The central proposition of this book is that the place of the dog in British society was a "live" question throughout the Victorian age, and indeed well into the twentieth century. Perhaps at no other time has the "dog question"—by which I mean, following late-nineteenth-century shorthand, the dog's place in British society—been so contested. As the animal advocate Lady Florence Dixie put it, "This dog question is really a very important one, quite a national question in fact."[10] This study follows these controversies, from the early Victorian years to the end of the century, exploring not only the place of dogs but also, of course, the place of their human companions. This period was crucial because the British faced, for the first time, some now familiar problems in the relationship between humans and animals. It is striking, in fact, when considering these Victorian and Edwardian debates, just how resonant they are today, when it might be argued that innumerable dog questions, if not *the* dog question, are regularly sounded. After a hundred years of relative quiescence, these questions even strike us with renewed vigor: as John Homans has recently written, "The dog world is in the throes of political and ideological convulsions of a kind not seen since Victorian times, when the dog as we know it was invented."[11]

I have defined the "dog question" above, all too briefly, as the issue of the dog's *place* in British society, and it behooves my background as a cultural geographer to treat this question of space both metaphorically and literally; indeed the two are hardly capable of being separated, as the fuller discussion below argues. The decisive contention here is one about *domestication*—the dog's *inclusion* in the home and the household, and its putative *exclusion* from public space, but I refer also to the dog's all-too-conditional citizenship in the "homeland" of Britain and "Britishness." The overall argument may be summed up in the assertion that a kind of *cultural* domestication of the dog was accomplished in these years. In this book I argue that the Victorian "invention" of the dog was at the same time a material and imagined geography of domestication, albeit one that was always partial, incomplete, and provisional. These struggles were in some measure eclipsed in the twentieth century—notably by the development of the trope of a "nation of dog lovers"—but with the aid of recent developments in the still young, and interdisciplinary, fields of animal and animality studies, I hope that I can convince readers of both the historical and the contemporary significance of this Victorian "dog question."

The historical study of animals has reached a maturity and acceptance that could barely be imagined only a few decades ago, when the idea was nothing more than a source of amusement, a satire on the faddishness of social history, and its ideological commitment to inclusivity.[12] Yet, as the Victorian animal rights campaigner Henry Salt observed, "the mockery of one generation may become the reality of the next."[13] So it has come about, but though we have clearly come a long way, animal history is barely a generation old all the same. The historian Asa Briggs, in the concluding part of his landmark Victorian trilogy, recognized in 1988 that animals were an important element in the "intelligible universes" of the Victorians, noting that "the role of animals in Victorian Britain—real or imaginary . . . —deserves a book in itself."[14] Harriet Ritvo had happily just supplied the very volume for which Briggs was searching. *The Animal Estate* was that rare thing, an instant classic that more or less invented a field—building on pioneering work by social historians on the human treatment of animals, for sure, but showing for the first time how central animals and animality were to Victorian society and culture.[15] Ritvo's book went some way beyond Keith Thomas's influential *Man and the Natural World*, for instance, in considering animals per se, rather than as wrapped up within the developing Victorian concern for nature and the environment.[16]

The history of animals has developed in directions unanticipated a quarter of a century ago, however. *The Animal Estate* emerged before the great explosion of interdisciplinary interest in "animal studies," and could not draw on the theoretical and philosophical debates that have since come to the fore. Moreover, its central thesis—that animals in the nineteenth century became newly significant "primarily as the objects of human manipulation"—needs nuancing if not revising given contemporary perspectives.[17] Asa Briggs had suggested that animals typically had to be treated anthropomorphically in order to become intelligible, and historical work on animals has largely—and understandably—focused on *humans* as a result.[18] The historical concern with attitudes toward animals, and their domination by discourse and human needs, is still a major theme—this book was indeed largely conceived of in this vein—but what has become known as the "animal turn" encompasses a much wider set of debates, many with significant implications for historical work.[19] These include (the list is not exhaustive by any means) the agency and capabilities of animals themselves; the nature of human agency and human being, and the ways these have been constructed in relation to animality; and the inadequacies but also the ever-present cultural work of anthropocentrism and anthropomorphism. In practical as well as academic terms, the animal turn also draws attention to the following concerns: relationships with animals that might go beyond, or at least complicate, the undeniable realities of objectification and domination; our ethical and political response to animal otherness and difference, as well as our responsibilities; the thorny question of the "rights" of animals; and the possibility of other ways by which we might represent or register animals' interests.[20]

Despite the contempt for the tame and the domesticated that we sometimes come across in critical theory, approaches to the history and the geography of animal-human relations have the signal power to challenge anthropocentric theory and philosophy.[21] While this is not a book about theory, or the animal turn, as such, writing historically about animals *now* does present an opportunity to draw upon this critical work. My preference is to try to wear this theory lightly, partly for fear of wearying the patience of the nonspecialist and the uncommitted, but also because I want to tell this series of stories as clearly as possible. I should add that, as a result, I have generally avoided the more critical, accurate, and ethically endorsed terminology in favor of the conventional terms such as "human" and "animal," "pet," "owner," and so on.[22] All the same, I hope that readers whose interest is in animal or animality studies may nevertheless take something from this book. In much of this introductory chapter, in addition to outlining the book and its themes, I try to set out my intellectual convictions and affiliations as straightforwardly as I can.

First and foremost is my background in cultural and historical geography. Geography's interest in animals—at least in a newly critical sense inspired by the animal turn—is of even more recent vintage than history's, still barely out of its adolescence, albeit growing fast.[23] While geography as a discipline has had a long-standing interest in human relationships with animals, all part of its fundamental concern with nature and the environment, this was long aligned more with natural history and ecology, as for instance with the study of animal distributions in the subfield of "zoogeography," or in its interest in domesticated livestock. Animals *were* considered within the remarkable post-WWII development of cultural geography, but this too was largely confined to those animals domesticated by human societies, with a strong anthropological and anthropocentric emphasis. The contemporary geographical study of animals only emerged in the 1990s, its principal aim being to consider how human-animal relations are played out in spaces and places, these locations and landscapes being at the same time solidly material and imagined or socially constructed. As Susan Pearson and Mary Weismantel put it, "We seek a social-geographic account of the shared and segregated spaces occupied by humans and animals within particular social formations."[24] These spaces—to repeat—are both material and imaginative: Chris Philo and Chris Wilbert defined the "new" animal geography as an attempt "to discern the many ways in which animals are 'placed' by human societies in their local material spaces (settlements, fields, farms, factories, and so on) as well as in a host of imaginary, lit-

erary, psychological and even virtual spaces."[25] This twin concern with
attitudes, imaginaries, and discourses, as well as with material geographies, is central to the field, with a focus on the *territorialization* of humanity and animality in the contemporary world, and on the historical
emergence of such modern socio-spatial regimes. We can readily agree
that "conceptualizations of space and allocations to 'appropriate' places
are fundamental to power relations between humans and other animals,"
but rightly or wrongly the emphasis has been on the ways in which humans *dominate* the animal world, seeing them as either in their right place
or else problematically "out of place."[26]

The most prominent, if not always the most considered, geographical
themes here are those of exclusion, marginalization, and enclosure. By
"exclusion" is meant the expulsion of the animal from the human world,
both conceptually and practically: the construction of cities and societies where, it is said, animals and "the animal" have been removed and
purged, either wholly or in part. Some have traced this attempt to *purify*
the human world of the pollution of animality to Cartesian rationalism
and/or Enlightenment science in the West, if not to even longer-term
histories: the exclusion of animals and the animal can be said to follow
"a more general logic and desire for classification and control of the nonhuman world," one that reaches a critical point in the nineteenth century with the emergence of mass urbanization and capitalist modernity.[27]
Marian Scholtmeijer's sobering assessment of modern literature's complicity in violence against animals asserts, for instance, the absolute "conceptual dissonance" between animal nature and the city.[28] Where such a
degree of separation of the human is not possible (and it has to be admitted straightaway that such a process is necessarily incomplete, at best),
animals have been physically and conceptually marginalized, removed to
the outskirts of the city, for instance, or forced underground—ignored in
large part, or made nearly invisible. Chris Philo and Diana Donald have
separately written, for instance, about the Victorian removal of London's
Smithfield Market, following unease about the effects on the public of its
"beastly sights" (not to mention its sounds and smells), to the outskirts
of the city: a metropolitan "improvement" that removed animals from
the potentially confusing urban throng.[29] This theme has been rehearsed
many times, but the end result has been summed up by the geographers
Jody Emel and Jennifer Wolch in the most emotive terms: "Artfully
hidden behind factory-farm gates or research-lab doors, obscured by
disembodiment and endless processing, and normalized by institutional

routines and procedures, the thoroughly modern instrumental rationality that characterizes contemporary human-animal dependency has rendered animals both spatially and morally invisible."[30]

Finally, where animals have remained a part of human societies, they have been enclosed in a variety of carefully controlled, thoroughly human-dominated spaces. The urban zoo is the icon of enclosure of the animal in human society: an imaginative act as well as an institution, a "mapping project" that functions to mark the boundary between humans and animals.[31] For, as the philosopher Jacques Derrida notes, these material spaces depend upon the conceptual enclosure that the very term "animal" represents: "Confined within this catch-all concept, within this vast encampment of the animal, in this general singular, within the strict enclosure of this definite article ('the Animal' and not 'animals'), as in a virgin forest, a zoo, a hunting or fishing ground, a paddock or an abattoir, a space of domestication, are *all the living things* that man does not recognize as his fellows, his neighbors, or his brothers."[32]

These incontrovertibly spatial themes were all rehearsed in the late 1970s by the art critic John Berger, who argued—in the very loosest of chronologies—that a world in which human beings and other animals lived alongside each other, as part of a peasant ecumene, began to be replaced in the nineteenth century by a modern, capitalist culture of alienated nature.[33] This was a process of both physical and cultural marginalization, in which animals were confined or expelled entirely, at least in the symbolic economy, and where real, physical, presences were replaced by signs, images, and the meretricious economy of the spectacle. In his recent discussion of the enclosure of animals in modernism, Steve Baker similarly argues that "the modern animal . . . is the nineteenth century animal (symbolic, sentimental), which has been made to disappear."[34] This process apparently leaves "man" (and the gendered language is entirely appropriate) at the center of his world, unmoored from nature, withdrawn into the solitude of the domestic, the private, and the familiar. For Berger, looking at animals in the zoo was the experience that prompted these bleak reflections, and the zoo remains the emblematic space in his vision of debased modernity, as it does for other critics, such as J. M. Coetzee's fictional animal advocate Elizabeth Costello, who conceives of zoo animals as nothing less than prisoners of war.[35] This emphasis on captivity, control, and disappearance is still an important framing argument for understanding what has happened to animals in the modern age. With regard to colonial South Africa, for instance, Lance Van Sittert and Sandra Swart have pointed to the inescapable alternatives of extermination and domestication: "The newly delicate sensibilities of the urban middle class ultimately also required the reordering of urban space to incarcerate or exterminate wild animals, displace domesticated food and transport animals to the periphery and make the public thoroughfares safe for the middle class and its pets."[36] Likewise, the geographer Michael Watts declares, "One might say that the relation between animals and modernity can be construed as a gigantic act of *enclosure*."[37]

These narratives of enclosure, marginalization, and exclusion of animals are potentially misleading, however, and they should not stand as an accurate summary of the arguments of historians and geographers as to the placing of the animal in modern societies. To take only the most obvious objections, we should note that closeness to nature and intimacy with animals in the age of improvement was hardly a guarantee against violence and abuse.[38] Moreover, the idea that human beings in the nineteenth century did, or even *could*, separate themselves in any significant sense from animals and animality is quite wrong.[39] The historical geographer Peter Atkins considers that it was not until the end of the century at the very earliest that we might talk of any "Great Separation" of human residence from animal production.[40] Before that time, as others have observed, cities and towns simply "teemed with animal life":

> Animals were ubiquitous in Victorian cities, as much or more of an element of daily life as they were in the country. There were the horses, the indispensable cog in the national economy, which provided transport and haulage; there were dairy cattle, which supplied milk to many city dwellers; there were the pigs which supported the domestic economy of the poor; the dogs which ranged the streets; the cats which feasted on the city's vermin; the caged birds which hung from many windows; the fowls, rabbits and pigeons which provided protein and pocket money to anyone who had a corner to keep them in; and the cattle, sheep and poultry that were driven to town-centre markets and slaughterhouses.[41]

Most obviously, the urban animal economy's dependence on horses only intensified in the nineteenth century: people continued to bump up against horses as draught animals and means of transportation well into the twentieth century.[42] Rats, too, were clearly never far from human beings, and their numbers grew, like horses, alongside the expansion of cities and societies and modernity itself.[43] Even the "exotic" was not easily contained or cordoned off, as captive animals were constantly on display, strikingly readily available for purchase; likewise, animal products derived from exotic animals were also exhibited at sites such as the South Kensington Museum.[44] Rather than seeing industrialization, urbanization, and "modernity" as leading to the physical distancing of people from animals, and only by way of compensation generating the humane movement, as Keith Thomas suggested, it can be argued that it was the increasing *proximity* of humans to animals that prompted the first waves of animal activism.[45] Rob Boddice has argued that "the city brought animals and humans closer, on a grand scale, than they had been before."[46] The same can be said of the awareness of the need for the more efficient urban regulation of animals, however haltingly this came about.[47]

One can still posit an intensified concern to *classify* animals, as in the fourfold taxonomy suggested by Atkins—that is, animals directly useful for consumption or as beasts of burden; as pets or companion animals; as wild but nevertheless welcome urban animals; or as marginalized and "out of place" vermin or "pests."[48] We might, with regard to the latter, reasonably talk of a process of abjection, in Julia Kristeva's sense of the violent casting out of nature from the symbolic order, or perhaps of purification, in Bruno Latour's theorizing of the attempt within modernity to purge "culture" of "nature."[49] An example: Conor Creaney sees the tableaux created by the Victorian taxidermist Walter Potter as emblematic of such a process, presenting, in miniature, domestic anthropomorphic idylls, which nevertheless acknowledge the discordant presence of death and the impossibility of bridging the divide between human and animal.[50] But the idea of the exclusion of nature and animals in the nineteenth century, and the reduction of real animals to mere signs and signifiers, once more attributes far too much agency to human beings and the power of their discourses. Latour insists on the futility of "purification" and of the equal importance of "translation," the paradoxical accompaniment of the belief that we have separated culture from nature being the need to recognize "hybrid" forms that acknowledge the entanglement of humans with animals.[51] The modern city, in this sense, was the locus of these intensified human-animal relations, with animals remaining simultaneously central and marginal.[52]

Pets or companion animals are one other obvious counterpoint to the notion of a general exclusion or abjection of nature and animality. The dog, in particular, was regarded as "the first and most intimate companion of man."[53] The Victorian journalist John Hollingshead talked of dogs as the "tribe" of animals "the most mixed up with man of all."[54] The importance of companion animals is discussed more fully below, but it is clear from the project of animal geography that the socio-spatial processes of exclusion are at least as significantly matched by those of *inclusion*, the bringing in of (some) animals (under certain conditions) within human society and its affective economy.[55] This in one reading might be just another form of enclosure, but at the very least it testifies to a familial, domestic kind of discipline, rather than the carceral complex envisaged by a too enthusiastic Foucauldian reading.[56] Even in the case of zoos — taken so straightforwardly as the limit cases of manipulation and control — these should be seen as "supremely domesticated social products" rather than merely enclosures of "wildness," and the responses zoos provoke in their visitors/viewers, who in turn have to be "domesticated" to their aims, are in any case far more various and complex than some critics have suggested.[57] Peter Sloterdijk's gloss on Heidegger (and on Nietzsche and Plato) recognizes the ways in which humans as well as animals are domesticated, such that the project of humanism and the practice of pet keeping are thoroughly reciprocal: "With domesticity the relationship between men and animals changed. With the taming of men by their houses the age of pets began as well."[58]

It is the complexities of these nineteenth-century animal geographies with which this book is concerned. Animal geography as a subdisciplinary perspective considers that nonhuman animals are "central agents in the constitution of space and place," but like animal studies in general it does so while questioning the dualisms (human/animal, nature/culture, and so on) that hamper any accurate understanding of the place and placing of animals.[59] The geographies that are increasingly being revealed are hybrid and heterogeneous, constituted (to use the language of the hour) by complex networks and assemblages of agents, actors, and things.[60] It is precisely this hybridity that is obscured by overemphasis on the work of "purification."[61] The perspectives opened up are various, and sometimes threaten to become "bewildering," but we may note the common ambition within a critical animal geography to dis-locate or "deterritorialize," to call into question, the conventional placing of animals. This means of course interrogating the place of the human, and our anthropocentric assumption of privileges; as Kari Weil puts it, "To deterritorialize is to become aware of the animal otherness within the human."[62]

The most important of the *placing* processes discussed in this book is the attempt to domesticate, to provide a home for, the Victorian dog. There are other stories about the animal to be told—as hunting companions, for instance, as working dogs, as entertainers, and so on—but I want to concentrate on the dog's role as a companion animal, installed so apparently comfortably in the family home. The central premise of this study is that it was only in the nineteenth century that the dog began to be "domesticated" in this modern sense, and only ever incompletely, provisionally, or perhaps better still, proleptically. It is in these years that the dog's *place*, not in some abstracted sense of modern life, but in the actual, onrushing modernity of the great metropolis, was proposed, debated, challenged, confronted—and ultimately accepted, albeit conditionally. The pet dog became literally *familiar*—iconic certainly, but also mundane and in many ways beneath notice. Since it requires an effort of will to defamiliarize ourselves, a return to this period may be justified by recognizing that the Victorians remain the authors of our present-day cultural attitudes and regimes. I am interested in this period precisely because the animal was not *yet* as fully "territorialized" as it would later become.

As a story to be set besides the (at least) ten thousand years of cooperation between species that has been the focus of zoology, evolutionary biology, anthropology, and archaeology, we can conceive of a "cultural" process of "domestication" concerning the ways in which animals—dogs in particular—came to be installed at the heart of the modern, Western, bourgeois household, in the categorical form of "pets."[63] Though the use and definition of the term is contested, the rise and acceptance of pet keeping in the last couple of hundred years, the encompassing and enclosing of the animal under the aegis of the family, in the private space of the home and household, and in the human-coded world of urban society, is clearly central. James Rubin writes that "the spread of pet-keeping to the middle classes and its association with emotional wholesomeness is a modern phenomenon."[64] And the case can be made that it is in the Victorian period specifically that the practice of keeping dogs as pets—with all its repercussions—developed most meaningfully. With the bourgeois phenomenon of pet keeping, Laura Brown asserts, "animals entered the space and consciousness of human beings in a distinctively new way."[65]

What we mean when we speak of domestication is clearly at stake here. The term is intensely problematic, and has had many definitions, but in a frequently quoted statement, a domesticated animal can be defined as "one that has been bred in captivity, for purposes of subsistence or profit, in a human community that maintains complete mastery over its breeding, organization of territory, and food supply."[66] It has been aligned in the past with a crude narrative of mastery over nature, the conversion of animals into property, and what the Victorians would unselfconsciously have called the emergence of civilization out of barbarism and savagery. However, this definition has become far less straightforward, not least as natural and social scientists have questioned the directionality of domestication, and emphasized the flexibility and variability of the distinction between wild and tamed nature: even for livestock, draught animals, and dogs, domestication no longer seems quite such a "one-way" process or "one-time" event.[67]

Moreover, the biological and economic emphasis of many of these earlier writers on domestication requires a complementary focus on scientific classification as a socially embedded, cultural-historical practice. Notably, in the eighteenth and nineteenth centuries, domestic animals were understood as *taxonomically* different from their "wild" peers, different in *kind* rather than the product of a contingent, prehistoric, cultural event.[68] More specifically still, we can note the contingency of definitions of "domestic" in its practical deployment: for example, animal protection legislation in the nineteenth century was typically reserved for "domestic" animals rather than "wild" ones, but with the actions of an organization such as the RSPCA initially limited to protecting "domesticated" animals such as horses and cattle rather than being extended to "domestic" pets.[69] Likewise, Scholtmeijer has recognized the "double-sided nature of domestication" evident in the different treatments of domestic pets and domesticated livestock: "Where ethical practice is concerned, the logic established by pets leads to full moral status for animals within strictly anthropocentric moral codes."[70] The term "domestic," in other words, remained and remains thoroughly unstable, an artifact of discursive and institutional practice as much as a distant event in natural and human history.[71]

Geography has been important to this re-theorizing of domestication, this production of a fuzzier, more complex, and more problematic relationship with the animal. In Kay Anderson's essential contribution, domestication becomes a process of "drawing animals into a nexus of human concern where humans and animals become mutually accustomed to conditions and terms laid out by humans."[72] Subsequent consideration of the process scales back the anthropocentric focus on human agency, such that we can better define domestication as "an experimental, contingent and contestable process that draws in culture and nature, human and nonhuman, mind and body, and that frequently exceeds human control and intentionality."[73] The locus of this inconstant, negotiated process of domestication is not incidental: as geographer Emma Power writes, this question is as much about "where" species meet as "when."[74] And here, the question of *home* is fundamental, as the central imagined and material site where animals like the pet dog are domesticated: that class of animals, in the words of Henry Salt, "who have become still more associated with mankind through being the inmates of their homes."[75] The anthropologist Rebecca Cassidy notes, "It is worth remembering that 'domestication' was originally defined as 'becoming accustomed to the household.'"[76] If we accept this definition of domestication, we arrive at the central importance of the geography of "home"—the "primary locus of security, dreaming and identity"—for human-animal relations.[77]

"Home" has an equally complex cultural history, one that also draws forth a critical geographical analysis.[78] For Alison Blunt and Robyn Dowling, "home" is "both material and imaginative, a site *and* a set of meanings/emotions."[79] The likes of Gaston Bachelard and Witold Rybczynski have influentially asserted that the idea or ideal of home conjures up feelings of comfort, privacy, intimacy, security, and belonging, these being associated with families and familiarity, and this is no less true for all that our *real* homes fail to live up to these expectations: the strength of the ideal may in some situations be inversely related to our experiences of domestic, family life.[80] John Gillis has contrasted the families we live *with* to the ones we live *by*—and this observation may be extended to the homes we live in and the homes we live by.[81] It is the *relation* of the physical and experiential space of the house or home to its associated "spatial imaginary" that is critical here. The home is about organizing space and bringing it under control, but it is also about "the realization of ideas."[82] As a "spatial imaginary," a home is always "a set of intersecting and variable ideas and feelings, which are related to context, and which construct places, extend across spaces and scales, and connect places."[83] It is not, has never been, divorced from the world of work—as feminists have long recognized—and to this end, criticism of the supposedly Victorian doctrine of "separate spheres," with its neat distinctions between home and work, male and female, public and private, must readily be accepted. Moreover, housework, or home-work, is critical to social reproduction, and thus to the political economies of capitalism, the state, and empire.[84] At one level, since much of the business of social reproduction, then and now, has been devolved upon women—sometimes on their own, sometimes as household managers—any critical geography of home needs to recognize the work of "domestic ideology" in conjuring up a false notion of the home as a space of interiority and security. In this respect, Bachelard and Rybczynski propagate not only a nostalgic but also a gender- and class-inflected view of home life, their admirable poetics obscuring the agonistic politics of the home.

It is not enough, however, merely to confront the ideal or the myth with reality and experience. It is clearly wrong to take the prescriptions of advice manuals for reality, but at the same time to refuse prescriptiveness and cultural codes any power at all is strangely self-denying, as if representations were not social facts too.[85] The pioneer discussions of "Victorian" middle-class domestic ideology may have mishandled the chronology, but they were far from naïve about the inability of households, even middle-class ones, to live up to the prescriptions of rhetoric.[86] Nor were those ideals ever as coherent and monolithic as critics of the focus on ideology have charged: domesticity was "a systematized body of concepts about human life and culture," but "separate spheres ideology was not a rigid set of rules internalized as natural and adhered to unquestioningly"; rather, "separate spheres were in the process of being constructed, rife with internal contradictions, and frequently challenged (both overtly and covertly)."[87] The most successful work that has been carried out in the investigation of public and private spheres, on women's and men's lives, and on the nature of domesticity, has not rejected the conceptualization of domestic ideology or ideologies out of hand, so much as reminded us that these were never hermetically sealed discursive systems, and that both male and female subjectivities were formed in a productive tension with the prescriptions of gender and class.[88] The ideological geography of public and private worlds was a creative fiction, for sure, always inadequate as a description of lived experience, but it contributed to the cultural work of identity formation all the same. Maps as mismeasures of reality may still produce real effects, even if these included anxiety and inadequacy, resistance and transgression. In a stronger sense still, we can follow the likes of Pamela Gilbert in insisting on the importance of the public and the private as boundaries mediated by the development of the "social" domain, so that liberal "governmentalities" could project thoroughly feminized domesticity as responses to the social problems of class.[89]

Equally ideological, equally creative and critical — productive as well as procrustean, we might say — is the separation of an interior world of human culture from an exterior world of "nature." We have to recognize that the domestic order of the nineteenth-century middle-class home was constituted *through* the public worlds of work, economy, and the market, and of politics, bureaucracy, and the state; but so too should we assert that the classed and gendered culture of the Victorian middle class was not sealed off from the natural world either. Home was far from a purified, exclusively "human" space. If "the domestic is created through the extra-domestic and vice versa," the relationship between culture and nature, humans and animals, is also crucial to its very definition.[90] Illustrations of family harmony, and the purported triumph of nurture over nature, were to be found, for instance, in the public presentation of "Happy Families," those street theater micro-menageries of dogs, cats, rats, and pigeons, "living amicably, or at least quietly, in one cage."[91] As George Behlmer notes, the people of the streets grasped the ideal of domestic harmony, even if they staged these microcosmic peaceable kingdoms in order to liberate the pennies of gratified passersby.[92] Within the home too, nature was brought in to the work of families. Russell Hitchings has argued, with contemporary society in mind, that the domestic is a place where "we can certainly make ourselves at home, but where we are always in the presence of an array of intimate nonhuman strangers," such that we never fully control or discipline either the home or the wider social world.[93] Victorian middle-class households were in similar fashion encouraged to incorporate nature within their domesticated idylls: "The power of visiting and studying a good menagerie is ever regarded as a pleasurable privilege; but the fact of having and holding a collection of living creatures all to one's self, is a precious possession for princes to boast of."[94] The prescriptive literature on household management normalized the keeping of animals for both utility and companionship. The Beeton brand endorsed, for instance, a thoroughly animated vision of domesticity alongside its conventional support of healthy homes for all classes: "To provide clean and pleasant cottages for the poor is properly considered an object of great importance. Inferior, perhaps, but akin to that subject, is the consideration of the wise and fit manner to manage the houses and the feeding of the live stock of the hutch, the dormer, the hen-house, the kennel, the beehive, the aquarium."[95] *Cassell's Household Guide* likewise offered its readers—among its myriad instructions—papers such as "Animals Kept for Pleasure and for Profit": advice on fattening chickens, on grooming horses and rearing calves, on feeding, killing, and curing pigs, on beekeeping, on cage birds and dovecots, on dog training, and so on.[96] In theory at least, then, caring for animals was a vital part of Victorian *house-work*. Work it was, for sure—labor that was presumably devolved much of the time to servants.[97] But the ideological emphasis on keeping "pets" acted to align them with an affective economy held at a distance from the world of work and the market.

In this regard, pet animals were not supposed to be supplementary workers in the household, as they might once have been. By and large, the only work that the pet dog was assigned was the cultural work of embodying and securing the home. Samuel Beeton considered, for instance, that some sort of apology was deemed necessary for the inclusion of dogs among "Home Pets" of more obvious *utility*, but he offered the following justification: "As regards the creature now under consideration, however, he claims the right to the title of Home Pet, —nay, as something infinitely more dignified, —as Home friend and protector."[98] Pet keeping as a practice thus brought nature into the home, albeit to reconfigure it as quite distinct from the animality to be found outside: companion animals like dogs were, from the nineteenth century, if not earlier, constructed as *familiars* —part of the family, if not *quite* family themselves.[99] And thus it is far from enough to say, as Mary Douglas does, that pets are placed at the bottom of a "protohierarchy."[100] Nor that pets are (only) objects of domination and discipline, particularly of the carceral kind.[101] As the cultural geographer Yi-Fu Tuan famously argued, pet keeping is structured as both dominance *and* affection, and the discipline and hierarchy of the family extended in any case to its human subjects as well as its animals.[102]

We need to recognize, particularly in the home, "the enchanting effect of human-animal encounters," even if we are tempted to see this affective investment largely in cynical terms.[103] There are important parallels, for instance, between the ways in which dogs and children were treated, for homes were places where dogs, like children, should ideally be cared for without reference to economic value. Both were precious, sentimental investments in "the emotional order of domesticity" constructed by nineteenth-century middle-class culture.[104] Jennifer Mason has argued that people's inclusion of the dog "within their literal circle of affection testifies to their commitment to the affective priorities of home life rather than the economic principles of the market."[105] Furthermore, dogs served a propaedeutic purpose, teaching middle-class children to care for animals, one of the first steps on the road to becoming successful, self-disciplined, respectable citizens:

> Bow-wow-wows—We are fond of you all
> You will play with us, and come at our call,
> You will not hurt us if we don't hurt you,
> We will not hurt you, now see if we do.[106]

In the new, Victorian, "domestic ethic of kindness to animals," pet keeping was a morally purposive act, socializing children to become responsible citizens.[107] The care and training of pets (and children too) was intimately linked to the discipline of the family, the discipline required to run the ideal middle-class household.[108] Pet animals' roles in the sentimental education of the home meant that they were always more than *just* property, more than simply "the first living possession of man beyond the limits of his own kindred."[109]

This book takes its stance, then, on a very literal reading of domestication, considering as a central theme the historical incorporation of the companion animal into the *domus* itself, as both material and cultural fact. Dogs became *familiar* because they came to be associated with the family, and with the private sphere of the home. These animals were welcomed into the *heart* of modern life, indicating the affection in which these animals were held, but also besides the *hearth*, welcomed as no other animal has ever been into the actual space(s) of the home.[110] We might consider the value placed on pet dogs' being actually inside the house, rather than being confined in adjoining spaces, particularly where their natural sense of the household hierarchy might be misdirected—for instance, to one of the servants:

> Dogs kept in stables or kennels cannot strictly be classed as "pet dogs," however worthy of the denomination. Masters consigning these creatures to what they term "the proper place for them," deprive themselves of the opportunity of observing those endearing qualities which render "pet dogs" so valuable,

independently of their external recommendations, and which
enlist the sympathy and regard that are shown in the kindness that is, however ill-advised, constantly lavished on canine
house pets by their proprietors. Kept in a stable, energetically
as a loving dog may display his recognition of the various
members of his owner's family, he must in reality look upon
the coachman or groom as his master.[111]

The *true* pet was welcome in the parlor rather than confined to the yard,
embedded in the leisurely heart of the household, the very embodiment
of home and its enfolding sentiments. In short, the dog became part of
a more-than-human, respectable, middle-class family.[112] As pet keeping
was established as more than simply a luxury pursuit, pets were domesticated, denaturalized, "saturated in subjectivity," even "bourgeoisified."[113]

Looking at the question of home or family "pets" is of further significance, however, because the question of domesticity was inevitably informed by what was characteristically portrayed as *not* the proper places
for "domestic" animals: that is, the streets and the slums of Victorian
cities. While dogs were increasingly placed and embedded in the modern metropolis, their presence in *public space* was always contentious, and
indeed increasingly so. As Kirsten McKenzie has noted, with regards to
the role of dogs in disordering colonial public space in early-nineteenth-
century Cape Town, "Dogs emerge as animals that are tailor-made for
cultural ambiguity. They are liminal figures that cross the boundaries
so central to the nineteenth-century bourgeois psyche. They disrupt the
division between the home and the wider world. At one and the same
time, dogs in early nineteenth-century Cape Town were valued members of the respectable household and sources of dirt and disorder on the
street. The division was dependent upon the dog's material location and
symbolic associations."[114]

The whole question of the "lost" dog and the "stray," for instance,
which I revisit throughout this book, turned inevitably on the definition
of the homes that these animals seemingly lacked. Much of the problem
may be encapsulated in the remarks of the Harvard paleontologist Nathaniel Shaler, drawing on his own experiences of the unhappy "stray":

> If by chance he becomes separated from his master and the
> other people with whom he is familiar, his bereavement is

> intense; but in most cases, at the end of a day or two, he is compelled to form new bonds, and he sets about the task in an exceedingly human way. I dwell in a town where dogs abound and where the frequent coming and going of the people puts many of the creatures astray. Perhaps as often as once a week, almost always late in the evening, one of these unhappy lost ones seeks to make friends with me. His advances toward this end always begin by his dogging my footsteps at a little distance. If I do not repulse him he will come nearer until he has made sure of my attention. A friendly word will bring him to my hand; but his behavior is never effusive, as it would be if he had found his rightful owner, but mildly propitiative and with a touch of sadness. There is, it seems to me, no other feature in the life of the dog which tells so much as to his moral nature as his conduct under these unhappy circumstances.[115]

The proper dog, we infer, is intimately attached to his owner, master or mistress. The homeless dog in Shaler's anecdote has an innate *moral* sense that tells him that he rightly belongs in the domestic sphere. Without that enfolding habitus, the dog is deprived and desolate, reduced to a kind of bare life: he is "out of place," certainly, but perhaps more than that, he no longer seems to have a place at all.

The inevitable corollary to this intense focus on placing the pet dog in the home is thus the problematization of the *public* dog. Dogs' presence in the public sphere became all the *more* suspect when a domestic hearth was assigned to them as a kind of right. There were certain reasons to be afraid of dogs in public: in Victorian and Edwardian Britain, the ever-present threat of rabies contributed to the fear of the uncontrolled and masterless animal of the streets, for instance. But rabies was also imaginatively linked to the rise of bourgeois pet keeping: in threatening to replace domestic propriety with dirt, disorderliness, and depravity, nineteenth-century rabies phobia "shattered the myth of the bourgeois interior."[116] Legislation against working dogs in the mid-century—representing their condition as an affront to their domestic destinies—also narrowed the options for the public dog. So too did attempts to round up "strays," not only to save them from suffering, but also to keep them out of the hands of the dog stealer and the vivisector. As Dorothee Brantz notes, strays "quickly lost their standing as pets and became recategorized as 'wild' animals, which in many instances also meant that their status shifted from that of an animal worthy of protection to one of an animal that had to be eliminated."[117] The RSPCA's initial public preference for policing cruelty in the streets rather than interfering with the privacy of the home was yet another marker of this dichotomous moral geography of concern, further bearing down upon the public animal. And when pet dogs were allowed out in public, their presence was accepted fearfully by some, and only grudgingly by others, conditional on their being in specified places, accompanied by human owners, restrained by the lead or the muzzle, always required to be demonstrably under "proper control."

In any event, any attempt to enclose and privatize the dog had to be a failure: because there continued to exist myriad street dogs, and because even the "bourgeois" dog in the streets was a source of anxiety, but also because the place of the dog continued to be a resoundingly public question. Indeed, all attempts to make the dog a "private" animal only served to exacerbate its problematic "public" career. This observation explains this introduction's subtitle, which is partly inspired by Stahl and Grandville's mid-nineteenth-century French satire *Scènes de la vie privée et publique des animaux* (translated and reworked in Britain as *Public and Private Lives of Animals*), but is more directly lifted from Karen Chase and Michael Levenson's exemplary discussion of the public life of the Victorian family.[118] Chase and Levenson show that the greater the power of the middle classes' "home fetish," the greater the "contradiction, resistance, refusal, and bewilderment" that results; their theme is "the public extension of a normative domesticity that then confronts, and indeed generates, trouble in paradise."[119] I want to endorse these insights but also to extend them to the attempt to privatize nature, with the resulting "bewilderment" my specific subject. All of the antinomies of bourgeois moral geography, familiar from the prescriptions of female propriety and the privileges of class, played themselves out with special force when it came to the place of the animal. None of this is accidental, because the pet dog came to be associated with a bourgeois domesticity that idealized women and placed them at some distance from unrespectable spaces and people. The "bad" dog—loose, dirty, dangerous, diseased, alien—was likewise linked to its human associates in the unrespectable and criminal classes. This reminds us again that the question of domestication is a city story, one that takes in the diversity and duality of the modern metropolis, its places and neighborhoods, its characters and types, human and nonhuman both.

This book covers some relatively familiar themes in the social history of animals (rabies and vivisection, for example) as well as some less familiar ones (dog stealing, dog walking, pet cemeteries). What I have tried to do throughout, however, is to look at the entangled histories of animals and humans from the perspective of my general thesis about the Victorians' cultural domestication of the dog. All of the chapters that follow have a focus on this domestication, however various — of dogs and their owners, of science, of heaven, and ultimately of the streets and the city itself. That this domestication is always a *process*, destined never to be completed, always riven with contradictions and conflicts, bears repeating. Domestication pitted at various times men against women, class against class, science against sentiment, and these contests reveal much about not only what the Victorian world was but also — I contend — what our world has become.

The structure of this book is broadly chronological, with a certain unity of place provided by a focus on London. The first substantive chapter, essaying the most general treatment of the question, considers the dogs in Charles Dickens's world — not so much his own dogs, or the dogs in his fiction, though these have their say, but rather the ways in which he was imagined and celebrated as a dog lover, and by extension how the country saw itself in regard to these animals. In this chapter I suggest both a *less* sentimental Dickens and at the same time a *more* sentimental one — Dickens's ambivalent celebration of domesticity, and domesticated nature, considered in relation to his propensity for the public world of the streets. I spend some time discussing Dickens's vision of the city, and of the place of dogs within it, as a marker of the range and tensions within Victorian attitudes to the public and the private animal.

The following essays are loosely paired. In chapter 2 I move to consider the contradictions and complexities of the "bourgeoisification" of the dog, as revealed by the phenomenon of dog stealing, a crime whose most famous victims were the poet Elizabeth Barrett and her pet spaniel, Flush. This was a practice that both reinforced and challenged the proprieties of Victorian moral geography, particularly insofar as it revealed the contested mapping of class and gender in the modern metropolis. Chapter 3 turns from the problem of these *private* dogs, led away in the streets by unscrupulous thieves, to the wider problem of the *public* animal, not just "lost" dogs but also the dogs of the streets that were deemed to be more or less without value. This chapter, which focuses on the work of the famous Battersea Dogs' Home, explores the seeming paradox of a sentimental investment in "rehoming" dogs combined with the policing of unwanted dogs from the streets, and their mass euthanization in the Home's gas chambers.

The next two chapters consider science and the responses to scientific materialism. Chapter 4 examines the relationship of dogs to evolutionary science, and wanders a few miles from the heart of Victorian London to Charles Darwin's home at Down House in Kent. Here, the theme is the way in which the reliance of modern medical science on vivisection violently dispensed with domestic sentiment, to the outrage of many dog lovers and Victorian animal advocates, but the chapter also takes in the ways in which the formally pro-vivisection Darwin contributed to the domestication of evolutionary science at the same time that his theories challenged Victorian moral geographies. Much of the anti-science, anti-materialist sympathies of eminent Victorian dog lovers informs chapter 5, on pet cemeteries, which takes in the short life and inevitable early death of pet dogs and discusses the most audacious feat of the Victorian moral imagination: the domestication of the afterlife itself. Some dog owners and dog lovers, notably middle- and upper-class women, rejected the blandishments of scientific, social, and religious orthodoxy, challenging the exclusion of animals from the next world.

The final substantive chapter considers the threat of rabies, and the response of self-professed dog lovers to medical and police assessments of the danger that dogs posed to human beings, particularly in the crowded streets of the metropolis. It concludes with an assessment of the provision of facilities for dogs and their owners, and the creation of what I have termed, in measured celebration, the "dog-walking city." This chapter is the most obviously theoretical, particularly in considering the agency of animals, and I return to the theme in the conclusion, reflecting also on the inclusion of dogs in the political community. Here, I emphasize the "conditional citizenship" of the dog and the incomplete work of national domestication. Before we accept too easily the notion that dogs became at home in Britain, we need to confront the political challenges to their domestication, themes that were apparent at the beginning of the twentieth century and at the beginning of our own. All the same, the possibilities for thinking of dogs as some kind of "citizens" are explored here, albeit in summary form.

The debates that are covered in these chapters all concern *where* dogs should be and how they (and their human companions) should *behave.*

Together, I submit, they add up to the "dog question"—British society's relationship with the dog from the early nineteenth century through to the end of the Victorian era. That the question of the dog should prove to have been so fractious, so shot through with representations of divisions within humanity, should hardly come as a surprise. Dogs, perhaps above all other animals, are inherently disruptive to the various spatializations and territorializations associated with what we presume to call the "social order," particularly in the ambiguous form of "pets." The discourses and practices of pet keeping were crucial to the construction of a civil society, for sure, but Edmund Leach acknowledged long ago that the "pet" is an improper or anomalous creature, representing a troublingly intermediate category between "human" and "animal."[120] Pet dogs were part of the material and mental furniture of Victorian Britain, specifically of the middle-class household—but they were not merely objects, and not all played ball with this version of the civilizing process.[121] At a symbolic level, dogs were always "troubling to middle-class discourse in the ways in which they slipped between categories of respectable and disreputable."[122] If the security and comfort of "home" is constituted through the troublingly public, "political" world, so too did the *extra-domestic* world of the animal contribute to the anxieties of this most famously domestic of cultures.[123] Dogs were symbolically as well as materially "messy." Whether or not we assign nonhuman animals "agency" (like most of my colleagues in animal studies, I emphatically would), their potential to transgress the boundaries associated with cultural codes and conventions should readily be accepted. And once again, the more that pet dogs became "the center of an influential cultural fantasy about the potential proximity of human- and animal-kind," all the more potential they possessed to pose a challenge to hierarchies and codes of propriety.[124] By doing so, by refusing to attend to the purported separation between public and private space, and by oscillating between alterity and intimacy, metaphor/difference and metonymy/similarity, respectability and unrespectability, these unerringly errant animals offer us a unique opportunity to question what being at home with animals really means.

CHAPTER 1

Dogs in Dickensland

At Home and Astray with the Landseer of Fiction

C HARLES DICKENS'S reputation as a lover of dogs was firmly established after his death. John Forster advised an audience apparently insatiable for personal details of the recently departed author that his interest in dogs was "inexhaustible."[1] In her reminiscences, Mamie Dickens averred that her father loved all animals, but that he reserved his strongest love for dogs.[2] Curiosity and affection were seen (as with his almost exact contemporary Charles Darwin) as mutually reinforcing: "This power of observation and description extended from human life to that of animals. His habits of life could not but make him the friend of dogs."[3] Even during Dickens's lifetime, however, this canophile characterization was being canvassed and given the author's seal of approval. The most elaborate and fulsome account comes from Percy Fitzgerald, whose acquaintance with Dickens came about through their common interest in dogs (in 1865 he presented Dickens with the ferocious and ill-fated Irish bloodhound Sultan). Fitzgerald was clearly keen to induct Dickens into the dog fancy, and he produced not only the earliest critical appreciation of "Dickens's Dogs," but also an epithet—"The Landseer of Fiction"—that stuck with the author, apparently much to his own satisfaction.[4] Fitzgerald's extended sketch, published in 1863, includes pen portraits of the most famous of Dickens's canine characters—Boxer from *The Cricket on the Hearth*, Dora Copperfield's Jip, Paul Dombey's Diogenes, Bill Sikes's Bull's Eye, the circus dog Merrylegs from *Hard Times*, and the dismal dancing dogs from *The Old Curiosity Shop* (figure 1). Beyond mere proof of affection for the canine race, however, Fitzgerald attributes an unheralded *political* significance to Dickens's powers of observation and description, a narrative of canine *emancipation* that will serve as an introduction to this book about the place of dogs in Victorian Britain.

Fitzgerald first acknowledges the march of moral sentiment in Britain, a humanitarian benevolence whose workings have freed the British dog from centuries of oppression and contempt. This address is worth reproducing at some length:

> One of the pleasantest workings of that enlarged philanthropy of our time, whose only embarrassment seems the discovery of sufficient grist—as it may be called—for its labour, has happily taken the shape of an enlarged sympathy for an oppressed and long-suffering class of fellow-creatures: the odious intoleration of centuries has been at last happily swept away, and the dog no longer skulks in caves and deserts, the Pariah and Cagot of a civilized community. The days of his persecutions have gone by. A price is no longer set upon his head: neither is he compelled to practise the rites of his peculiar worship—whatever that may be—in the perilous secrecy of the blind alley and the

Figure 1. Walter Crane, composite of illustrations for Fitzgerald, "Dickens's Dogs." (Reproduced by kind permission of the Syndics of Cambridge University Library)

lonely *cul de sac.* Nor is he any longer cast out into the Coliseum a canine martyr—butchered, as it were, to make a Saxon holiday. His is not a proscribed tribe—the Israelite caste of the animal world—driven into the kennel ghetto—spat upon—pelted with mud and stones by youthful Arabs of the Streets, who are yet Christians and believers. They do not skulk along timorously, with averted eyes and slavish gait, grateful for the withheld kick, or the stone unlaunched, or even for the poor gift of life, which any believer had the privilege of taking from them. The grand day of their redemption has come about. Liberal men of large hearts have agitated that the blessings of a free constitution might be extended to them.[5]

The familiar narrative of animal welfare—the theory of moral evolution that Roderick Nash terms "ethical extensionism"—is here presented as a kind of *civic* inclusion and domestication.[6] References to the "freedom" extended to animals were not uncommon—the *Times* in 1860 referred to Martin's Act of 1822 as "The Magna Charta of the brute creation," for instance.[7] But Fitzgerald's elaborate vision of canine "emancipation" is notable for putting in pride of place not the work of an avowed agitator such as "Humanity Dick" Martin, but rather that of Charles Dickens, albeit alongside the other great master of animal portraiture, Sir Edwin Landseer:

> Much of this altered tone and liberal toleration is, no doubt, owing to a happy change in the feeling of society. That the old, low canine bigotry is out of fashion, and a more enlightened sentiment has come in its place, must be, no doubt, set to the account of what is called the spirit of the age. But for the thorough propagation and wholesale popularization of these views, their extension through the length and breadth of the land, two persons—two incomparable artists each in his own walk—are more directly responsible. To Mr. Charles Dickens and Sir Edwin Landseer a grateful canine posterity, if ever it should reach to the necessary development, shall set up the bronze statue or commemorative pillar!

If Fitzgerald's conceit is to treat the development of the humane movement as a kind of canine enfranchisement, an achievement of citizenship and civil rights comparable to the great political and social struggles of the recent past, Dickens and Landseer appear, startlingly, in the place of a William Wilberforce or a Daniel O'Connell. But while ranked together, it is Dickens who is claimed as the *greater* artist, and by implication the greater emancipator: for though Landseer's animal portraiture is praised for its precision, Dickens's stories are regarded as both more various and more authoritative, more deeply knowledgeable of "the interior working of the motives and emotions of the tribe."[8] Dickens is praised for his portrayal of *characters*, rather than merely the superficial impression of *character*.[9] Fitzgerald claims that Dickens's unique and *uncanny* ability to understand dogs set him apart even from the greatest animal painter of the age: "[Dickens] takes the newly-enfranchised animal within the charmed circle of his characters, sets him down at the fireside and chimney-corner, and furnishes him with quaint reflections of the whims and humours of humanity, playing on them with delicate touches which seem almost earnest, until they really mount to the dignity of a character."[10]

It is implicit in Fitzgerald's argument that Dickens's art cannot be detached from its ideal performance in a *domestic* setting, in the little theater of the home, where the lessons of heart and hearth can be more effectively learned. The narrative of political inclusion is thus inseparable from the literal, familial domestication of the dog. Dickens's portrayal of the most domestic of domestic animals is in this sense entirely in accord with the work of his novels, which "speak not just for but from the hearth, creating the occasion for their own consumption in the domestic sphere."[11] Once more the novelist is said to have the advantage over the artist, for "the one preaches from the wall; the other, with a far greater command of eye and heart, from a pulpit by the fireside."[12] This portrayal of Dickens as a famous dog lover and even a liberator of animals is plausible because it is of a piece with his paeans to domesticity, the love of animals being wrapped up in the observation that the great novelist's nature was, from his earliest childhood to the day of his death, "home-loving."[13] In the memory of a grateful and gratified public, Dickens's virtues seem naturally to embrace both the love of dogs and of the home.

What should we make of Fitzgerald's arresting claim that it was none other than Charles Dickens who led the Victorian movement for animal "liberation"? If we sidestep the humor and hyperbole in Fitzgerald's account, the significance of Dickens's relationship with dogs and other animals is still worth revisiting—not because he is somehow representative of the humanitarian *geist,* but precisely because he is regularly *represented* to us as such. Dickens matters because he remains central, however misleadingly, to our very *idea* of the Victorians. For good or ill, Dickens has lent his name not only to the age but to a country besides: the place that Chesterton affectionately but accurately called "Dickensland."[14] Moreover, because in his lifetime and long after, Dickens has been made to *perform* as just such a representatively "humane" figure, his love of dogs has been written into the narrative of the Victorian animal welfare movement. We might cavil at the notion of Dickens being the O'Connell of a Canine (rather than Catholic) Emancipation, but his affection for dogs has nevertheless come to stand in for the ripening Victorian moral conscience toward animals.

Dickens loved his dogs, then: but in what sense can he really be called a friend and defender of animals? Certainly, Dickens has been pressed into such service, more than a few times. The nineteenth-century animal welfare movement was ever ready to recruit supporters from the arts, to claim the likes of Dickens and Landseer, and many others, as allies in the fight against animal cruelty. Chien-Hui Li has usefully reminded us of the creative appropriation of literature by humanitarians, the attempt "to place the animal defense movement within a laudable humane literary tradition and strengthen its affinity with the literary sphere."[15] In Dickens's case it was readily believable because his irrepressible humanitarianism seemed paradoxically to transcend the bounds of humanity, enfolding animals—and especially dogs—within his energetic, passionate, often angry benevolence. At the same time, moreover, Dickens's love of the home readily appeared to encompass all of its members, human *and* nonhuman.

So on the one hand, Dickens can be portrayed as a proactive figure in the animal welfare movement: a prominent RSPCA member; a campaigner against public slaughterhouses, dog fighting, and bull baiting; a critic of the mistreatment of horses by cabdrivers; and a prominent antivivisectionist. Dickens's "outspoken opposition to animal suffering" makes him "a pioneer in raising the issue of humans' unjust treatment of animals."[16] This concern for animal welfare paralleled his plaint against the victimization of vulnerable human beings, particularly children. Thus Ruth Richardson has recently noted Dickens's comparison in *Oliver Twist* of the treatment of humans and animals by the master sweep Mr. Gamfield: this man of "ingrained inhumanity" beats his donkey as a

prelude to handing Oliver over to the not so tender mercies of the workhouse.[17] In the case of the orphan Oliver, it is the lack of a loving and
secure family that distresses, and it is the same sentiment that appears
to motivate Dickens's interest in abandoned animals. Home love, as well
as a love for justice, impels Dickens's sympathies toward man and beast
alike.

Most significantly in this regard, Dickens has been widely identified
as an ardent and enthusiastic supporter of the North London dog shelter that would later become famous as the Battersea Dogs' Home. In a
widely quoted article, "Two Dog Shows," published in 1862 in Dickens's journal *All the Year Round*, the work of the Dogs' Home is characterized, and defended against Gradgrindian critics, as a peculiarly English
response to the suffering of animals, one based on feeling, on heartful,
humanitarian charity. The Dogs' Home is described as "an extraordinary monument of the remarkable affection with which English people
regard the race of dogs; an evidence of that hidden fund of feeling which
survives in some hearts even the rough ordeal of London life in the nineteenth century."[18] Given Dickens's enthusiasm for domesticity, it comes
as no surprise to contemporary commentators that he should have supported the Dogs' Home, for it aimed to provide for animals a version
of the domestic life that is for Dickens the goal of every journey, "the
prospective haven from the alienation and cruelty of homelessness."[19] As
Cynthia Curran notes, "The use of the word 'home' is significant because
it reflects the belief that a dog's proper place was in a domestic setting;
these stray dogs came to be seen as having fallen from security."[20] Critics
concur that this concern to find homes for lost and abandoned dogs is
entirely in accord with Dickens's "philosophy of practical benevolence,"
and that the treatment of humans and the treatment of animals perfectly
align.[21] The same ideals of restoration and redemption can be found,
for instance, in Dickens's involvement with Urania Cottage, the refuge
and reformatory for prostitutes and other unfortunates he founded with
Baroness Burdett-Coutts; if Urania Cottage was an assertion of Dickens's "domestic will," so too seems to be the Home for Lost and Starving Dogs.[22] Grace Moore has argued most forcefully for the parallels
between "lost" dogs and "fallen" women, seeing these "homes" as exactly
analogous institutions.[23] The significance of the Dogs' Home and the
links to domestic ideology are explored in a subsequent chapter, but for
now it is enough to note that Dickens's apparent support of the Home
appears to establish beyond doubt his inveterate love of animals.

The corollary of this advocacy of domestic reclamation of dogs (and humans) is the problematization of the *public* animal. Dickens would not have been the first nor the only commentator to see the problem of the "stray" as comparable with that of the indigent pauper and the vagrant poor. Most pathetically, *Bleak House*'s street sweeper Jo does not even know what the word "home" means.[24] We might recall also the simpleton Barnaby Rudge, abruptly forced to take to the road, weeping at the prospect of abandoning the dogs he has befriended, and imagining their finding only a closed door to greet them; Barnaby's sensitivity to their plight carries "such a sense of home in the thought" that it brings tears to his mother's eyes.[25] In just such a way Dickens seems ever to be pleading for proper homes for street dwellers, human or animal.[26]

Moreover, Dickens characteristically contrasts the security of the home with the nightmarish qualities of life on the streets. At the same time as he is eulogizing domesticity, Dickens portrays a public world that can be viscerally unsettling in its thoroughgoing confusion of humanity and animality. Jon Mee has characterized this Dickensian treatment of the public sphere as a "visionary excess of metonymy," inimical to the integrity of the bourgeois self.[27] The cattle market is the inevitable icon of this unimproved and unsettling London: Jeremy Tambling notes that the presence of cattle in the streets, and the raising of the alarm of a "Mad Bull" in the market, in *Dombey and Son,* evoke the simultaneity of the modern and the unmodern in the heart of the metropolis.[28] Tom Pinch in the marketplace at Salisbury similarly observes "a great many dogs, who were strongly interested in the state of the market and the bargains of their masters; and a great confusion of tongues, both brute and human."[29] But it is Oliver Twist's encounter with the chaos of Smithfield Market (before its mid-Victorian removal and reformation) which serves as the *locus classicus* here: with its barking of dogs, bellowing and plunging of beasts, bleating of sheep, grunting and squeaking of pigs, Smithfield is the synecdoche of a city reduced to a "nightmarish slaughterhouse."[30] Indeed, in the year that *Oliver Twist* was published in book form, the animal welfare journal *The Animals' Friend* laid open the "disgusting details of the slaughterhouse" to a horrified public.[31] As we have already noted, the most heinous offense of the old, unreformed Smithfield was its propensity to erode the proper distance between man and animal: "The anticipation was that these people would be debased, bestial in their habits and strangely similar in disposition to the animals with which they shared their spaces."[32] And Oliver is of course a lost lamb to the slaughter, caught up in a disconcerting and dangerous world where humans may at any moment turn into animals.[33] The other side of Dickens's domestic idyll is thus this terrifying *eidometropolis* (to use Jeremy Tambling's term) where humans are constantly in danger of being transmogrified into beasts and brutes.[34]

Street dogs are emblematic of this *undisciplined*, transgressive, anthropomorphic public sphere. Dickens's early writings present a host of errant and undomesticated dogs, denizens of the rookeries or of the highways, all to various degrees rendered out of place by the dictates of middle-class moral geographies. To crib Henry Mayhew, we might divide these canine "types" into dogs that *will* work (such as the circus dog Merrylegs and his fellow street and public performers, or the guard dogs that accost Quilp) and those that will *not* (above all, Bill Sikes's criminal companion, Bull's-eye, who shares in his master's villainy almost to the end).[35] The streets of Dickensland abound with dogs incompatible with the requirements of disciplinary modernity, animals whose moral condition is critically compromised by their sharing of the city with human beings. So common indeed are dogs in this Dickensian vision that the unreformed city sometimes verges on being given up to the animal altogether, such that animals are transformed into humans as much as the other way round.[36]

In one of his characteristic journalistic tramps around London's "shy" or disreputable neighborhoods, for instance, Dickens's uncommercial traveler visits and observes the "lower" animals of its backstreets and byways, noting the company these animals are said to keep. Goldfinches, cats, dogs, and donkeys—all are revealed as at the same time unapologetically demoralized but yet also shamefully self-conscious of their poverty and of the failings of their human companions. In some cases, as with the birds of the locality, it is the *denaturing* of these animals that Dickens finds striking: "That anything born of an egg and invested with wings, should have got to the pass that it hops contentedly down a ladder into a cellar, and calls that going home, is a circumstance so amazing as to leave one nothing more in this connexion to wonder at."[37] In others, as with the feline tribe having a "strong tendency to relapse into barbarism," it is a kind of *reversion* that seems to be at play. But it is the dogs of the working streets that most hold Dickens's attention, as these animals, with no trace of a natural destiny left to them, opportunistically and anthropomorphically take on the tone of their underclass milieu. The dogs of these neighborhoods are a mix of the honest and the disreputable, the industrious and the idle, but it is the latter that predominate in Dickens's sketch, for they "avoid work . . . if they can, of course; that is in the nature of all animals."[38] Populating the city's streets with their vagabond human companions, these dogs exhibit an agency that inverts the accepted order while maintaining a focus on the low and the disreputable:

> We talk of men keeping dogs, but we might often talk more expressively of dogs keeping men. I know a bull-dog in a shy corner of Hammersmith who keeps a man. He keeps him up a year, and makes him go to public-houses and lay wagers on him, and obliges him to lean against posts and look at him, and forces him to neglect work for him, and keeps him under rigid coercion.
>
> There are a great many dogs in shy neighbourhoods, who keep boys. I have my eye on a mongrel in Somerstown who keeps three boys. He feigns that he can bring down sparrows, and unburrow rats (he can do neither), and he takes the boys out on sporting pretences into all sorts of suburban fields.
>
> There is a dog residing in the Borough of Southwark who keeps a blind man. He may be seen, most days, in Oxford-street, haling the blind man away on expeditions wholly uncontemplated by, and unintelligible to, the man: wholly of the dog's conception and execution.
>
> At a small butcher's, in a shy neighbourhood (there is no reason for suppressing the name; it is by Notting-hill, and gives upon the district called the Potteries), I know a shaggy black and white dog who keeps a drover. He is a dog of an easy disposition, and too frequently allows this drover to get drunk. On these occasions, it is the dog's custom to sit outside the public-house, keeping his eye on a few sheep, and thinking.
>
> The dogs of shy neighbourhoods usually betray a slinking consciousness of being in poor circumstances—for the most part manifested in an aspect of anxiety, an awkwardness in their play, and a misgiving that somebody is going to harness them to something, to pick up a living.[39]

This is an amusing vision, and it helpfully functions to remind us of
the etymology of "rookery," but though it deploys the topoi of conventional morality with a kind of affectionate satire, its image of indigent and
work-shy canines "keeping" their supposed human masters also carries a
distinct disciplinary charge. These passages follow the accepted doctrine
of canine plasticity, in which dogs inevitably take on the "habits" of their
keepers: the conviction that "dogs kept by the vicious, become vicious in
their habits; while, on the other hand, dogs who live with persons of mild
manners and regular habits are always mild in character."[40] But it also
recapitulates the assumptions of "moral environmentalism," such that
humans are recognized as creatures of habit and habitus too—and in
their ultimate demoralization, all hierarchy, order, and discipline, including the proper distance between human and animal, is lost.[41] In full-on
homiletic mode, Dickens speaks directly about the dangers of such bes-
tialization: "And, oh! ye Pharisees of the nineteenth hundredth year of
Christian knowledge, who soundingly appeal to human nature, see first
that it be human. Take heed it has not been transformed, during your
slumber and the sleep of generations, into the nature of the Beasts."[42]

Of course, a straightforward conclusion follows: the need to redeem
these brutes from the degrading environments of the city, to rehome
them and hopefully to restore them to respectability. The dogs, "un-
distinguishable in mire," and the horses, "scarcely better," described in
the celebrated mud- and fog-bound introduction to *Bleak House* attest to
this wholesale breakdown of social and natural order.[43] The demands of
humanity as well as of hygiene and public order require their removal
to proper domestic spaces where they can be enclosed and properly
disciplined. The rescue and rehabilitation of Oliver Twist (latterly dis-
covering a bourgeois pedigree, however compromised) is in this sense
no more than a recapitulation of a domestic ideology that functions as
an adjunct of disciplinary society.[44] Just like Oliver, the true, honest,
crypto-bourgeois canine citizen secretly *desires* to be removed from the
vicious streets to the safety and comfort of the home. In just the same
way, Victorian naturalists constantly reassured their readers that the dog
was an *innately* private animal, that he "attaches himself to humanity, and
is never so happy as when domesticated, and a sharer of his master's toil
or pleasures."[45]

The direst implications of what happens to the dogs—and the people—
who are, despite this yearning, left abandoned and homeless is made quite
clear in Dickens's 1853 essay "Gone Astray." Here, the young Dickens is

significantly placed alongside a "self-interested dog," one that he equally significantly names "Merrychance." Robert Douglas-Fairhurst comments on the most sinister undertones of this encounter — for the narrator first feeds the dog some German sausage but comes to fear that he is only inciting its appetite for a human meal: first "frisking about me, rubbing his nose against me, dodging at me sideways, shaking his head and pretending to run backwards, and making himself good-naturedly ridiculous, as if he had no consideration for himself, but wanted to raise my spirits," but subsequently, "his mouth watering, and his eyes glistening, . . . he sidled out on the pavement in a threatening manner and growled at me."[46] Douglas-Fairhurst notes that Merrychance's behavior mirrors the form of the essay, alternating as it does between delight and danger. But the latter is never far away, even if the ultimate degradation is reserved for much later, in *Bleak House,* with the street sweeper Jo (a "wounded animal that had been found in a ditch") losing his humanity completely, becoming equivalent to the dog that accompanies him in listening to some street musicians.[47] Jo is equally inconsiderable, "a thoroughly vagabond dog," albeit "an educated, improved, developed dog, who has been taught his duties and knows how to discharge them." Jo's exquisite agony is "to see the horses, dogs, and cattle, go by me, and to know that in ignorance I belong to them, and not to the superior beings in my shape, whose delicacy I offend!"[48] So, while the young Dickens is merely menaced by a dog, "Jo is viewed as little more than a dog — one that can walk on its hind legs and perform a trick with a broom, but a dog nonetheless. Shuffling around on his crossing, he is not lost, because he has never been missed. He is merely a stray."[49] And like a stray, we might add, belonging to no one, he is abjectly disposable. Ivan Kreilkamp has remarked that dogs, as the most minor of minor characters, constitute a "sub-proletariat" of the novel, "possessing no solid claim to recognition or memory on the part of the narrator or any other character"; to *be* a dog is to be subject to non-novelistic temporalities, to lack narrative, so that one's passing leaves little or no trace.[50] The "homeless" dog of the streets, like the "houseless rejected creature" that Barnaby Rudge's father has become, or like that "hunted dunghill dog," Magwitch, is only the most anonymous and most vulnerable to the constitutive violence inherent in the novel and in society itself.[51]

It is easy to make the case, then, that Dickens's interest in dogs reproduces and reinforces the intimate connections between the cult of the dog and the cult of domesticity, presenting the home as a disciplined and ordered space in contrast to the transgressive animality of the public world. It is reasonable to infer an interest in animal welfare from Dickens's humanitarianism and his love of home. As we have seen, dogs had long come to be regarded as naturally embodying the domestic virtues, enabling them to play a full part, as pets, in the Victorian sanctification of the family: "Victorian pets," notes Adrienne Munich, "expressed themselves within domestic spaces resembling ideal Victorian homes."[52] In the sentimentalization of domesticity, the faithful dog represented coziness and security, as well as the antithesis of the competitiveness and materialism to be found in the "public world."[53] More than merely an icon, the dog was a preeminently "family-constituting being."[54]

Far from uncritically celebrating this domestication of the dog, we have long come to acknowledge the troubling aspects of this concern to rehome the "stray." That such domesticity was a form of familiarized discipline is impossible to deny: pet keeping helped to inculcate habits of kindness, for sure, but we should remember that this was "kindness in the service of a more effective and efficient control."[55] The darker side of such domestic training, as close as any shadow, is particularly obvious in the wake of decades of feminist criticism of Victorian patriarchal attitudes. Adrienne Munich's brilliant essay on Queen Victoria's domestic life notes, for instance, that many of Landseer's famous animal paintings—particularly those of dogs—assert the human ability to socialize, rather than banish, the animal other, and that such representations of successful domestication could in turn legitimate other forms of authority, such as the patriarchal. The taming or domestication of Bella Wilfer in *Our Mutual Friend* has become emblematic of this domination, for not only animals but adult women too were trained to accommodate themselves to the proprieties of the Victorian parlor: "Was it not enough that I should have been willed away, like a horse, or a dog, or a bird?" the as-yet-unbroken Bella protests.[56] Similarly, the fate of *Little Dorrit*'s Tattycoram and the revealingly named "Pet" Meagles suggests that the home, even one run by a loving family, is little more than a cage. Tattycoram is treated like a dog or a cat, even to the extent of being renamed at the whim of her new "owner."[57] "Enriching one's home by bringing in other people to share it can be almost as manipulative as the actions of a parasite," argues Frances Armstrong; "invasion can take the form of inclusion." This insight is easily extended to "pets" as well as people.[58] Even as resistant a subject as Ebenezer Scrooge can, ultimately, be treated as a domesticated animal:

> "Here is a new game," said Scrooge. "One half-hour, Spirit, only one!"
>
> It was a Game called Yes and No, where Scrooge's nephew had to think of something, and the rest must find out what; he only answering to their questions yes or no, as the case was. The fire of questioning to which he was exposed elicited from him that he was thinking of an animal, a live animal, rather a disagreeable animal, a savage animal, an animal that growled and grunted sometimes, and talked sometimes, and lived in London, and walked about the streets, and wasn't made a show of, and wasn't led by anybody, and didn't live in a menagerie, and was never killed in a market, and was not a horse, or an ass, or a cow, or a bull, or a tiger, or a dog, or a pig, or a cat, or a bear. At every new question put to him, this nephew burst into a fresh roar of laughter; and was so inexpressibly tickled, that he was obliged to get up off the sofa and stamp. At last the plump sister cried out: —
>
> "I have found it out! I know what it is, Fred! I know what it is!"
>
> "What is it?" cried Fred.
>
> "It's your uncle Scro-o-o-o-oge!"[59]

If Dickens preached from a fireside pulpit, then, as Percy Fitzgerald claimed, the effects of his exhortations of domesticity can readily be taken to reinforce the notion that the woman's place, like the pet's, was in the home: in Urania Cottage, Rosemarie Bodenheimer writes, "in place of religion, he preached the doctrine of Home—which for Dickens meant order, punctuality, neatness, and good housekeeping."[60] It is persuasive enough to read Dickens's interest in dogs *primarily* as a counterpoint to his sentimentalization of the home, with all that this suggests for the place not just of children but also of women and the other classes of subordinate humanity. Dickens's philanthropic interest in both animal and human welfare can be portrayed, albeit crudely, as both conforming to and complicit with the dictates of a hegemonic "domestic ideology." Thus Nancy Armstrong, focusing on *Oliver Twist*, sees the novels of the early Victorian era as representing disruptions of domestic order, including "the destruction of boundaries between nature and culture," but only as a preliminary to the restoration of the household and the reconstitution of the family, a domestication of desire with the home reduced to little more than a prison.[61]

There is, however, another side to this story, which is after all far too suspiciously neat in its recapitulation of classic feminist and Foucauldian themes.[62] Does Dickens, like Landseer, really suggest that animals must succumb to the "power of domestic absolution"?[63] Perhaps: but we must not take this *bourgeoisified,* sentimental, animal-loving, domesticating, and domineering Dickens too far, too easily, or too literally. One plank of this interpretation of a simultaneously home- *and* animal-loving Dickens may be dismantled straightaway. Despite the invocation of Dickens's support for what would become the Battersea Dogs' Home, the article noted above is not his work at all.[64] The likely author of "Two Dog Shows" is in fact the journalist and essayist John Hollingshead, as Beryl Gray has pointed out. Since Hollingshead was a regular contributor to *All the Year Round,* and since he consistently supported the Home in print, for Dickens to have written this article is—to borrow Gray's aptly amusing words—in the line of his keeping a dog and barking himself.[65] The Dogs' Home never had the public support of the country's most famous writer and its most famous extoller of the domestic virtues. There is nothing to indicate—beyond speculation and inference—that he considered the work of the Dogs' Home to be a parallel to the project of domestication he supervised at Urania Cottage and advocated in his fiction.[66]

Moreover, Dickens's mobilization of the concept of home is evidently more ambiguous than a monolithic presentation of "domestic ideology" suggests. As has been noted many times, there are few unimpeachably happy homes in Dickens's fictions, domestic spaces instead often appearing "threatening, uncanny, and very far from providing a safe haven."[67] The dog kennel without a dog to animate it, recalled by David Copperfield, suggests the great lack of just such a "family-constituting" pet in his formative years; instead, David himself, whipped like a dog by Murdstone, responds with a bite, both man and boy being animalized in mutually degrading corporal discipline.[68] In such dramatically unhappy families as these, some animals might indeed figure as consolers and cajolers: thus Diogenes plays his part in bringing Florence Dombey back to life, "an unromantic dog who instantly does his bit to make the house a home, caring nothing for appearances and creating minor chaos as he vigorously offers and receives affection."[69] But Dickens's dogs are also more messily ambiguous than their role as home helpers suggest, and not simply (like Dora Copperfield's Jip) as icons of domestic incompetence. Thus the exuberant Boxer—for all Caleb the toymaker's dolls' houses and Noah's Arks, the latter barely large enough for even the smallest birds and beasts—refuses to be contained by this "fairy tale of home," dashing in and out as he does "with bewildering inconstancy."[70] Likewise, in Dickens's very first published story, the boisterous and uncontainable family dog does his best to subvert a family's plan to extract a legacy from their rich cousin Augustus Minns.[71] Unfortunately for them, Augustus has an unmingled horror of both children and dogs (especially hydrophobic ones): "He was not unamiable, but he could at any time have viewed the execution of a dog, or the assassination of an infant, with the liveliest satisfaction. Their habits were at variance with his love of order; and his love of order, was as powerful as his love of life."[72] Douglas-Fairhurst tellingly sees this story as "a modern pantomime," "where every dog is guaranteed to misbehave."[73] Any predilection for cleanliness, neatness, and domestic order is effectively trumped here by young Dickens's delight in Minns's farcical comeuppance. In a different register, Betsey Trotwood's obsession with keeping donkeys off her lawn is evidence only of the "self-defensive nature of orderliness."[74] And when Dickens writes that dogs should perhaps, like spoiled children, be placed in the class of "public nuisances," the heavily underlined irony undercuts Nancy Armstrong's suggestion that the work of such fiction is to police public and private disorder through the domestication of desire.[75] Here, the joke is surely on those who *fear* the exuberance and messiness that animals bring into the household from the outside world; it is a satire on neatness and on the bourgeois boundaries of the self.

Most important, though, is Dickens's lifelong fascination with the life of the streets, which encompasses its nonhuman denizens, and which in similar fashion cannot be made to fit with the paeans to domesticity, unless it is to observe with Chesterton that Dickens had the key to the streets as another man might have the keys to his home.[76] Dickens's attraction to the street never fades, and a chronological division, with the breakdown of his own family as the tipping point, does little justice to the ever-present tensions between the longings for home and the longings for the world, in Dickens's life as well as in his art. For Bodenheimer, as with all of Dickens's critics, there is a constant tension to be observed between Dickens's disciplined striving and his vagrant instinct.

Dickens pictured himself as "the descendant at no great distance of some irreclaimable tramp," the antithesis of those "steady-going people, who have no vagrancy in their souls."[77] Moreover, Dickens presented himself specifically as the kind of "lost" animal that might fall prey to the dog stealers or become the unwitting object of the charity of the Home for Lost Dogs: in 1839 Dickens's youthful esprit saw him advertising himself as just such an animal, in a letter to William Behnes, for whom he was to house-sit:

> Left his home
> On the evening of Tuesday the Thirtieth of April last,
> A remarkable Dog
> answering to the name of
> Boz.

> He had on at the time a white collar, marked with the initials "C.D." (in marking ink) and was last seen, in company with some other dogs, lying on the banks of the Thames at Richmond.[78]

Near the end of his life, Dickens was also delighted in the story he was told about a dog whose recurrent absences his mistress eventually discovers as owing to his presenting himself in a public house for his regular pint.[79] Dickens's joy in this anecdote derives directly from his recollection of his boyhood life on the streets, when he too presented himself to a publican with a request for the house's "VERY *best* ale."[80] It is impossible not to read this anecdote in terms of the quintessential Dickens mixture of thrill as well as trauma in the memory of his abandonment to the life of the streets, his lifelong homelessness.

The fact that Dickens kept a bronze figure of a "dog fancier" (perhaps even a dog stealer) with "lots of little dogs in his pockets and under his arms," on the writing desk in his study, also suggests this acknowledgment of the pathos of the public animal, the longing for home and at the same time the lure of the street.[81] Dickens, in one register, disavowed the vagrant, putting a distance between himself and the "vagabond savage" identified by Henry Mayhew. Like the dog of the naturalists' description, Dickens wanted to be a "permanent inmate" of English homes, his great ambition being "to live in the hearts and homes of home-loving people."[82] But like Mayhew, he recognized the latent predisposition to vagrancy (of the benign "harum scarum" sort) even in the most civilized and domesticated heart.[83] Much of his tramping portrays the streets as a "nightmare of a world without interiority," but there is a disdain for domestication too, an only half-humorous "loathing" for the settled and secure domestic hearth. Dickens would surely have agreed with Foucault, that man is but an "erratic animal."[84]

Of course, Dickens has long been understood in terms of dualism and splitting, "self-division," "conflicting impulses," and "persistent self-contradictions," and it is not too difficult to see these in terms of more general paradoxes.[85] What is significant is how these tensions, the delight and the despair, are accommodated and managed.[86] *Staged* might be better still, for the theatrical resonances in the sentimental presentation of the home are unavoidable for the great impresario of domesticity.[87] Dickens's stage management of the home seems to encompass his portrayal of animals both inside and outside the security of its walls. There is little comfort here in the recognition that Dickens disposes his animal actors and sets them in motion, like so many Merrylegs, or worse still the distinctly un-merry performing dogs encountered by Little Nell outside the "Jolly Sandboys," dancing away to the mournful tune of their organ grinder, Jerry.[88] In just such a way, in Dickens's fiction, "the four-footed actors play their little parts, and in a pleasant, complimentary manner become as essential to the piece as the more leading human men and women."[89] Percy Fitzgerald's memories of Charles Dickens indeed light on the fact that what brought them together was not just their shared interest in dogs, their "common delight in the honest tribe," but also their love of the theatrical dog *act:* "the old association of the dog as a performer on the melodramatic stage."[90] Fitzgerald was thinking here of the heroic feats of "Carlo, the Performing Dog," or the vengeance of Dragon, the "Dog of Montargis," stock characters in London's illegitimate theatrical repertory.[91] Dickens's sentimentalization of home and his horror of homelessness might perhaps be felt to derive from this *melodramatic* strain.

Dickens's love of *pantomime,* melodrama's great rival, attests, however, to a markedly less sentimental response to the world, one more alive to the messy vitality and indeed animality of the metropolis.[92] Pantomime's staging of the encounter between human beings and their recalcitrant milieux, with an emphasis on metamorphosis and mutability, revels in the breakneck confusion of the modern metropolis just as Dickens's early fiction and journalism does. If melodrama presented life as it ought to be, pantomime largely sidestepped these stock conventions and resolutions, taking its delight instead in dramatizing the tensions and ambiguities in the encounter between human beings and nature.[93] In the figure of Orson, the "wild man," for instance, "savagery" was staged as a contest between violent tenderness and innocent destructiveness, the gentle and the diabolical.[94] Likewise, Clown, pantomime's most celebrated protagonist, was a child of nature, "a morally ambivalent character, neither entirely civilised nor wholly savage," entirely lacking in self-discipline, acting on animal impulse, and with a childish taste for mayhem.[95] These animalized figures are notably resistant to anthropocentric reassurance, and the instability of the human self was played out in pantomime's staging of the natural world. Joseph Grimaldi, for instance, the most famous personification of Clown, recruited both animals and inanimate objects in his celebrated performances. These animal "properties" (what we now call props) can be seen in Cruikshank's illustration for Grimaldi's *Memoirs*, as edited and fashioned by Dickens (figure 2). Improvised for a Birmingham engagement, Clown, front stage, carries on these "live properties," while Harlequin, Columbine, and Pantaloon play out their drama in the background: "He dressed himself in an old livery coat with immense pockets and a huge cocked hat, both were—of course—over his clown's costume. At his back, he carried a basket laden with carrots and turnips, stuffing a duck into each pocket, leaving their heads hanging out, and carried a pig under one arm and a goose under the other."[96] This is a reminder that the theater reflected and reinforced the menagerie of the streets, with melodramatic resolution often overturned by the force, or the line of flight, of farce.

Jane Moody has persuasively portrayed pantomime as "a theatrical form that dramatized the pleasures, fears and absurdities of urban life," and there is much of this tradition that recalls Dickens's treatment of the ever-present urban animal: the Dickens not of sentimental domesticity, that is, but the Dickens who had a special relationship with pantomime and indeed with Grimaldi himself.[97] This was a world in which "Everything is capable, with the greatest ease, of being changed into Anything."[98] Clown reveled in this mobility, and mutability, taking the urban miscellany of the street as props for his comic improvisation, and, like the wild man Orson, subverted the boundaries separating nature and culture.[99] In pantomime, the animals that pervaded the public sphere, capering through the city's streets and into its homes, were all grist to his

Figure 2. George Cruikshank, "Live Properties," from Dickens, *Memoirs of Joseph Grimaldi.* (Reproduced by kind permission of the Syndics of Cambridge University Library)

mill, as they are indeed to Dickens, who incorporates them—assembles them—in a "turbulent democracy of things."[100] Animals here serve as a reminder to the bourgeois self of the absence of providence, the limits of his or her discursive and practical ability to exert authority over the environment. An unlikely voice of reason, admittedly, but Montague Tigg points out that even Hercules "can't prevent the cats from making a most intolerable row on the roofs of the houses, or the dogs from being shot in hot weather if they run about the streets unmuzzled."[101]

So we have on the one hand the Dickens that delights in the bustling vitality and animality of the streets and on the other the Dickens that preaches the quiet domestication of human (and animal) nature. Critics have long noted these warring tendencies in Dickens. George Levine argues for the parallels with a *Darwinian* vision of the world—"Species are not fixed but endlessly varying. All the stable elements of our gardens, our domestic animals, our own bodies are mysteriously active, aberrant, plastic"—even if he accepts that in the end Dickens comes down to the un-Darwinian themes of essentialism, stage melodrama, teleology, and conventional morality.[102] Jonathan Buckmaster comes to a similar conclusion, specifically recalling Dickens's representation of Grimaldi's life: on the one hand noting Dickens's interest in pantomime's concern for external performance rather than interiority, for effect rather than affect, ambiguity rather than authenticity, but arguing that Dickens's focus on the feeling, suffering self ultimately reconciles the narratives of theatricality and sensibility.[103] We might recall here John Westlock's wish for rampant horses, lions, bears, and mad bulls to draw an affrighted Ruth Pinch back into his arms: so might Dickens's disorderly public realm, including its undisciplined animals, serve to *shepherd* us back to the higher claims of sentiment and the domestic resolution of melodrama.[104]

Still: for all the putative triumph of *feeling*, the power of pantomime's portrayal of a radically contingent urban world allowed a part of Dickens, the part that adored pantomime, to delight in the chaos and messiness that animals brought, their transgression of public and private space and their subversion of anthropocentric reason. Accepting David Trotter's definition of "mess" as "contingency's signature," this Dickensian vision of an uncontrollably animated city disrupts the conventional pieties and proprieties. Animals are "messy" (and not simply productive of "waste," stuff that might be cleaned up and usefully recycled in a commercial economy, like the dog dung, or "pure," that street sweepers like Jo collected), but in the sense that they contributed to the "unstable, contingent, spectacular world" staged in the pantomime.[105] However, whereas Trotter only considers animals as dead objects—like the taxidermy in Mr. Venus's shop in *Bleak House*—we, like Dickens, need to recognize animals as living and breathing participants in the enterprise of urban life.[106] Dickens's dogs—preeminently the dogs who "keep" human companions in the shy neighborhoods of the city—refuse to be deadened and disciplined by domesticity. They offer a marked *resistance* to the authorized placing of animals, and Dickens—again, part of Dickens—acknowledges and delights in their presence in the streets. The presentation of the animality of the public world therefore need not always be a frightening and troubling vision. With the help of pantomime, with "the hurly-burly transformative optimism of theatrical experience," Dickens captures the desires as well as the nightmares of the Victorian metropolis.[107]

What do these ambiguities tell us about Dickens as an animal lover, and also about the desire (ours as well as the Victorians') to induct him into the pantheon of animal protection? We cannot doubt that he cared for his dogs: "the tender relations that existed between the novelist and his canine companions" are repeatedly attested.[108] But there is of course a vast difference between kindly attitudes and any serious recognition of the "rights" of animals. Many men and women kept dogs but in no way supported the various aims of the nineteenth-century animal welfare movement. Many men and women found it easy enough to compartmentalize their feelings for some animals from any sense of their responsibilities to others. Indeed, Gary Francione considers our entire cultural attitude to animals as a form of "moral schizophrenia."[109] This kind of dualism is not hard to find in Victorian Britain, as we shall see, with the distinction between the private "pet" and the public "stray" the readiest reckoner of moral concern, or indifference.

We can see this in Dickens, I think, and, if we take a turn in "Dickensland," in "Victorian" attitudes more generally. If we return to Percy Fitzgerald's exuberant account of Dickens's role in the humanitarian emancipation of the British dog, it is made quite clear that there are, nevertheless, "bad" as well as "good" dogs. For Fitzgerald, the proper dog has to earn the citizenship he has been granted by man (and is to be strictly separated, in Fitzgerald's distinctly colonial rhetoric, from violent dogs equivalent to the coarse and rebellious Irish):

> The newer and healthier tone of society in this regard, encourages him to raise himself from a debased condition not of his own making; to let the schoolmaster go abroad in his ranks; to develop intelligence; to subject themselves to moral and decent restraints; to check those bursts of agrarian violence and outrage—that species of rude Whiteboyism, as it were—for which the barbarian code of society was in itself only too responsible —to cultivate, in short, the virtues of health, strength, and

washing. These things have the new philanthropists and the
friends of the dog preached and preached effectively.[110]

Fitzgerald makes it clear that there are *some* dogs who after all *never*
will be able to enjoy the benefits of their emancipation, and furthermore
that the citizen dog himself needs to maintain a clear distance from this
canine underclass:

> There may be seen, too, loose outcasts upon the streets — pau-
> per creatures, who, without protest on the part of the humane
> and those who can feel, are treated with reproach and con-
> tumely. But these, it is well understood, are the pauper spend-
> thrifts, the rakes and *mauvais sujets* of their order, who have
> taken to evil courses and spend their all, and who are now
> eking out a precarious livelihood by shifty ways and dishon-
> est tricks — specially in the neighbourhood of butchers' stalls,
> where police are inefficient — have forfeited that fair esteem
> and protection to which a righteous course of life would have
> entitled them. And as an instance of the way in which correct
> public opinion sets itself in protest against such conduct, mark
> how the respectable tax-paying citizen dog, hurrying down
> with his master — the well-fed, well-clad, canine industrious
> apprentice — mark with what reprobation he hunts, utterly
> routs, the trembling, cowering outcast, and disreputable va-
> grant. And yet he is wholly justified in such conduct; for is not
> that other a pure canine scamp, whom no dog of station could
> decently know, and who has brought discredit on the cloth?[111]

The cur as well as the poor will always be with us, then: we will see
this separation of respectable and unrespectable dogs many times in this
book. To what extent Dickens agreed with his friend's characterization
we cannot know, but it is surely unlikely that Dickens considered all
dogs as worthy of equal consideration, let alone was willing to put them
anywhere near on a par with humans. Animal welfarists who have attempted to recruit Dickens as a comrade in arms have signally ignored
the fact that Dickens specifically criticized Richard Martin — "Humanity
Dick" — precisely because the elevation of the animal implied for him the
derogation of the human being: "It was a pity he could not exchange a
little of his excessive tenderness for animals for some common sense and

consideration for human beings!"[112] Dickens surely did not share Trollope's scorn for those whom he termed "philanimalists," but nor was he one himself.[113] Dickens's condemnation of single-cause issues, such as vegetarianism, suggests that he adopted a pragmatic rather than a principled approach to animal suffering, and wholly avoided the notion that there was a kind of continuum of cruelty between humans and other animals. Kate Flint has argued, with regard to *Great Expectations*, that Pip's maturation sees him elevated from any animalistic characteristics, clearly distinguishing Dickens from any Darwinian notions of kinship with the animal—and indeed from the likes of Magwitch.[114] Chesterton's great commentary on Dickens's humanism is equally apposite here: "Men feel that the cruelty to the poor is a kind of cruelty to animals. They never feel that it is justice to equals; nay, it is treachery to comrades."[115] The extension of a common sympathy for animals and humans, or rather a common repugnant pity, is in this view a kind of *refusal* to extend rights to the human poor as fellow citizens: placing the likes of Jo among "the other lower animals" to whom we must extend protection is merely to continue to deny him his benison of humanity.[116]

For all of his domestic homilies, Dickens was also surely less uncomplicatedly sentimental in his attitudes to dogs than is claimed in the presentation of Dickens as an animal lover. Dickens's role in the "execution" of his dog Sultan (the gift of Percy Fitzgerald) shows, for instance, that Dickens could exhibit perfect sangfroid when killing an animal was deemed necessary.[117] Sultan's crime—biting a child—was heinous and capital, one that could not be excused in the manner of a Quilp: "He bit a man last night, and a woman the night before, and last Tuesday he killed a child—but that was in play."[118] Bowing to the inevitable, Dickens had Sultan taken out to be shot, a sad end for a favorite animal, but a fate that Dickens nevertheless narrated twice to correspondents, several months after the event:

> You heard of his going to Execution, evidently supposing the Procession to be a party detached in pursuit of something to kill or eat? It was very affecting.[119]

> The big dog, on a day last Autumn, having seized a little girl (sister to one of the servants) whom he knew, and was bound to respect, was flogged by his master, and then sentenced to be shot at 7 next morning. He went out very cheerfully with the half dozen men told off for the purpose, evidently thinking

that they were going to be the death of somebody unknown.
But observing in the procession an empty wheelbarrow and
a double-barreled gun, he became meditative, and fixed the
bearer of the gun with his eyes. A stone deftly thrown across
him by the village blackguard (chief-mourner) caused him to
look round for an instant, and he then fell dead, shot through
the heart.[120]

Michael Slater reads these comments merely as poignant, but Dickens
cannot help disguising his feelings with ironic detachment or even a joke,
or else by perfecting the mise-en-scène, erasing the animal by turning its
death into something like literature, or theater.[121] Sultan, the big Irish
bloodhound who hated the sight of a soldier as much as any Whiteboy,
had clearly reverted from respectable citizen to rude Irish savage, and
he had to go. Sultan's execution shows Dickens not so much as briskly
unsentimental, as Simon Callow suggests, but as what we might call
ruthlessly sentimental. We might generalize this attitude as a Victorian
version of what Arnold Arluke has called the "caring-killing paradox,"
for people may care deeply for animals, but accept the responsibility that
they may have to kill them.[122] Dickens's love for the dog was perfectly
compatible with a sense of the animal's limited rights, his conditional
citizenship, and the necessity of killing.[123] One is reminded of Dickens's
facility with killing fictional children, that mixture of "sentimental regret
and ruthless efficiency" recognized by Robert Douglas-Fairhurst—and
perhaps not in the end all that far from Augustus Minns's lively satisfaction.[124]

I end this chapter with Sultan's death because this execution is so
strikingly *unhomely*, so at odds with portrayals of an animal-loving Dickens, or, for that matter, animal-loving Victorians. The notion that humane
sentiment triumphed ultimately over hard-heartedness and hardhead-
edness cannot be allowed to stand: this is a fable of Dickensland. As
readers of Dickens, and as observers of the Victorian age, we have to
confront head-on the cultural contradictions that are exposed here: not
just the alternate layers of "violent brutality and sweetness" that we observe in Dickens's novels as well as Landseer's pictures, but also the key
distinctions between the home and the street, the private and the public, the "good" dog and the "bad," the cherishable and the disposable.[125]
Dickens often fervently resists the blandishments of domestic ideology,
celebrating rather than condemning the "live properties" of the pub-

lic world, and his dogs appear as disruptive agents of contingency and undisciplined desire. But the subsequent idealization of Dickens as the "Homer of the home" works to valorize the dog's domestic destiny, to the detriment and expense of the animal of the streets.[126] Like poor Sultan, where such animals could not properly be domesticated, they found themselves liable to the full penalty of the law, the recurrent victims of not just Dickens's but also the age's ruthless sentimentality.

CHAPTER 2

Flush and the Banditti

Dog Stealing in Victorian London

O N THE first day of September 1846, the poet Elizabeth Barrett, who was at the time making plans for her secret marriage to Robert Browning, stepped out of a shop in Vere Street in the heart of London's West End, and into her carriage, only to find that her beloved cocker spaniel, Flush (figure 3), had been caught up from under the wheels and spirited away by thieves. For a third and final time, Flush had fallen victim to the dog stealers who made their living from abducting pet dogs and holding them for substantial ransoms. Elizabeth Barrett's reaction, as twice before, was a mixture of alarm and resignation. There was nothing to be done except to pay the ransom the dog stealers were sure to demand; she would be informed that an "intermediary" might be able to locate her dog, and, for a price, his recovery might be effected. And if not, she should expect the worst, as the dreadful tradition went in her neighborhood of one lady who had refused the dog stealers' demands, only to find her dog's head sent to her through the post. Elizabeth Barrett, who would countenance neither her father's nor Robert Browning's advice to face down the extortionists, insisted that all must be done to procure Flush's swift release. And in the end it was she who made the extraordinary journey to the criminal underworld of Whitechapel, to negotiate with a Mr. Taylor, the head of the dog-stealing gang, or the *banditti*, as she called them. It would be five long days before Flush was returned to the Barretts' home in Wimpole Street, the "archfiend" Taylor having extracted six guineas for his release.[1] In all, Flush had cost his mistress some twenty pounds' ransom to the dog thieves. But safe he eventually was, and within a week of his return, Elizabeth

Barrett had married Robert Browning. Barely another week had gone by and she had left Wimpole Street forever, making her way with Robert and Flush to the continent, and finally to Italy, to a new life, a world away from London and its dog-stealing fraternity.[2]

What do we know of her spaniel in his captivity? Fortunately, we have Virginia Woolf's *Flush: A Biography*, and her reconstruction of his traumatic experience in the dog stealers' lair:

> Flush was going through the most terrible experience of his
> life. He was bewildered in the extreme. One moment he was in
> Vere Street, among ribbons and laces; the next he was tumbled
> head over heels into a bag; jolted rapidly across streets, and

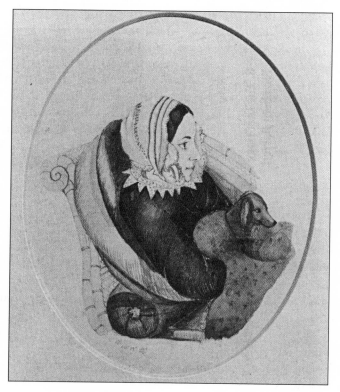

Figure 3. Elizabeth Barrett Browning and Flush, watercolor by Alfred Moulton-Barrett, 1843. (Reproduced by kind permission of the Provost and Fellows of Eton College)

at length was tumbled out—here. He found himself in complete darkness. He found himself in chillness and dampness.
As his giddiness left him he made out a few shapes in a low
dark room—broken chairs, a tumbled mattress. Then he was
seized and tied tightly by the leg to some obstacle. Something
sprawled on the floor—whether beast or human being, he
could not tell. Great boots and draggled skirts kept stumbling
in and out. Flies buzzed on scraps of old meat that were decay-
ing on the floor. Children crawled out from dark corners and
pinched his ears. He whined, and a heavy hand beat him over
the head. . . .

Whenever the door was kicked open he looked up. Miss
Barrett—was it Miss Barrett? Had she come at last? But it
was only a hairy ruffian, who kicked them all aside and stum-
bled to a broken chair upon which he flung himself. Then grad-
ually the darkness thickened. He could scarcely make out what
shapes those were, on the floor, on the mattress, on the broken
chairs. . . . A stump of candle was stuck on the ledge over the
fireplace. A flare burnt in the gutter outside. By its flickering,
coarse light Flush could see terrible faces passing outside, leer-
ing at the window. Then in they came, until the small crowded
room became so crowded that he had to shrink back and lie
even closer against the wall. These horrible monsters—some
were ragged, others were flaring with paint and feathers—
squatted on the floor; hunched themselves over the table. They
began to drink; they cursed and struck each other. . . .

The room was dark. It grew steadily hotter and hotter; the
smell, the heat, were unbearable, Flush's nose burnt; his coat
twitched. And still Miss Barrett did not come.[3]

Virginia Woolf's purpose in writing a biography of a Victorian pet is
satiric, of course; it is designed, at least in part, as a distancing commentary on a Victorian age that was still too close for comfort.[4] In point of
fact, it mimics and perhaps mocks Ouida's novel *Puck* (1870), which has
its dog-hero experience, among several "strange tyrannies," capture by
the capital's dog stealers:

These men smoked and drank; and swore and gambled, in the
lowest and coarsest fashion that they could; and were espe-

cially hilarious when one of them had brought in a valuable
animal, for whom its master would be certain to offer fabulous
rewards, or a priceless little pet dog, that could be slipped in
a pocket and carried out of the country before its owner had
scarcely discovered its loss.[5]

That Woolf, by sticking superficially to such a script, is critically commenting on the "Victorianism" of these animal narratives is hard to deny.
Woolf faithfully captures something of the Victorian temper, as well as
something of her own time and experiences.[6] *Flush: A Biography* should
certainly be read as a fable, like *Puck* and its ilk a way of apprehending
human society from the perspective of the animal world, but it has a
greater place among animal satires.[7] It is a way of reimagining the Victorians and their world, their values, and it is also a commentary on the
way in which that world could be appropriated and written, one that is
necessarily revealing of the assumptions and prejudices of its own age.
In the passage quoted above, for instance, Flush's status as hero and biographical subject is counterpointed to the anonymous beastliness of his
abductors, the brutalized denizens of Whitechapel. Woolf is merely more
archly self-aware than Ouida on this point. In Woolf's story, the "aristocratic" Flush is rudely thrust among thieves; a dog whose mistress had
tried to teach him to count and to play dominoes is here relegated once
more to the animal kingdom. Like all good fables, beasts and humans
have swapped places, turning the world upside down. This kind of inversion is no idle or ironic anthropomorphism, but a serious strategy for
reimagining the shared history of people and beasts in the Victorian age.
Like other animal narratives, Woolf's *Flush* evokes "a random movement
through a diverse world—a movement by means of which imaginary
animals create the opportunity for human speculation about boundary,
diversity, and transcendence"; so too, "they lead the reader to a critical
view of human-kind and, beyond that, to the contemplation of another
realm of existence."[8] For all these reasons, Flush's experiences, and the
world of the dog-stealing banditti, lay a special claim on our attention.

We can borrow Flush's story (both as real life and as textual strategy) to take up the challenge of the "animal turn" I have set out in the
introduction, "giving precedence to the animal perspective" in order to
tell a fable about a nineteenth-century world in which neither animals
nor humans quite yet know their place.[9] This approach allows us to re-
imagine the entwined *geography* of these human and nonhuman worlds,

for the *places* of Flush's nightmare ordeal among the dog stealers are central to this story and its significance. Virginia Woolf is keen on her part
to emphasize that this narrative of pet abduction is properly an urban
narrative, a story about the ways in which — again turning the world upside down — London's poor might be understood to exploit the rich, with
Whitechapel or St Giles's preying on the comfortable bourgeoisie of
Wimpole Street and the West End. Susan Squier's excellent analysis of
the sexual politics of Virginia Woolf's London points us in the right direction here. In particular, she alerts us to the symbiotic relationship that
existed between neighbourhoods only apparently worlds apart.[10] "The
terms upon which Wimpole Street lived cheek by jowl with St. Giles's
were well known," as Woolf wrote: "St. Giles's stole what St. Giles's
could; Wimpole Street paid what Wimpole Street must."[11] For Flush and
for bourgeois pet-owners in general, the public city was a place of danger
and anxiety, not simple, confident mastery. London's others, the thieves
and the banditti who shared public space with the bourgeoisie and their
pets, were never in truth very far away. The phenomenon of dog stealing gives us a glimpse therefore not just of human and animal relations,
but also of the complex geographies in which, and by which, relations
between different sets of people in the Victorian city were played out.

While dog stealing was hardly a new phenomenon, it was the spread
of pet ownership among the urban bourgeoisie that called up the opportunities for a crime that so directly attacked bourgeois sensibilities.
Animal-related discourse had certainly always extended to both sentimental and economic relationships, but pet stealing encompassed and
linked the worlds of companionship and commerce.[12] This was, quite
literally, trading in affection. It is easy enough to see why, economically,
such a crime should arise. By the Victorian era, astounding prices, up
to 150*l.*, were paid for breed dogs, particularly fancy dogs like span-
iels, constituting an alluring temptation to men living in a world where
that amount might easily represent several years' wages. The emotional
value of such pets, in any case, might far exceed their sale value: a terrier worth at most 5*s.* might fetch, so it was said, as much as 14*l.* when
ransomed.[13] Dog stealing could thus be a highly profitable business, a
criminal profession or a lucrative sideline for men who might earn a considerable sum by snatching and successfully ransoming a favorite pet.

 The dog stealers' modus operandi was a simple one, as Henry Mayhew informs us, a matter of prowling the metropolis for a likely dog out

in public with its master or mistress, in order to follow it home, and to wait for an opportunity to lure it away with a piece of coarse liver—fried and pulverized, mixed up with tincture or myrrh or opium—or perhaps with a bitch in heat.[14] A few years earlier, the racy London journal *The Town* suggested two alternative, and peculiarly precise, recipes for the "pudding" that dog stealers carried for this purpose: either "a piece of the liver of a bitch killed at a particular time" or, where this could not be obtained (and one presumes that this was a little more likely), "a portion of a bullock's liver, prepared for the purpose of being boiled with a red herring."[15] Picturing the "dog nipper" as a representative London character or type (figure 4), *The Town* portrays "nippering" or dognapping as something of a modern, metropolitan art:

> The *nipper* generally has a *pal,* who accompanies him with a piece of baize, for the purpose of covering the dog as soon as *nippered.* If a lady is walking along with a pet spaniel of value, attached to a string, one of the *nippers* dexterously contrives to cut the string, while his pal picks the dogs up and pops the baize over it, walking slowly onward; they never turn back, because they know how natural it is for persons to look behind for a dog. When the animal is secured, their business is to look out for the *chaunt* (*i.e.* advertisement;) when this appears, if they do not consider the reward liberal, they send a dog or two similar to the one described, to tantalize the parties, and to induce them to offer a further reward. If the dog be a favourite, this plan sometimes succeeds, and then they set to work to steal it for a second time. Wherever a good reward is given for its restoration, the animal is sure to be *nippered* again.[16]

Mayhew's great survey of London trades, licit and illicit, describes in similar terms the practice of a typical "lurker" by the name of "Chelsea George," who was said to clear 150*l.* yearly through his dog-stealing activities:

> Chelsea George caresses every animal who seems "a likely spec," and when his fingers have been rubbed over the dogs' noses they become easy and perhaps willing captives. A bag carried for the purpose, receives the victim, and away goes George, bag and all, to his printer's in Seven Dials. Two bills

Figure 4. "The Dog Nipper," *The Town* 51, 19 May 1838,
1. (Reproduced by permission of the British Library)

and no less—two and no more, for such is George's style of
work—are issued to describe the animal that has thus been
found, and which will be "restored to its owner on payment of
expenses." One of these George puts in his pocket, the other
he pastes up at a public-house whose landlord is "fly" to its
meaning, and poor "bow-wow" is sold to a "dealer in dogs,"

not very far from Sharp's alley. In course of time the dog is discovered; the possessor refers to the "establishment" where he bought it; the "dealer makes himself *square*," by giving the address of "the chap he bought 'un of," and Chelsea George shows a copy of the advertisement, calls in the publican as a witness, and leaves the place "without the slightest imputation on his character."[17]

The dog stealer was always hidden in this way behind the figure of the "restorer" or go-between who offered to help return the stolen dog. In this connection, Elizabeth Barrett's "Mr. Taylor," resident of Manning Street, Edgware Road, or of Shoreditch, or perhaps of Paddington, crops up time and time again in police and parliamentary reports on the dog-stealing trade. An owner of a Scotch terrier eventually restored for 4*l.* was referred to this same Mr. Taylor, who is said to have replied, "with surprising familiarity," "Ah, and you have got a valuable greyhound; I heard a man say he should have that too before long." Nominally a shoemaker, this Mr. Taylor was only the most notorious associate of the numerous thieves said to exist in places as far apart as Bayswater, Bethnal Green, Paddington, and Hammersmith.[18] The Metropolitan Police Report for 1837 identified as many as 141 dog stealers in the capital, of whom 45 lived wholly by the trade, 48 augmenting their ostensible occupations, and 48 being associates.[19] The corresponding figures for stolen and lost dogs, with prosecutions and convictions, for 1841–43 are given in the same report, and reproduced by Henry Mayhew (see table).

According to estimates provided by William Bishop, the Bond Street gun maker, dog fancier, and champion of a society formed for the prosecution of dog stealers and their confederates, up to July 1844 there were

Metropolitan Police: Recorded incidents relating to dog-stealing

	Dogs stolen	*Dogs lost*	*Persons convicted*	*Persons discharged*	*Persons charged*
1841	43	521	51	19	32
1842	54	561	45	17	28
1843	60	606	38	18	20

Source: Mayhew, *London Labour,* 1968 edition, 50.

151 known victims of the dog stealers, 62 of whom had paid out ransoms in 1843 and the first half of 1844. These persons altogether had paid the dog stealers nearly a thousand pounds at an average of 6*l.* 10*s.* each. From these same figures, Mayhew listed 36 specially prominent individuals who had paid 438*l.* 5*s.* 6*d.*, an average of upwards of 12*l.* each, and he suggested that over 2,000*l.* a year was pocketed by the fifty or sixty professional dog stealers in the city. These dog stealers' victims included such illustrious names as the Honorable William Ashley, Sir Francis Burdett, the Duke of Cambridge, Sir Richard Peel, and the French ambassador for good measure. The dog stealers were clearly no respecters of titles or status, as this account of the future solicitor-general attests:

> One of the coolest instances of the organization and boldness of the dog-stealers was in the case of Mr. Fitzroy Kelly's "favorite Scotch terrier." The "parties," possessing it through theft, asked 12*l.* for it, and urged that it was a reasonable offer, considering the trouble they were obliged to take. "The dog-stealers were obliged to watch every night," they contended[,] . . . "and very diligently; Mr. Kelly kept them out very late from their homes, before they could get the dog; he used to go out to dinner or down to the Temple, and take the dog with him; they had a deal of trouble before they could get it." So Mr. Kelly was expected not only to pay more than the value of his dog, but an extra amount on account of the care he had taken of his terrier, and for the trouble his vigilance had given to the thieves![20]

There were several things that were specially striking about dog stealing as a criminal activity. The first was its apparent professionalism and organization: even if we may reasonably doubt the account of the London dog stealers as a "regularly constituted club," with their own office and secretary, the sense that this was a systematic attack on bourgeois property and propriety is notable, befitting Elizabeth Barrett's banditti or "confederacy" of dog stealers.[21] This professionalism extended to the surveillance of bourgeois homes with valuable pets, a neat reversal of the usual relation between the bourgeoisie and the city's poor. As in the case of Fitzroy Kelly, Elizabeth Barrett's home was reported to have been watched for some time before Flush was first snatched. Furthermore, the role of the go-between, and "the burlesque dignities of mediation" that went with it, to use Robert Browning's words, meant that men like Taylor were virtually immune from prosecution.[22] Few observers failed to comment on the ingenious and alarming system of extortion that was the result:

> Obviously there is great art in dog stealing. The skulking vag-
> abonds whom one meets in the streets, carrying puppies under
> their arms, are too clever for the general public. They belong
> to a society. If they sell a dog, they know how to regain it in
> less than a month. They suffer a sufficient interval to elapse for
> the owner to become attached to his purchase, and then the dog
> is safely lodged at the office of some "society." In due time the
> inevitable advertisement appears, the reward is secured, and
> the dog is returned. . . . Thus we see how it is that people gain a
> livelihood by dogs. They are perpetually on the lookout for fa-
> vourable specimens of that interesting tribe. They know exactly
> when a handsome dog may be picked up at any moment.[23]

Dog stealing was in this way portrayed as a direct attack on the home, with the Englishman's castle not only under surveillance by the dog stealers, but ultimately invaded by the impudent "restorer" when he came to negotiate the agreed ransom:

> We are compelled thus, for the restoration of our property,
> to admit into our confidence the most notorious thieves in
> the metropolis, who, by adventitious circumstances, gain an
> entrance at all times into the houses of the wealthy, rendering
> their victims perfectly defenceless and subservient to their will;
> whilst they practice the most glaring extortion and cruelty,
> over which the police, the *protectors* of the public, declare they
> have no control.[24]

The second notable element was the viciousness, implied or actual, of the dog stealers' trade. As well as Elizabeth Barrett's story "of a lady . . . having her dog's head sent to her in a parcel," we might note the experience of a Miss Mildmay whose dog was threatened with ill treatment if she did not pay a ransom of 6*l.*, or the Miss Brown of Bol-ton Street who came "in great terror" to William Bishop saying that "to have the poor dumb animal's throat cut was a very frightful affair," and who was supposed to have subsequently quitted the country as a result.[25] Such casual cruelty was visited in cases like these on women made vulnerable precisely by their acknowledged capacity for emotion and tenderness, and on their dogs too, themselves noted for their loyalty and nobility.[26] It is not hard to see why the dog stealers came to be so reviled.

The class and even racial significance of dog stealing ought also to be immediately evident. The 1840s were revolutionary times, of course, and, as markers of class distinction, pets were functional to the symbolic economy of the bourgeois city. The dog stealers in their turn figured equally as a class enemy and as an alien threat—thus, note Barrett's use of the words "banditti" or "philistines" when referring to these representatives of London's criminal underworld.[27] Dog stealing may be taken to represent the specter of class conflict, something that the relationship between Wimpole Street and Whitechapel also suggested forcefully. We might also see, in the whole dreadful business, the threat of regression as well as revolution, for if Turner is right to argue that compassion for animals "quelled the fears of man's bestial past" and "served as an emblem of the heart and an example to the human race," so that kindness to animals was the sine qua non of civilization itself, then dog stealing threatened to take this civility away and bring to the surface the tensions induced by human kinship with animals.[28] Dog stealing ultimately registered the inversion of social hierarchies, putting human dependence on animals on trial; people were dominated and exploited through their own affections and sentiments, which could not be excluded wholly from their otherwise rational, modern lives. Dog stealing was a phenomenon that called into question conventional assumptions about human relations with animals; it recognized that, as in Dickens's *Great Expectations*, "the uncivilized may be banished but may return."[29]

Dog stealing, then, was portrayed as systematic, professional, cruel, heartless, and virtually beyond the reach of the law. The *Times* concluded that "in the nature of dog-lifting[,] the 'great fact' which meets the public eye is, that nobody can keep a dog that is worth anything, or for which they can be ascertained to feel any affection." "On this phenomenon of the day," it continued, "policemen, dog-dealers, and the losing public are wholly agreed, and Parliament bestirs itself to probe the evil."[30] As the *Times* noted, the problem was acute enough for Parliament to sanction a Select Committee to consider changing the law to make it more effective in combating the dog stealers. One of the major obstacles here, however, was that it was not at all clear what *kind* of crime dog stealing actually was, and the ineffectiveness of the existing law resulted precisely from this legal ambiguity. The whole question turned on the difficult problem, in English law, as to the value of dogs as *property*.[31] Given a dog's liability to stray, for instance, in contrast to most other possessions, it was difficult to draw sharp legal distinctions between stealing, receiving, and simply "finding," "lost" dogs. As the Metropolitan Police commissioner Richard Mayne reported to Parliament, "A dog is that sort of animal, allowed such liberty, and that runs about in that kind of way, that he may be enticed away in a manner that no other property can be. It is not possible for a horse or a sheep, or any such animal, to be enticed away like a dog. You do not find them straying about as dogs do."[32] The dog was, as the Radical MP Joseph Hume informed the House of Commons, a very peculiar and ill-defined "species of property."[33] Moreover, it was difficult to assess the *value* of a pet dog. While long-standing tradition insisted that animals were to be understood in terms of their *utility* for human beings, the notion of "aesthetic utility"—pets as sources of pleasure pure and simple—was difficult to reconcile with traditions derived from a more bluffly pragmatic rural society. In this vein, a dog such as a toy spaniel was particularly difficult to justify on grounds of utility alone, all the more so in that it was stereotypically a woman's pet.[34] So while Harriet Ritvo can assert that "nineteenth-century English law viewed animals simply as the property of human owners, only trivially different from less mobile goods," it is clear that there was nothing simple about this.[35] Indeed, whether one could even have dogs as property was a legal problem of some complexity.[36] From Tudor times, certain animals such as dogs, cats, and animals kept for sport, as well as certain types of landed property, were specifically excluded from the larceny statutes and their brutal penalties. Judges predisposed to leniency could propose that certain types of stolen goods, if they could not be undervalued in the defendant's favor, might be taken as formally without value in law.[37] This "strange doctrine of pricelessness," as the legal historian Sir John Baker puts it, was designed to mitigate the rigors of a notoriously vengeful penal code.[38] Scruples over the theft of objects of luxury, things of "pleasure," that is, rather than things of "profit," might be extended even to such items as jewels and banknotes, but the classic examples were birds, hawks, and—especially—hounds.[39] Though this was a legal fiction, and strictly a question of value rather than of property, by the nineteenth century the argument based on lack of utility remained central. Unlike working animals or animals consumed as food, because of their lack of obvious usefulness some dogs were systematically undervalued as property. According to Blackstone, it was a felony to receive any money for the restoration of stolen property; but only animals that served for food were recognized as such, not creatures kept for whim or pleasure. Civil actions for loss were therefore acceptable, but not those for theft. For the rising barrister and future Metropolitan Police commissioner Richard Mayne, it was, as a result, absurdly inconsistent to make dog stealing only a misdemeanor while the taking of rewards for recovery would be a felony subject to the maximum penalty of life transportation.[40]

In the middle of the nineteenth century, however, there were still many who felt that these distinctions made by the law with respect to property remained wise and beneficial, and that to alter them would be a bad day for criminal jurisprudence. They felt, for instance, that to add to the felony statutes was inappropriate given the nature and worth of the animals involved, and also because such a move was contrary to the reforming spirit of the age. In the debate over the proposed dog-stealing bill, the Liberal MP for Kinsale objected to a sentence of up to eighteen months "even if a person stole all the dogs in England."[41] Another MP pointedly asked why dogs should be singled out for special treatment: "A person did not commit felony by stealing a ferret or any such animal," he noted, "and he would wish to know what distinction could be drawn between a favourite cat and a favourite dog, that would justify them in making the stealing of one a larceny, while the stealing of the other was not larceny."[42]

The dog bill's supporters did their best to assert the unique honor of the canine tribe. First of all, they argued, the distinction based on utility was misleading, because dogs may be said to be equally as useful as those animals who provide food for human beings. The promoter of the bill, H. T. Liddell, pointed to the example of drovers' dogs, watchdogs, and sheepdogs. Secondly, the definition based on utility was represented as deeply unsatisfactory. The bill's antagonist, Joseph Hume, taking a strict stand on the principle of utility, would, as the *Times* noted, "by the same rule, license a thief to take a lady's necklace, whilst he protected her watch because it told her the time of day."[43] Finally, it was argued, dogs ought to be recognized, irrespective of these legal niceties, as the valuable property they clearly were for the benefit of the Exchequer, and thus deserving of the protection of the law: one letter writer thus insisted that "those who indulge their fancy by keeping dogs pay a heavy tax to

Government for that indulgence, and I cannot see why they are not to be equally protected as horses, or any other property which we may keep for our pleasure or amusement."[44] The resulting *Report from the Select Committee on Dog Stealing* similarly based its arguments on the intrinsic worth of dogs that might, in the case of a beautiful spaniel, fetch a hundred guineas on the open market: "However extravagant these prices may appear, Your Committee conceive that the value of any description of property must be measured by the price which such property will fetch in the market."[45]

The irony here, in that this reliance on market valuation mirrors the free trade in affections so complained of in the practice of the dog stealers, is nowhere apparent to the bill's authors: the argument is simply deployed to the effect that any doubts as to dogs being valuable *property*, in the legal sense, should be removed. Crucially, the Home Secretary, Sir James Graham, was won over by these arguments, straightforwardly insisting that "the possession of a dog was a possession recognised in law."[46] Graham likewise noted the absurd legal anomaly by which an offender might be transported for stealing a collar, as a felony, but not for stealing the dog that wore it: "A very short time ago, the penalty of death was attached to the larceny of a sheep; and it was now transportation for life. The same state of the law applied, he believed, to the stealing of a jackass: and he would wish to know why they were to transport a person for life for stealing a jackass, or for seven years for stealing a dog-collar worth 7*s.* 6*d.*, while no indictment could be preferred for stealing a dog worth 20*l.* and upwards?"[47]

The dog-stealing bill duly passed into law in 1845 (8 & 9 Vict., c. 47). Dogs were now clearly identifiable as property, and offenders could be visited with the full rigor of the law, with the hitherto untouchable receivers now liable to punishment for misdemeanor.[48] This seemed to be effective enough in curbing their depredations. Though the *Times* continued to report dog-stealing cases throughout the nineteenth century, Mayhew could report at mid-century that while "there might still be a little doing in the 'restoring' way . . . it was a mere nothing to what it was formerly," with only some half a dozen Londoners remaining in the professional dog-stealing line.[49] Mayhew was premature to consider the practice moribund: there is no doubt that dog stealing continued, as it still does.[50] But even if legislation did not mean the end of the dog stealers, what the Act accomplished was the decisive recognition that domestic dogs were *private property* and should be valued as such. Furthermore, this brought with it the important corollary that dogs in *public* should be identified as ideally *belonging* to someone. The older doctrine of "stray" animals being a kind of *common property* had to give way, in order to protect the owners of domestic "pets." The doggerel of the *Illustrated London News*, celebrating the passing of the dog bill as well as poking fun at the lawmakers who had spent parliamentary time on the cause, noted in passing this change:

> And idle dogs that go astray,
>> Must all go home, says "Solon";
> For though they may have stolen away,
>> They never can be stolen![51]

The attempt to combat dog stealing was thus aligned with the other forces of cultural domestication in Victorian Britain, working to take dogs off the streets and to install them in proper homes. We shall trace the significance of this public/private distinction at length in the rest of this book, but it is worth underlining the principles of the cultural geography that the country's lawmakers had created. By emphasizing the pet dog's status as *property*, its place in public, paradoxically perhaps, became ever more precarious.

While the essentials of the problem are easy enough to sketch in, dog stealing cannot be fully understood without appreciating this wider cultural geography. We should remember that the principal *spaces* with which the crime of dog stealing was concerned were the private spaces of the *home*, from whose protection pet dogs were abducted, and the *public* spaces in which they were most vulnerable. These were not, of course, the rigidly separated spheres of Victorian bourgeois ideology. However much they tried, the bourgeoisie could never prevent these spaces from mixing and merging. Nor could it be the case that the domestic sphere allowed the pressures of the market economy to be temporarily suspended and provisionally resolved.[52] As the literary critic Jeff Nunokawa has astutely emphasized, the zones of circulation associated with the public world of the marketplace were intimately connected to the zones of possession associated with the home.[53] Property, being ephemeral and vulnerable, flew in the face of the protocols of propriety that the Victorians taught as the virtue of the home. The domestic sphere, in other words, was never a refuge from the market, as the Victorians liked to imagine.

It was both a prop to the workings of the public world of men and the market place, and constantly, necessarily, infused with the values of the market economy. The concept of domestic security, presided over by the female "angel of the house," was nothing more than an elaborate ideological fiction that attempted to shield the Victorian bourgeois imagination from the forces of commodification associated with the world of property.[54] Domesticity was a decisively *gendered* discourse that marked out a particular bourgeois world that stood for values *beyond* price, at the same time as it was constantly shot through and threatened by a world in which everything was shown to have a market value. Dog stealing brought both this threat to domestic virtues, and the exposure of the market value of domesticity, uncomfortably and cruelly to the surface: it testified to the vulnerability of domestic property and the siege mentality that characterized the Victorian discourse of domesticity. As Nunokawa puts it, resonantly, "Everywhere the shades of the countinghouse fall upon the home."[55]

The gendered nature of the parliamentary debate about dog stealing is particularly revealing of these ambiguities surrounding the issues of domesticity, utility, and property. While supporters of the dog-stealing bill did their best to pose the problem as an outrage against *men's* property, with Liddell insisting that "no man's dog was safe a moment—and the more valuable it was the more certain it was to be stolen," the bill's opponents were quick to express their reservations about legislating in what they presented as the realm of womanly sentimentality.[56] In a general chorus of resentment at the ridiculousness of extending protection "to the poodles and lap-dogs of the metropolis," unsympathetic MPs insisted that dog stealing was already punishable by fine, imprisonment, and whipping, "and surely that was enough to protect the pug-dogs of the old ladies of England."[57] Dog stealing was difficult to combat, then, precisely because the question of property, founded on the principle of utility, was preeminently a gendered issue.[58] This was not simply because lapdogs, the most "useless" and vulnerable of pets, typically belonged to women. More than this, the association of non-useful animals with women confined to the house as domestic essence and ornament was particularly telling.[59]

The bourgeois ideal of domesticity, so crucial to constructions of femininity, was at the center of these concerns. Indeed, the link between the ideal of domesticity and the highly charged social-symbolic process of animal domestication deserves to be underscored.[60] The keeping of dogs as pets was a powerful emblem of this domestic ideology, as we have seen. The dog was regarded as instinctively understanding the concept of "family," and the pet dog became part of a household whose domestic geography was central to its sense of security. What is more, we may note again the attempted removal of animals such as dogs from the public spaces of the city to the domestic confines of the bourgeois home. Pet dogs became more important in the city as an object of non-utilitarian "fancy," far removed from the canine working classes of the countryside, but just as important is the fact that the working dogs of the city increasingly disappeared from view. London's dog carts, for instance, were banned in 1840 after considerable lobby arising from anti-cruelty sensibilities and from a concern with urban nuisances and sanitation (figure 5).[61]

Ironically, and despite the portrayal of canine celebration, this meant the destruction of many of London's working dogs: one publication from 1882 looked back on the fact that dogs were killed by the very act of Parliament meant to rescue them—"Within a month there was scarcely one of these useful dogs to be seen in the streets of London."[62] Dogs came off public, working streets, in other words, and into the bosom of the bourgeois home in the explicitly "useless" form of "pets." Those that did not—street dogs and strays, for instance—were increasingly regarded as out of place and ultimately disposable, as the following chapter will elaborate. This process closely paralleled the removal of other animals from the city streets to specialized and marginalized spaces—meat markets and slaughterhouses, for instance—except in this case the business of animal removal is a quite literal process of "domestication."[63]

Once more, in the "bourgeoisification" of dogs we can see a specific geography of exclusion and inclusion to set against the ancient histories of animal domestication. Dog stealing clearly threatened the domestic security of the household and its property. But it did much more than this: by actively trading on the sentiments of the household, and particularly those of its female members, dog stealing *reconnected* the geographies of sentiment and economy that Victorian bourgeois ideology attempted, through its public/private and masculine/feminine distinctions, to hold apart. Dog stealing was an innately vicious response to the effects of the practical and ideological separation of these geographies. The reversal of bourgeois polarities—the servility and subordination of the owner forced to pay a ransom for his or her dog's restoration, the passivity and helplessness of an owner held to ransom by his or her own sentimental attachments to a "useless" pet—was desperately cutting. It left the owner,

Figure 5. "No Dog Carts." (Source: E. C. Ash, *This Doggie Business,* opposite
p. 74; reproduced by kind permission of the Syndics of Cambridge University
Library)

whether male or female, in the "feminine" role associated with emotion,
attachment, and tender-heartedness. That is why both Robert Browning and the men of the Barrett household advised Elizabeth to defy the
demands of the dog stealers, this representing a "manly" refusal to parlay
that would put an end to the endless cycle of ransom and abduction. Dog
stealing, moreover, put a price on things—sentiments, attachments, domestic companionship—that should have no price. As a leading article in
the *Times* put it in reference to a stolen dog that might be valuable either
in monetary or emotional terms, such a dog "may be the companion for
years, which are not to be calculated by the rule of 'Just so much as it
will bring in market overt.'"[64] The *legal* fiction of pricelessness, which
shielded the dog stealers and their trade, was matched by an equivalent
domestic fiction that both made the trade possible and prompted bourgeois outrage. A correspondent to the *Times* summed up the problem
succinctly:

> Of all the combinations of rascals which infest this mighty city,
> there is not one, in my opinion, more hateful than the dog-
> stealer. Other thieves take our property,—these rob us of our
> friends. . . . They make trade of our affections. They take from
> us one whose good qualities we should be happy to recognize
> in many of our human friends; and they compel us to a course
> of sordid bargaining with a knife at our favourite's throat.[65]

That this is a thoroughly gendered question, shot through with the bourgeois ideal of domestic womanhood, is made plain by the parliamentary
Report: "A worse plan could not be laid, even to set fire to premises, than
is laid to get possession of dogs, such as pet dogs belonging to ladies."[66]

What made dog stealing such a dreadful activity, we might thus
conclude, was that it mixed up in a peculiarly outrageous way, for the
connected norms of gender and class, the worlds of sentiment and the
market, the private and the public worlds. The central problem was
putting a price on love and affection, forcing the owners to assess the
monetary value of a pet to them and to their families. In Flush's case,
Elizabeth Barrett fiercely rebuked Robert Browning for advising defi-
ance of the dog-stealers and their demands, arguing to him that "[a] man
may love justice intensely; but the love of an abstract principle is not
the strongest love—now is it?"[67] Stealing dogs put that "feminine," emotional argument dramatically to the test, revealing pets to their bourgeois
owners as a special form of property rather than just innocent domestic
companions. The phenomenon of dog stealing revealed nothing less than
the boundaries of an affective or sentimental economy in which capitalism and culture were complexly intertwined. Things that were not supposed to be valued in monetary terms could be revealed as intimately
penetrated by market values, so that the simple domestication of animals
could act as a marker of the terrible vulnerability of the domestic realm
to the public world of cash, commerce, and calculation.

The most critical aspect of this penetration of the values of the market
into the very world that was supposed to be shielded from it is arguably
the position of women within a patriarchal society. Dog stealing dis-
closed not just the absence of domestic security but also the ambivalent
status of women within that household, a status that women shared with
their pets.[68] Squier in this regard has amply demonstrated the elision in
Victorian society of women and their pets, both of whom were "routinely
relegated to a marginal position in modern urban society."[69] For Squier,

in direct reference to Woolf's *Flush: A Biography,* Elizabeth Barrett and her dog were alike victims of a patriarchal society that confined them to a suffocating domestic captivity. The removal from Wimpole Street, in Flush's case involuntarily, and in Barrett's case firstly in the daring expedition to the dog stealers' Whitechapel lair and secondly in the escape from the Barrett household altogether, takes on signal power accordingly. Of course this is why the escape to Italy, for both Flush and Elizabeth Barrett Browning, is so significant. Italy—Shelley's "Paradise of exiles"—represented a breakout from the confining class, gender, and racial oppressions of Victorian London. Flush, in Italy, is shorn of his coat, a Paradise for fleas as well as an unnecessary burden given the climate, but he is also divested of his "aristocratic" pedigree, and all the classed and racialized fantasies of breeding and superiority. Freed from dog stealers and from patriarchal tyranny alike, he, like Elizabeth Barrett Browning, and like her great creation Aurora Leigh, is given access to a new type of city life: democratic, affective, "marked by equality between genders and classes."[70] Ironically, in the home of the real banditti, in a land of mongrels, there was nothing to be feared from dog stealers. Without domestic oppression, the menace of the dog stealer simply melts away. As Flush himself realizes, "Where were chains now? . . . Gone, with the dog-stealers. . . . He was the friend of all the world now. All dogs were his brothers. He had no need of a chain in this new world; he had no need of protection."[71]

Flush's capture by the dog stealers betrays not only the vulnerability of the Barretts' domestic refuge in Wimpole Street, but also the symbiotic male domination of Mr. Taylor's den of brutal banditti and the Barrett household itself. As Virginia Woolf points out, in Florence there were no dog stealers—and no fathers either.[72] For Elizabeth, the abduction of Flush may be taken to speak to her own domestic circumstances quite directly: "The Whitechapel episode is a temptation scene; forced to choose between winning the approval of her male counterparts and saving Flush, Barrett is also being asked, symbolically, to choose between two systems of morality—one masculine and impersonal, the other feminine and personal."[73] That Barrett chooses to ransom her pet dog, whatever the cost, is thus of tremendous personal and political significance. Since "Flush's value to patriarchal society is analogous to women's value," the message of the dog-stealing episode was that women, like pets, are worth only what their masters will assign to them; and it is this realization that connects the serio-comic *Flush* with the gravitas of a feminist epic like Barrett Browning's *Aurora Leigh*, preoccupied as it is with the victimization of women within Victorian society.[74]

To those who might still cavil at regarding dog stealing as a feminist issue, we can point to a painting by the genre and animal painter Briton Riviere—in his day regarded as second only to Landseer—entitled *Temptation* (1879), in which the dog stealers' challenge to domesticity, and the concession of the vulnerability of property, domestic security, and even woman's virtue, are neatly illustrated (figure 6). This painting captures the key moment before the abduction of a prized spaniel. In the words of one critic, "An untrustworthy-looking individual is trying to win the confidence of a King Charles Spaniel with a seductive bit of liver. The drama is unfinished. Whether fidelity or gourmandise will turn out the stronger passion we can only guess."[75]

In this picture, the open doorway to an otherwise solidly prepossessing domestic fortress represents the ideological fiction of domestic security.[76] The ragged "lurker" preys upon the dog's trusting affections, one hand offering temptation, the other poised to grab his quarry and thrust it into his coat pocket. And the dog, with its bow, is clearly feminized, both in reference to its position as a lapdog and in its possession by a doting mistress. There are few better illustrations of the vulnerability of property and the siege mentality of the Victorian bourgeoisie. It is not difficult, moreover, to read the painting as denoting dog stealing but connoting sexual temptation and the vulnerability of domestic female virtue. A picture like *Temptation*, with its resonant title, and its emphasis on the fragility of domestic security, points in fact to two forms of patriarchal tyranny. We have here a fable of woman and pet caught between two worlds—the private space of the domestic hearth, and the public space of the streets and the criminal underworld.[77] There is a political geography to dog stealing, therefore, not just in the exploitation of the rich by the poor, of Wimpole Street by Whitechapel, but also because the geography of bourgeois domesticity cannot be divorced from the domination inherent in the gendered geography of "domestication" itself.

Few would in fact disagree that domestication is closely related to several strands of domination in these ways. For Ritvo, the Victorian age marked the working out of "a fundamental shift in the relationship between humans and their fellow creatures, as a result of which people systematically appropriated power they had previously attributed to animals, and animals became significant primarily as the objects of hu-

Figure 6. Briton Riviere, *Temptation,* 1879. (Private collection; from David Hancock, "In Cavalier Style," *Dogs Monthly* 16, no. 9 [1998]: 10–13, 11.)

man manipulation."[78] But "domestication" is hardly confined to human-animal relations alone: relations of domination are also evident in the "domestication" of human beings. Adrienne Munich comments in this vein that women and servants (including non-Europeans) were similarly patronized and domesticated, victims of a sadoerotic kind of power that reduced humans to the status of "pets."[79] And the cultural geographer Yi-Fu Tuan makes this same point most insistently, by extending the definition of "pets" from animals to people and even to landscapes.[80] But if affection and domestication are linked, in this *geography* of domesticated nature, then dog stealing cannot be seen simply in terms of criminal opportunism and bourgeois vulnerability. Flush's horrible experiences point, as several critics have noted, to victimization at the hands of the dog stealers *and* in the protective space of the bourgeois home from which he was abducted. The equation of dog stealers and domestic tyrants is indeed central to Woolf's biography of Flush, and it should make us pause when considering the ultimate significance of dog stealing. The invalid Elizabeth Barrett in Wimpole Street was as much a hostage as poor Flush in Whitechapel. If dogs like Flush are vulnerable in public spaces when off the leash, their chains forgotten in a moment of woman's weakness, as Woolf points out, so are women let out into the public space of the streets largely under the restrictions of propriety and fear. Woolf's *Flush* is abundantly illustrative of how an instinctive love of freedom can be turned in patriarchal society to domestic anxiety and confinement: these are the lessons of Victorian bourgeois morality.[81] Just as Whitechapel and Wimpole Street are connected, just as the geographies of affection and commerce are inseparable, just as property and propriety are linked in zones of circulation and possession, so too in a terrible way is the dog stealer revealed as an *associate* rather than an antagonist of the bourgeois patriarch. Dog stealing is not (just) an attack on the home; it might be taken to actively bolster domestic ideology, acting to usher women, like pets, to the safety and security of the household. Flush's brutal transportation from domestic hearth to criminal rookery is a challenge to the moral geography of the bourgeoisie specifically in the ideal of domesticity for which pets were such potent symbols. The phenomenon of dog stealing tested the limits to this domestication, revealing the vulnerability and ambiguity of the bourgeois domestic world by putting a price on its interior world of affection and sentiment, and by revealing the patriarchal domination at the heart of both the domestication of animals and the ideal of domesticity itself.

CHAPTER 3

Finding a Forever Home?

The Home for Lost and Starving Dogs

ATTERSEA DOGS' HOME is the oldest and most famous animal rescue charity in the world. Founded in late 1860 in the mazy north London backstreets of Holloway, by the equally obscure Mary Tealby, the advent of the "Temporary Home for Lost and Starving Dogs" was greeted with derision. The *Times*, commenting acidly on the fashion for providing "homes" for ever-proliferating categories of the "homeless," still "expected that human benevolence would have its limits, and that those limits would be marked somewhere within the regions of humanity, as far as mere sentimental interference was concerned." Why should there not be a home for rats, it wondered?[1] Others asked—missing the point still further—why not a home for lost and starving elephants?[2] The familiar objections against animal welfare were trotted out early on: the investigative journalist James Greenwood recalled that "people shook their head and sneeringly demanded to be informed whether the last little boy or girl had been fished out of the kennel to which the vice or poverty of its parents had consigned it—whether it had been set on its little legs, and cleansed and clothed, and sent to school, and permanently provided for,—that these humanitarians felt at liberty to extend a succouring hand to mangy little puppy dogs and prowling curs generally orphaned and in distress."[3] For such critics, the prior claims of humanity—always, inevitably, unmet—precluded the extension of humanitarian concern even to those "closest" and most "domestic" of companions.[4]

Clearly, the charity needed all the friends it could get, and the Dogs'

Home has made much of its debt to Charles Dickens for his early, generous, far-sighted support, rising far above the prejudices of the day.[5]
As we have seen, this attribution is mistaken, but the argument for the
power of sentiment is still significant. To John Hollingshead, the real author of "Two Dog Shows," the idea that anyone could have dreamed up
such an institution—one of the "queerest" in the metropolis—was both
curious and charming: "An institution in this practical country founded
on a sentiment . . . I think it is rather hard to laugh this humane effort to
scorn."[6] It bears repeating that the Dogs' Home is described as "evidence
of that hidden fund of feeling which survives in some hearts even the
rough ordeal of London life in the nineteenth century."[7] It is as though
the boosters of the Home had tapped into an aquifer of kindness and generosity lying not too far beneath the hard asphalt of the city's streets.

The *domestic* ethos of the new enterprise was always central to its reception. As Hilda Kean has remarked, it was of crucial importance that the
new charity was promoted as a "Home," with its constellation of reassuringly familial references: "The status of dogs was inextricably linked
with the respectable family. A home was simply the dogs' proper place."[8]
The Home was largely taken on its own terms, as a domestic refuge for
the "homeless" dog. In an early encomium, for instance, Ireland's *Freeman's Journal* set out the aim of the Home as follows: "This valuable asylum is intended for the reception of eratic [*sic*] members of the canine
family who have been unfortunate enough either to have strayed from
home or who have been banished by cruel and unfeeling masters."[9] It
was portrayed elsewhere as a "refuge for canine wanderers" and a "comfortable house of accommodation."[10]

   The Dogs' Home may therefore be aligned with the host of philanthropic institutions—rescue homes, refuges, reformatories—that sprung
up in mid-Victorian Britain, all designed to reclaim and re-domesticate
their inmates. Grace Moore has made a particular identification of the
work of the Home with the Magdalens for penitent women; and although the specific link with Dickens, and with Urania Cottage, is spurious, some kind of general association with reformatories is plausible
enough.[11] In these spaces, a moral transformation was to be effected,
taking the distressed poor, those at the margins of the social body, and
returning them to a life of respectability. The Dogs' Home, at least in
its public promotion, was the "animal equivalent" of such philanthropic
ventures.[12] In one of the very earliest of its appeals to subscribers, for in-

stance, one of the Home's supporters emphasized the domestic character of the dog. Unlike the rat or the wild elephant, the dog's unblemished history of companionship and its unconditional acceptance of the household hierarchy made it the fitting object of such a charity:

> Surely no one will venture to deny that the dog deserves this care at our hands, for, of all animals in the creation, the dog, I think, may unhesitatingly be pronounced the most domestic, the most intelligent, and the most exclusively devoted to man. He is entirely dependent upon us, and gives up his whole life, with all its energies and all its instincts, to our service. His master possesses his whole heart. He attaches himself with the most unselfish love to him and to his family, and treats all others with the utmost indifference, unless so far as he discovers them to be enemies of his master, and then his indifference is immediately changed into the most active and aggressive hostility. No other animal so entirely deserts all other society, even that of his own species, for the society of his master: be that master who or what he may, a king or a beggar, happy or miserable, kind or cruel, it is enough for this affectionate animal to know that he is his master, and no change of circumstances will affect his fidelity, no neglect will alienate his love, no cruelty will drive him from him.[13]

What is more, the dog *instinctively* understood and valued the home, household, and family. In contrast to, say, Dickens's Tattycoram, there was no resentment at being taken up and patronized, no shame in being an object of charity, or a second-class member of the family. Deprived of the loving protection the family offered, the dog was doomed to either slow starvation or sharp abuse—the victim of vicious street boys and their casual cruelties. The naturalist William Kidd thus proposed the Dogs' Home as the solution to the problem of the street dog: "These poor wanderers are, for the most part, homeless, and in a state of semi-starvation," he wrote, picturing the arrival of the dog at the Home in terms of becoming "a member of this happy family." The reward for humankind was the sight of "numberless happy (and funny) dogs, their funny (and happy) tails wagging in endless gratitude and glee for the liberality bestowed upon their ill-used race."[14]

The contrast between the homeless dog of the streets and the happy intimate of the Home is perfectly brought out in the work of the artist John Charles Dollman, who visited the Dogs' Home in or around 1875, soon after it had removed to Battersea. Dollman's pathetic portrayal of a street tyke, "supported by voluntary contributions," as one of his prints has it (figure 7), may be juxtaposed with the loving tenderness shown by the keeper and his daughter toward the dogs exercising in the yard at the Battersea Home (figure 8).

Figure 7. John Charles Dollman, "Supported by Voluntary Contributions," *Illustrated London News*, 15 December 1875, 20. (Reproduced by kind permission of the Syndics of Cambridge University Library)

Figure 8. John Charles Dollman, "The Dogs' Home," *Pictorial World,* 27 February 1875, 522. (Author's collection)

The street dog, deprived of the comforts of home, is portrayed as paradoxically behind bars in the public streets—a prisoner of want and neglect and abuse. This argument is made quite explicit by the supporters of the Home, as the words of the RSPCA member quoted above make clear: "I feel sure that not one of the readers of this pamphlet, if he knew that a poor little dog was deserted and shut up in an empty house, without the possibility of obtaining food, would refuse to rescue it. He may rest assured that the lost dog, though having all London to wander about in, is as effectually starved to death, and that too with the constant sight of food before his eyes, as if he were in the condition of that shut up prisoner."[15] The Dogs' Home, in this vision, offered the lost or abandoned animal nothing less than salvation—a new life with a new family, in (to use the parlance of contemporary rehoming institutions) a "forever home."

It is worth reminding ourselves, however, what kind of a "home" this was, and just who these "homeless" dogs were. This was not a *rest* home, of either the short-term or the permanent variety; to give a parallel example of Victorian animal welfare, the Home of Rest for Horses, founded in 1886, started as a "rest cure" for overworked dray horses, subsequently morphing into a "retirement" home in more recent times. By contrast, the Holloway, later Battersea, institution was always intended as a *temporary* home for lost and starving dogs, as its full title reminds us. The secretary James Johnson early on drew the public's attention to the specific remit of the Home: "The Committee are anxious to impress upon the public the fact that this institution is not intended to be a permanent home for old and worn out favourites, nor an hospital for the cure of gentlemen's sick dogs, but simply what it professes to be, a place to which humane persons may send really homeless and famishing dogs *found in the streets*."[16] The notion of the "homeless" dog was not quite as straightforward a category as it may seem, however. The Dogs' Home was intended for two different and wholly incommensurate categories of dogs. Setting aside an abortive experiment in taking in canine boarders, the Home was aimed at the two distinct classes of "lost" and "starving" dogs. "Lost" dogs—like the pampered Hajjin in Frances Power Cobbe's *Confessions of a Lost Dog* (1867), rescued by the Home and returned to his grateful owner—were those who had strayed or otherwise become separated from their human companions. The Dogs' Home was there to enable owners to quickly locate their domestic companions and "restore" them to their families.[17] On the other hand, the "starving" or "famishing" category denoted the street dwellers who were either more or less feral or more or less abandoned by their human "owners" to roam the streets at will. For these dogs, the Home set out either to "rehome" them with suitable human owners, or else to put them out of their misery.

The resulting mixing of classes and categories of dogs is captured again by John Charles Dollman, in his 1879 painting *Table d'Hôte at a Dogs' Home*, which was worked up from earlier engravings (figure 9). The metaphor of the table d'hôte—the bane of the middle-class traveler forced to share a dining table with the hotel's patrons, whatever may be their condition or character—gives Dollman the chance to imaginatively present the various classes of rescued dogs at the feeding trough: from the fancy greyhound and spaniel, too disdainful or polite to tuck in, to the variously proletarian terriers with no such qualms about filling their hungry faces.[18]

The classification of rescued dogs was always imbued in this way with class-consciousness. The ardent professions of the supporters of the Home were one thing—"I may here just make a passing remark, that no distinction is made; every homeless dog, be his race or condition what it may, is received into the Asylum when brought there"—but the practice was always very different, particularly when it came to rehoming rather than admission.[19] Dollman's picture suggests how critical the "class" distinction remained, with "useful" and refined dogs such as the spaniel and the greyhound separated by a kind of "physiognomic determinism" from the rough and savage bulldog.[20] Of course, Dollman's portrayal is heightened and carefully manipulated—but it is in keeping with journalists' accounts of the social organization of the Home.[21] Most of the rescuees were not privileged pets such as Cobbe's Hajjin, but far less respectable "strays." John Hollingshead's "Two Dog Shows," so supportive of the work of the Home, recognizes that its inmates were "not conspicuous in the matter of breed."[22] Like Dickens, Hollingshead was not a sentimentalist, and for all that he acknowledged the declassing and homogenizing effects of poverty and misfortune—the "fellowship of misery"—he emphasized the durable distinctions between "lost" and "starving," as a subsequent essay, "Happy Dogs," makes quite clear:

> It is a melancholy fact, and one not at all peculiar to animals generally, that the most worthless dogs have the largest appetites, and make the most noise. The keeper knows about a dozen of his large-headed, thick-limbed, gaping, shambling pensioners by the title of the "wolves," and, to use his own words, "they are a precious sample." They form the "dangerous classes" of the Refuge; they do nothing but eat and yell, are never likely to be reclaimed, and belong to that family of gift dogs which people never will look in the mouth.[23]

The renowned social investigator James Greenwood also marked the preponderance of the canine poor among the occupants of the Home, reading into the behavior of the animals their background and destiny. In his account of a visit to the Dogs' Home, ethology as well as physiognomy is a basis for classification of the "genuinely lost dog":

> Very many there were—and these the first and most eager to rush to the bars—who barked with a purpose. These, no doubt, were the genuine lost dogs—the animals who somehow or another had lost sight of a well-loved master in the street, and after searching miles and miles, and all round about to find him again, were discovered muddy and miserable, and with

Figure 9. John Charles Dollman, *Table d'Hôte at a Dogs' Home,* 1879. (Courtesy of National Museums Liverpool)

worn and bleeding feet, and conveyed unresisting to the home.
But it is not a question of paunch and kennel with this kind of
dog. Other dogs, contemptible curs, all teeth and belly, may
endeavour to pursuade [*sic*] these honest creatures that nothing can be more foolish than to thrust themselves forward to
be owned out of such snug quarters, retired from the cares and
anxieties of the world, and nothing to do but to eat and sleep;
but the really faithful tyke turns a deaf ear to all such perni-
cious counsel. He has pined for him night and day ever since
he has been an inmate of the Refuge, and whenever he hears
the outer gate slam, his heart is in his mouth lest it should be
he. If one had a clever ear for dog language, he might note the
various emotions that disturb the poor brute by the various
tones in which he utters his "bow-wows." "Bow-wow-wow! I
hear him, I verily believe! It is'nt [*sic*] his footstep exactly, but
perhaps he has come in his slippers! Bow-wo-ow! Ah, no! it
is'nt him, nor anybody I ever recollect seeing with him. Bow-
wo-o-ow! Will he never come and fetch me out of this?"[24]

These "good" dogs may be contrasted with their infectiously vicious
or disreputable peers. For Greenwood, there were some dogs, "with a
dash of better breed" in them, just enough to turn an honest dog's head
"from his proper jog-trot concerns, and set him hankering and wandering after improprieties of the vicious town." Nor are these "misguided"
dogs the worst of it; they are still set apart from the wholly irredeemable street dogs who are *never* to be found in the Home, that is, the "accomplished cadgers" who have the wherewithal to make a living in the
London underworld, presumably somewhere in the vicinity of Dickens's
"Shy Neighbourhoods":

> The dog that does not put in an appearance at the institution
> is the out-and-out gutter-bred street cur. The keeper remarks
> this, and evidently saw something singular in the fact; so do
> not I. I know that dog, and can answer for him that he is the
> artfullest villain that walks on four legs. This is the dog that
> has his regular beat, and attends it with ten times the diligence
> and punctuality of any policeman of the force. He has his
> coffee-shop, where working-men go to breakfast early in the
> morning; he has his public-house tap-room, where working

men dine, to investigate at noon; and come the dusk of evening, he finds leisurely and profitable employment in "snatching" from unguarded butchers' boards and laxly-watched tripe-shops.[25]

Grace Moore insists that Greenwood is here referencing the *prostitutes* of the metropolis, bolstering her thesis on the association between street dogs and "lost" women, but it is clear from the above that these "accomplished cadgers" are habituated rather with the work-shy, casual, undeserving poor, the professionally unemployed, the beggars, and the vagrants.[26] These are the "incorrigibles" who refuse, and are refused in their turn by, Victorian charity. As Seth Koven has noted, the "casual" poor were "literally members of a savage race because they existed outside the seat of domesticating, moralizing, and civilizing influences: the home."[27] The dogs pictured by Greenwood, those that reject home life in preference for the streets, are the exact equivalent of the unsocialized, undomesticated beings that Pamela Gilbert has characterized as *anti-citizens*: "wanderers, without home attachments, and therefore without potential for citizenship."[28]

What is particularly striking, then, is that the inmates of the Dogs' Home were understood via the discursive tropes regarding the *human* vagrant, at a particularly important juncture for Victorian social policy. The work of the Home was never a matter of private charity alone, nor of merely the burgeoning generosity of British sentiment toward animals: it always encompassed the great public questions of political economy and moral reform. Koven has astutely noted that most of the intrepid investigators of the slums should be seen as "urban housekeepers," both thrilled by disorder and desiring a more rigorous policing of the boundaries of private home and public streets.[29] Journalistic visits to the Dogs' Home are surely a direct extension of this social politics of "slumming." They helped make sense of the condition of humanity, just as "slumming" helped to construct the definition and materialization of "society" itself. Anthropocentrism being a two-way street, however, we should not simply read such statements as "really" being about people; rather, they participated in an ongoing discussion about the nature or status of human and animal "vagrants," involving the animalizing of the human as well as the humanizing of the animal. Just so, in George Augustus Sala's "The Key of the Street," the flâneur-narrator takes on the role of a houseless, hopeless vagrant, undergoing a transformation from human to dog: "I feel my feet shuffle, my shoulders rise towards my ears; my head goes on one side; I hold my hands in a crouching position before me; I no longer walk, I prowl."[30] Vagrancy carries with it the taste and the taint of transmogrification, the fear and the thrill of "becoming-animal."[31]

Most important, though, the Dogs' Home's status as an analogue of the institutions designed to remove the indigent poor from the streets of London raises questions about the Home's relationship with the state and with the police. Sala could conceive of the human vagrant "becoming-animal," but he nevertheless insists that the human being was in a *worse* condition than the homeless dog, for the latter will at least not be bothered by the police. Observing a mongrel dog, Sala's vagrant persona remarks:

> I know he is a dog without a bed, like I am, for he has not that
> grave trot, so full of purpose, which the dog on business has.
> This dog wanders irresolutely, and makes feigned turnings up
> by-streets — returning to the main thoroughfare in a slouch-
> ing skulking manner — he ruminates over cigar-stumps and
> cabbage-stalks, which no homeward-bound dog would do.
> But even that dog is happier than I am, for he can lie down
> on any doorstep, and take his rest, and no policeman shall say
> him nay; but the New Police Act won't let me do so, and says
> sternly that I must "move on."[32]

Sala was writing in 1851; a mere decade later, however, with the active assistance of the Dogs' Home, the dog's presence in public space *would* become a matter of government and police, of what Kimberly Smith calls "political rule."[33] What secured the future of the Dogs' Home was the support of the Metropolitan and City police commissioners and the Home Secretary. Koven's observation may then be readily transferred from the human to the animal poor: "Activities that began as forms of charitable slumming now became essential components of the state's apparatus to care for poor citizens."[34]

In one of the first issues of the RSPCA's new monthly, *Animal World*, the relationship between the police and the stray dog population of London is mythologized in the story of "Charlie, the White Sergeant," a stray adopted by the Bow Street police station. Turning up at the doorstep,

refusing to be moved on, and eventually taken in by a kindly policeman, Charlie became a mascot and honorary peeler, rewarding his res-
cuers with years of faithful service. *Animal World* added that "if 'Charlie'
rewarded the humanity of his benefactors, does not his history point a
moral which favorably reflects upon the usefulness of the 'Temporary
Home for Lost and Starving Dogs.' Could he speak, 'Charlie' would be
the first to say that hundreds of equally deserving animals have been
cast upon the streets, and require only the kindly patronage of man to
make them useful and happy."[35] This story puts the happiest and most
sentimental gloss on the relationship of "lost" dogs to the Metropolitan
Police, however. For the most part, dogs did not turn up announced,
demanding to be given a commission; rather, they were rounded up and
reluctantly dragged off the streets (figure 10). This is arguably the most
important element in Victorian society's attempt to remove such animals
from the public sphere and to find them a "proper" place. The vocation
of the Battersea Dogs' Home lay in establishing an enduring relationship
with the Victorian policeman-state in carrying out this project of discipline and domestication.[36]

The problem of the "stray" had in fact exercised the British public for
years, but in the 1860s the most drastic of solutions were being regularly
essayed. "There can hardly be a greater nuisance than the London cur,"
the *Times* opined, nodding once again to the issue of utility, "snapping at
restiff horses, tripping up decrepit foot-passengers, barking at boys with
baskets, pilfering from the counters of provision-shops, and serving no
useful purpose whatever."[37] Changes to the dog tax were proposed as a
solution to the problem, but the tax was blamed by others for leading to
greater numbers of disowned dogs. One correspondent was led to ask,
"Would it be too much to ask that the police should be ordered to destroy all these wild ownerless dogs without waiting for them first to bite
some one?"[38] The Metropolitan Streets Act of 1867 had already empowered police with what the *Times* leader writer called a "despotic jurisdic-
tion over dogs"—allowing the Metropolitan Police to seize, detain, and
destroy, after three days, all apparently ownerless dogs; these powers
were reaffirmed in the Dogs Act of 1871, which extended them to England and Wales, and which added further specification on the treatment
of dangerous and rabid dogs.[39] But the practical implementation of these
powers was a matter of more pressing concern for the police: want of
space at detention centers, the disturbance that these dogs made to the
peace of their neighborhoods, and the offensiveness of these duties to the

Figure 10. "The Home for Lost and Starving Dogs, Battersea—Bringing in a New Comer," *Graphic*, 8 October 1887, 392. (Reproduced by kind permission of the Syndics of Cambridge University Library)

police themselves, all made these measures barely workable, as I shall discuss in a later chapter.[40] In this grave situation, police commissioner Mayne and his City of London counterpart, Lt. Colonel Fraser, desperately sought a partner in the work of clearing the streets of "wretched curs whose seizure is not the most pleasant part of a policeman's work."[41]

Fortuitously, these debates over the problem of the "stray" dog were paralleled by discussions within the Home as to how it might continue its charitable work. From as early as spring 1861, it was clear to all that the Home could not continue as a temporary refuge for "lost" dogs and a rescue center for the "starving." Ever increasing admissions, strictly limited space, and the impossibility of expanding the Home any further in its present location forced the members of the committee to formulate a new set of rules, wholly unenvisaged at its foundation only a few months previously. A new order was brought in, that any dog brought to the Home not identified and claimed within fourteen days from the date of its admission was to be sold to pay expenses, or otherwise disposed of. This was apparently such a radical change that the motion was only passed "with the utmost reluctance on the part of the Ladies present."[42] The Home, which had been begun with Mary Tealby taking in abandoned dogs and nursing them in her own house in Victoria Street, Islington, now committed to a policy by which the unreclaimed were to be sold or, failing that, "otherwise disposed of."

Whatever the qualms of the ladies, the managers of the Home came to an agreement that the Metropolitan Police would bring dogs to Holloway (and subsequently to Battersea) for detention and destruction. Informal assistance to a police campaign of action seems to have been in place in 1869, with the *Luton Advertiser* reporting that "during the five months of the police raid against wandering curs, 12,465 dogs were taken to the 'Home,' where a gentle quietus was administered to the halt, blind, maimed, and diseased; and the rest were either restored to their owners or placed with new ones."[43] The apparent success of this campaign seems to have led to a police order enacted on the 6th of June 1870, by which it was agreed that all stray dogs would from now on be sent to the Dogs' Home. The Metropolitan Police reported the following year that this arrangement was working "very satisfactorily," that "the nuisance previously caused to residents at Police Stations, and to persons living in the neighbourhood of Police Stations, has been almost entirely removed."[44]

Effectively, the Dogs' Home became an auxiliary branch of the Metropolitan Police forces, a subcontracted agency receiving a fee of 3*d.* for each dog taken to the shelter, nominally for food and maintenance.[45] In 1887 the Home's secretary, John Colam, argued that this was something of a bargain for the state: "The police and the metropolis therefore have their work done practically for nothing, including registration at the home, restoration to owners, &c."[46] Nevertheless, this payment from the police was clearly crucial to the Home's fortunes: Garry Jenkins writes that "the Home's arrangement with the Metropolitan Police would safeguard its future" on the basis of this subvention alone.[47] The sum was supposed to be repaid when dogs were returned to their owners or sold, but there was no mention of what would happen to this money in the event that the dogs were put down. Presuming that the Home kept that 3*d.* in these circumstances, minus of course the cost of feeding and caring for a dog for three days, and expenses involved with destruction and removal, these monies must have been a considerable source of income for the Home, certainly representing the kind of financial lifeline that

Jenkins suggests. Moreover, and perhaps just as important, the new arrangement "legitimized the Home in the eyes of not just the police but other authorities."[48] The Dogs' Home became an important adjunct to the policing of the public sphere, rather than being merely a celebration of the private and the domestic. To put it in Pamela Gilbert's terms, it is precisely the "social problem" represented by the presence of the street dog that "produced, mystified, mediated and monitored" the boundaries between the public and the private.[49]

The figures for dogs seized by the police show a steady growth in the numbers of dogs sent to the Home, punctuated with a number of spikes, such as in the later 1870s, in 1885, and again in 1896. These years were particularly associated with rabies' scares, but surges were also associated with changes in regulations and greater rigor in enforcement. The late 1870s, for instance, saw new orders issued under the Contagious Diseases (Animals) Act, empowering the police still further to impound any dogs they regarded as not under proper control. It must be the case that this kind of policing had the most impact upon the working people of London, those who had most to lose from having to pay the dog tax, and those with the fewest resources in terms of looking after animals generally. Their dogs were likely to end up as "strays" to be rounded up, detained, and destroyed. While praising the utility of the clauses contained in the Contagious Diseases (Animals) Act relating to stray dogs—indeed, he referred to this legislation as the "Stray Dogs Act"— the Superintendent of T Division in London (Kensington) pointed out, for instance, the puzzling fact of apparently well-cared-for dogs ending up in the Home but remaining unclaimed:

> This order appears to have been of great service in freeing
> the streets of ownerless curs. I am convinced that some other
> mode of enforcing the Dog Licenses is necessary. In nearly
> every case when persons claim dogs which have been seized
> by Police, a license is produced, whilst in the greater number
> of cases in which dogs, seized within the Metropolis, are sent
> to the Dogs Home, it is evident from the appearance of the
> dog, that it is not "ownerless" and has been well fed, and it is
> but fair to assume that the owners do not hold licenses, or the
> dogs would, I think, be claimed in more instances than at
> present.[50]

We may perhaps wonder how many of the animals taken to the Dogs' Home could reasonably be described as "starving," "ownerless," or "homeless." Many "rescued" dogs must have been without licenses, with their human companions unwilling or unable to pay to get them back. Poorer dog owners may have resorted to letting dogs roam either on a daily basis or when it came to the period at which license fees were due. In effect, the work of the police—and by extension that of the Home— was to penalize the working classes, precisely because they were not able to establish ownership of their dogs as legal property, and because they could not provide homes of the kind that domestic propriety demanded. Almost by definition, then, the poorer classes could not claim to keep "pets," for they could not house them to the satisfaction of Victorian moralists. In this regard, it is suggestive that the police complained that their work was not always welcomed by the general public and by the street children in particular: "This duty is performed by Constables in uniform, who are frequently subject to derision, and sometimes followed a long distance by hordes of children to a Station, commisserating [*sic*] the unfortunate dog. The occasional employment of Constables in plain clothes (as may be required) would be desirable for this work, and I do not hesitate to say that it is a disagreeable duty to carry out in uniform, and objectionable to most men."[51]

Time and again, too, questions of value and property crop up in the operations of the police and the Dogs' Home. As with the phenomenon of dog stealing, the attempt to domesticate the lost and abandoned dogs of the metropolis is pervaded by considerations of the market. The managers of the Home tried exceptionally hard to distance themselves from considerations of venality—perfectly aware of the charges that might be leveled against them—but every aspect of their operations created difficulties with regard to the *worth* of dogs: for animals could only be taken up in the streets if they were classifiable as *lost property,* or alternatively if they had *no* worth at all. Moreover, restoration and rehoming could only take place if the title over an animal was previously, and unequivocally, transferred to the Home; and, lastly, whether dogs were destroyed or not, or how expeditiously, was unapologetically assessed on the basis of their "value."

These questions were foreseen at a very early stage, even by opponents who now look heartless and out of temper with the spirit of the age. It is worth emphasizing that not all the opposition to the Home was mounted on the grounds of the ridiculous sentimentality of silly women. The *Times* also drew attention to the fact that the operations of the market, the invisible hand, made the Home's philanthropy redundant:

> Any "*valuable*" dog found and brought to this "Home" will be restored to its owner. A "dog of that description," not owned, will after a reasonable time be sold, and the proceeds of the sale will be applied towards the support of the Home. Here, again, the old aristocratic landmarks are recognized. The King CHARLES' owns an enchanted life—the turnspit or mongrel may be turned into sausagemeat without a tear over its untimely grave from our Lady of Islington. The gross partiality of this provision apart, is it not wonderful that any person with a small experience of London life should propose such a scheme as the establishment of a refuge for lost valuable dogs? Why not a "Home" for 5*l.*-notes dropped in the streets? Why not an office for the reception of valuable deposits without security or guarantee? A "valuable" dog is worth something which varies between 1*l.* and 20*l.* Now, this sum of money does not commonly run about the streets of London for any considerable time without attention. The difficulty is to keep the "valuable" dogs—not to find a home for those which may have gone astray. There are plenty of gentlemen lounging about the streets of London, with long coats and keen wits, who will take ample care that no "valuable" dog shall undergo any kind of canine suffering. Such an animal is the great nugget of the London streets. He is met with occasionally in the shape of mere flotsam and jetsam, but in ordinary cases he is the subject of a long series of manoeuvres from the London dog-stealers.[52]

The *Times*'s jibe about "lost" five-pound notes is strikingly similar to the Chicago School mantra concerning the likelihood of five-dollar notes in the streets going unclaimed: the argument is that *homo economicus* will see to it that any valuable "lost" dogs will not be unclaimed for long—they would be cycled through the informal economy and its intermediaries and eventually returned, for a fee, to their owners. All of which logically left as the right and proper subject of the Home not these valuable "lost" dogs at all, but rather the *unwanted* and *valueless* street dogs and strays.

The mission of "rehoming" dogs was further tainted by commercial considerations, however, because the Home *sold* dogs, to defray the expenses involved in keeping them for the statutory period, and also, in the case of the most valuable dogs, to contribute to the finances of the institution. But dogs could only be sold if they were the Home's property to sell, a point on which the Home's managers and the police had to insist: "It must be distinctly understood that a person bringing or sending a Dog to the 'Home' resigns all right to it from that moment."[53] The problem was that some merely "lost" dogs might end up being sold to new owners if their old ones did not act quickly enough. The Home might thus act as a kind of fence, allowing the transfer of title over stolen property, enabling London's dog stealers to buy up a prized dog for less than its sentimentally determined worth. For these reasons, one correspondent to the *Times* complained that "owners of dogs in London ought to be warned that the Dogs' Home might prove to be their most dangerous enemy": his dog was stolen, taken to the home, sold for 2*l.*, and when the dog was discovered, the new owner refused the offer of expenses, and claimed that purchasers from the home were assured of good title. As a result, "the home may be made use of by the professional dog-stealer, and it is somewhat of an anomaly that the police, from whom alone the home derives its title to the dogs, should be actively engaged in the search for lost property, and at the same time should supply the only barrier that can prevent its restoration, when found, to its rightful owner."[54] This aggrieved dog owner was at pains here to question the right of the institution to call itself a "Home" at all, as the repeated scare-quotes indicate:

> The reason for the line of passive indifference at present adopted towards those searching for their lost property is not difficult to find, as the sale of valuable animals to strangers gives less trouble and a surer profit than the restoration to their owners, while the skins of the worthless probably produce enough to cover the expense of their brief sojourn at the "Home." It has not been my wish unduly to decry the "Home," but to point out that the indiscriminate use of the power possessed by that institution of giving with the dogs it sells an indisputable title, irrespective of all antecedent circumstances, does work great injustice and may be put to very evil uses by the professional thief, and also to warn those who lose favourite or valuable dogs and fail to recover them within the first

few days that they need not look for active assistance from the "Home," but must be prepared to make a bi-weekly pilgrimage to Battersea during certain prescribed hours of the day if they wish to prevent their property being destroyed or sold for a tenth of its value, and themselves debarred from all right to recovery.[55]

The dog stealer thus cast a very long shadow. From its very beginnings, the Dogs' Home made strenuous efforts to keep separate its animal welfare responsibilities from the taint of money and the market, from "mercenary inducement," as Kidd put it.[56] Toward the end of the century, the institution claimed, disingenuously, that it was not at all responsible for the seizure of dogs, but acted simply as "a trustee of public property."[57] But such attempts to marginalize or contain the market could never fully succeed as long as dogs remained not just property, but such a peculiar species of property. Given the long-standing equation of privacy with property, it is clear that the status of the "homeless" animal was intensely problematic: the public animal was not a common resource, but instead at best a troublingly *im*proper kind of property.[58] The *Times*, in 1866, made this clear when it distinguished between dogs and horses: "There is, however, an important distinction between dogs and horses in respect of 'domicile.' Horses may be said to have a fixed abode, and the number which each man keeps must be tolerably well known to his neighbours. Dogs, on the contrary, are wont to range freely about, and in many instances are the legal, or, at least, the ascertained, property of no one."[59] Far from being securely contained as private property, the dog was an all too public animal. As we have seen, this vagrant propensity played straight into the hands of the dog-stealers. But it also made animals vulnerable to being taken up, and taken off, by apparently more altruistic agents.

Take, for instance, the experience of William Bishop in 1863—the same William Bishop whose campaign against the capital's dog stealers won him such accolades two decades previously. In a spectacularly ironic turn of events, Mr. Bishop's ten-year-old dog became the victim of an overzealous associate of the Dogs' Home, a Miss Eliza Hicks, who peremptorily identified the animal as a distressed street dog, ordered it to be summarily put out of its misery, and had it dumped in a nearby dustbin. Miss Hicks was described as a "friend" of, and a "nurse" at, the

Dogs' Home, and the press made much of the paradox involved in her humane destruction of Mr. Bishop's favorite: "She is a lady connected with an institution called the 'Dogs' Home,' an institution, one would suppose, intended for the preservation, not the destruction of canine life."[60] Bishop promptly summonsed Miss Hicks for "wilful murder" of his dog, explaining that having alighted from his cab near Gray's Inn Square, he had left the dog to wait for him, only for Miss Hicks to intervene with such tragic consequences. The police court had initially refused the suit, accepting that Miss Hicks had acted out of a mistaken spirit of kindness. Undeterred, Bishop took the case to the Westminster County Court and, despite the difficulty of estimating the proper value of the dog, was ultimately awarded nominal damages of 5*l.*[61] As one reporter put it, "His Honour marked his sense of the services the defendant was rendering to the owners of pet dogs by giving judgment for the amount claimed."[62]

What is remarkable in the reporting of this unfortunate case is not only the extravagant affection that Mr. Bishop felt for his dog, who was described as "his life" and "his love," but also the acerbic commentary on the workings of the Dogs' Home, whose malign influence was portrayed not as confined to Holloway but rather as pervading the public streets. The *Leicester Chronicle*'s take on "The Great Dog Case" emphasized the ways in which dogs might be peremptorily assessed as worthy of the Home's charity, or alternatively summarily dispatched:

> Unfortunately for both dog and master, there was a lady promenading in the neighbourhood, whose compassion toward distressed members of the canine race was manifested after a somewhat peculiar fashion. However well-intentioned her sympathies towards dog kind in general might have been their result was fatal to this one, who, for some reason, was not considered a fit subject for the "Home." The defendant fancied the plaintiff's valuable little dog exhibited signs of distress. Without further ado, she called to a man, who appears to have been chief executioner to the Home, and gave him directions to take the wretched dog and forthwith dispatch it, never troubling herself about either its own or master's opinions on the sentence. The executioner was to receive sixpence as his fee. He accordingly took the dog, and after some trouble killed it.

When the plaintiff discovered his loss he caused minute search to be made, when the corpse of the animal was found ignominiously thrust into a dust bin.[63]

Attention was also drawn to the fact that Bishop, recently fêted as one of the greatest benefactors of dogs for obtaining the celebrated Dog Act, "under which so many of the fraternity of dog-fanciers, *alias* stealers, have been brought to book," should have suffered in this way: "To think that his dog, of all others, should be the subject of such an outrage! Enough to make a cynic of him!" But the class-based operation of the law was also highlighted, for Miss Hicks had destroyed a dog that was very far from being an outcast:

> Did she merely destroy poor, wretched, half-starved dogs such as one meets in the street, looking as though it would be the height of charity to make an end of them outright, one might have had some excuse to make for her. There are certainly many such mendicants without any ostensible means of subsistence, and this lack we know, in the case of human destitutes, has been proposed as a qualification which should bring such persons under the supervision of the police and the coercion of the law. Dog-kind must expect the same treatment as their betters at the hands of our active reformers, although it is more than doubtful whether dogs have not an affection for life in common with other higher animals, many of whom, though said to be endowed with reason, are yet not more intelligent. But, allowing that it is lawful and right to destroy houseless dogs, the present case is aggravated by the fact that the subject of this lady's attention was a well-to-do dog—a dog, in fact, whose residence was Bond-street, and whose master was in the habit of taking his darling, as he affectionately called the animal, for airings in a cab.[64]

This little incident is as resonant in its own way as Flush's abduction, though the result this time was tragedy rather than triumph. A fancy dog and a favorite was not safe in the streets after all. For all that the dog possessed a fine home in a fashionable neighborhood, it was vulnerable to predation in public. Instead of being taken to the domestic refuge of the Dogs' Home, Mr. Bishop's dog was "sent to his long Home," dispatched in public and in the most brutal and undignified way.[65] Despite being valuable property, the dog ended up in a common dustbin, transformed to chaff or waste, and only posthumously restored to property status by the fiat of the Westminster magistrates.

We can argue that the restoration and rehoming of dogs were *always* subject to the intrusions of the market economy. Matthias Colam, secretary of the Dogs' Home, stated unequivocally in 1889 that "we are not influenced by the market value of dogs."[66] But the Dogs' Home inevitably became a very important *dealer* in dogs, "a perfect mart for buyers."[67] The charge that the Home profited from the business of dogs, particularly from their contract with the police, and from the destruction of strays, would not go away. The novelist and animal advocate Ouida, focusing once more on the transformation of animals into waste, remarked at the height of the rabies scares, that once the disease was eradicated by the new preventives available, this would "enable the managers of the Dogs' Home to resume their profitable manufacture of sensitive living creatures into manure."[68]

One correlation of the interpenetration of the Dogs' Home with the market economy was the simple fact that dogs assessed as "valuable" were also the ones seen as viable, worth keeping, worth being kept alive, or for longer. They were allowed to live while the "untrained, ill-bred, deformed, neglected, starving, diseased, and consequently worthless animals" could be made to die.[69] How was value measured, however? Clearly the pedigree/mongrel distinction was crucial: "When a stray dog is now found in the streets he is taken to the Home for Dogs and mercifully killed, unless he is of rare breed."[70] But judgment seems to have been at least partly aesthetic, with an eye to which dogs might be sold to prospective owners. The *Newcastle Courant* put it in the plainest of terms: "Good-looking dogs are kept to be sold; the remaining are destroyed by a dose of hydroceanic acid."[71] Greenwood also noted that a dog at the Home had been kept for seven months, far longer than would have been the norm, "a great brown dog, curly and handsome."[72] *Some* dogs, then, identifiable by their appearance and behavior as "valuable" and domesticated property, might find themselves given an extended grace period not accorded to the low-born and the ill-favored. Constantly under pressure, the Home's managers had to assess—in a ruthlessly sentimental equivalent of triage that is at the same time a distinct type of emotional labor—not just the health and behavior of incoming dogs, nor even sim-

ply whether they were to be considered street dogs or lost pets—further
to this, they had to decide whether dogs were likely to find purchasers
and be gathered up to domesticity. If not, they had to be killed as quickly
as possible after the statutory period of a few days. The mission of the
Dogs' Home was after all to restore property, or else to turn strays into
property. The future for any animals that could not undergo that transformation was bleak. Since it was "a capital crime to be an unowned
creature," the only alternative was death.[73]

Understandably, Battersea's official histories recognize but do not
dwell upon the vast numbers of dogs euthanized in the Home following its establishment as an authorized depot for strays. Jenkins refers
to such deaths as "a sad but necessary and accepted practice," and more
precisely to the "dark side" of the figures for rehomed animals, to wit
that 75 percent of dogs never left the home at all.[74] The difficulty is that
such acknowledgment is often bound up with the fact that ill and severely malnourished dogs had to be put down, or alternatively with the
acute crisis represented by the several rabies scares. Linda Kalof thus
notes that the dogs that were taken in by Mary Tealby's shelter were
the "lucky" ones, considering the thousands of dogs that were "regularly
slaughtered by authorities on suspicion of rabies during the 1800s."[75]
But from around 1870 the *normal* work of the Home was to put down
dogs, in their thousands every year, the overwhelming majority of admissions. Figures are incomplete, and I have not been able to consult
the Home's archives, but taking out the total of rehomed animals (which
include those restored to owners or sold to new ones), the kill rate looks
typically to be around 80 percent, climbing to perhaps as high as 90 percent in exceptional years.[76] Put plainly, the purpose of the Home, belying
its restorative and rehoming functions, was systematically to destroy the
"worthless" dogs seized by the police. As Secretary Colam put it, "The
inhabitants of this great metropolis chiefly benefit by our institution,
both as regards the recovery of lost dogs and the riddance of stray dogs
in the streets."[77]

This killing took place within the Home, in private rather than in
public, as quickly as possible in order to reduce the suffering of the animals involved, and with an eye to necessary efficiency. The lethal chamber developed by the famous surgeon Dr. Benjamin Ward Richardson,
a man committed to the alleviation of pain in domestic animals, was a
major breakthrough in this regard. His gas apparatus (see figure 11)
was commended for being able to kill 100 dogs at a time, in under three

minutes, and the crematorium disposed of the remains with equivalent expedition. Nodding to Browning's antivivisection poem, the *Sun* admired the fact that "the crematorium performs its destructive functions with equal results [to that of the lethal chamber], only a few incinerated bones remaining to mark the untimely if necessary end of 'poor dog Tray.'"[78]

Unlike the tramps applying to the casual wards of the metropolis, London's destitute dogs could be summarily disposed of. Theirs was a fatal breed of worthlessness:

> There are some dogs whose life is of no value to themselves
> or to anyone else. When a fellow of this good-for-nothing de-
> scription has enjoyed the bounty of so liberal an institution
> without paying for it, being in fact a pauper, and having no
> master to reclaim or employ him, then he is gently invited to
> retire from existence; for human science has invented several
> easy and painless devices to relieve an unlucky dog, cheaper
> than permitting him "to eat his own head off." It would,
> indeed, be unjustifiable, as a matter of social and political
> economy—worse than the toleration of monkery or beggary
> in the Middle Ages—to undertake to support all the idle dogs
> in London as long as they chose to live at the public expense.
> Their consumption of food, which, though not of the same
> kind as human food, has yet a value no less certain and ap-
> preciable, must compete ultimately with the wants of the two-
> legged population.[79]

To complain of such killing may appear anachronistic as well as unfair, but that this was not universally accepted is evident from several sources, as the remarks of Ouida cited above show. If we are to believe Hollingshead, there was also a certain level of dissension over the introduction of this policy at the Home:

> So far, the Refuge appears to be popular and well managed;
> but the committee is not altogether of one way of thinking.
> Some, perhaps the most humane portion, insist upon placing
> all the animals in the Refuge on an equal footing, and object
> to any dog being destroyed, rejected, or given up as incurable.
> Others, perhaps the most practical members, see the neces-

Figure 11. "Sketches at the Dogs' Home, Battersea," c. 1886. (Courtesy of London Metropolitan Archives, SC/P2/BT/004/007)

sity which exists for checking the increase of the "tykes;" the "rest;" the standing balance which "eats its head off," never moves on, and becomes surplus dog population. Here the old workhouse difficulty, with hopeless paupers, is reproduced on a small scale, with animals performing the parts of men. How it will be got over, time alone will show, and the dissension, if the practical party carry the day, may probably cost the society a few subscribers.[80]

A second marker of dissent is the controversy aired in the pages of the *Morning Post* in 1876 between a correspondent known only as "B.G." and the secretary of the Dogs' Home, James Johnson. For "B.G.," the scale of the killing of dogs made it impossible for the word "Home" to be used: "A real Home for lost and starving dogs would command the sympathy of every benevolent person. It is because I thought and still think that the establishment at Battersea is not such a Home that I have called attention to it."[81] For "B.G.," not only did these inconvenient truths put the lie to the name of the Dogs' Home, they put its work at odds with the law. For while the police may have powers to take possession of dogs, "B.G." insisted that the keepers of the Home had so such authority; the ambiguous position of the private Home vis-à-vis the state, and the ambiguity of its claim to full title over the dogs, as property, were noted. For "B.G.," the Home was no better than the dog haters who were currently occupied in carrying out a very public campaign of euthanasia of dogs in west London: "In the eye of the law they stand on precisely the same footing with the dog poisoners who are at present engaged in creating such havoc in the suburbs of London. Like them, they are equally amenable to punishment under the Act of Geo. IV. for the protection of domestic animals. As far as a dog is concerned it can make no difference to it whether in the course of a stroll it bolts a piece of poisoned meat or is dragged off to this Home at Battersea, to be disposed of a few days later."[82]

Finally, there were a few journalists who refused the lure of easy sentimentality and the clichéd comparison with human institutions for paupers and indigents, recognizing that the material violence of rendering fell, in wholly incomparable fashion, on nonhuman animals alone.[83] One such reporter, in 1870, gave short shrift to the blandishments of domesticity, seeing the Dogs' Home as not merely a prison, but one constituted of condemned cells:

Condemned criminals are what they amount to; for they are
only kept at the Home a certain number of days to see if their
owners come to claim them, and then they will be mercifully
and quickly killed! A few, indeed, of likely breeds, are allowed
to live a little longer, in case people in want of a dog should
apply to choose one (as many do;) but how can we expect
intelligence and happiness from dogs who have had their day,
and who have only been brought to this cheap harbourage by
Samaritans polite enough to pull a preliminary bell, or, failing
that, agile enough to give a strong fling over the official wall
and take a good long run far away directly after?[84]

The animal advocate Annie Thomas (Annie Hall Cudlip) similarly represented the "harrowing spectacle" of the Home in carceral rather than
domestic terms: "They are prisons to the free and fetterless spirits of the
mongrels, which chiefly abound here; in a word, they are workhouse
wards, and different as possible to anything that these unhappy dogs
have hitherto understood when the word 'home' has been mentioned in
their presence."[85]

The domestic image of the Battersea Dogs' Home thus helped to paper
over its normal functions of policing, incarceration, and execution. In nu-
merical terms, the Home was centrally concerned with killing rather than
saving animals. Battersea Dogs' and Cats' Home, to apply contemporary
terminology, was the world's first "open-admission" or "kill-shelter," not
so much an asylum as a mausoleum.[86] Despite the emotive language, this
is not meant to take Battersea Dogs' Home especially to task. Rather, we
need to delve behind what I think is the commonplace view of dog welfare institutions, to consider when and why they emerged, and what was
their rationale. Perhaps the most obvious point—but only obvious when
we consider the workings of such homes and refuges in comparison with
what happens elsewhere, as the geographer Krithika Srinivasan has recently done—is that dogs in modern Britain, in order to be assured of
life, have to belong to someone, to be owned, to be *property*. The comparison with the Indian "street dog" shows straightaway that the Western
"stray" is a particular legal and spatial construction. "Dogs in India can
be in the absence of a human owner," observes Srinivasan, but "strays"
(and "lost" dogs) in Britain are by definition *out of place*.[87] If they are not
obviously property, not obviously domestic, these dogs are vulnerable to

an ethico-political marginalization that allows them to suffer a kind of ordinary rendition from public space, and to be euthanized in private, to take only the most modern and humane manifestation of a purification of space that operates primarily and not incidentally through the killing of nonhuman animals.

Curiously, this is at the same time a *domesticated* killing, not simply because it is hidden away from public scrutiny, nor because the principal victim is an animal properly thought to be domestic, but also because it is wrapped up in an ethos of care and responsibility. Garry Marvin's conception of "domestic killing"—that is, the orderly, "culturized" killing of domesticated animals in "specialist places of death"—is an important reference here; Marvin contrasts this form of killing to the "disorderly" extermination of "pests" and the killing of wild animals by hunters.[88] But his characterization of such killings as non-individualized "cold deaths," brought about by working professionals maintaining proper emotional distance and discipline, is not entirely convincing. The euthanizing of dogs is not typically carried out with a clinical detachment devoid of emotional significance.[89] In this sense, at least, it might be better to consider these deaths to be "domesticated" rather than merely "domestic"— a domestication of killing, bringing death into the family, as it were, and if not quite the great Victorian ideal of the "good death," then as good a death as could be envisaged for an animal companion in such dire straits.

Donna Haraway has recently foregrounded the importance of killing responsibly, a recognition of the necessity of killing in what she terms the ontological choreography of shared suffering. This is very well, and those who give their time to care for animals even to the extent of caring them out of existence will understand the physical and emotional entanglements of such "killing well." However, while Haraway goes on to confront the impossible idealism of "Thou shalt not kill" with a more realistic, and to her mind respectful, "Thou shalt not make killable," it is precisely the historically and geographically situated contingency of *killability* that she ignores in her strictures: the ways in which we ("we" at least in the West) have made the "hopeless, homeless cur" into an animal that has only a bare life, an animal that like as not cannot be found a "forever home," at least not an earthly one.[90]

CHAPTER 4

The Descent of the Dog
Domesticating and Undomesticating Darwinism

*I*N THEORY, natural selection changed everything. By demonstrating that humans and animals were kin, that they shared "a common progenitor" with beasts, that their differences were only ones of degree, and that they were subject to the same natural laws, Darwin's discoveries promised to eliminate "the unbridgeable gulf that divided reasoning human being from irrational brute," and potentially to expand the space for moral considerations of the claims of animals.[1] In practice, not only did anthropocentric attitudes and practices change remarkably little, the impact of "Darwinism" was surely not to sap but to shore up arguments for human exceptionalism.[2] Darwin himself bridled at the suggestion that he had put humans on the same plane as animals. The more forceful Huxley maintained that "no one is more strongly convinced than I am of the vastness of the gulf between civilised man and the brutes; or is more certain that whether from them or not, he is assuredly not of them."[3] The "enormous abyss, of an immeasurable width" between humans and other animals remained resolutely unspanned.[4]

What part did domestic animals, and the most domestic animal of all, play in the failure of Darwinism to close this chasm between humans and the rest of the animal kingdom? In this chapter I argue that Darwin leaned heavily upon the domestic dog in the working out and presentation of evolutionary theory. The dog was a close companion in what we can call Darwin's domestic science, principally by grounding evolution in the everyday world of the Victorian home. The dog belonged to a domestic "living laboratory" that was reassuringly familiar to the scientist and his readers.[5] But this compact between science and the home could not hold for long, threatened as it was first by the controversies over vivisection, into which Darwin reluctantly became drawn, and secondly by the development of experimental science—alienating and distinctly *unheimlich* as it was to the Victorian public. By the end of the century, we might even say that the Victorian dog had completed its journey from being a companion in a domesticated form of scientific inquiry to a mere research tool and instrument, reduced to the status of the experimental or laboratory animal—still living, but no longer vital.[6] This *descent* of the dog (and I mean by this poor pun the dog's falling away in social as well as scientific status) confirmed the anthropocentric orthodoxies of the late Victorian era. It indicates, I argue, an abortive scientific attempt to domesticate the Victorian dog.

I want to begin this argument by registering the fact that dogs were "anomalous animals," thoroughly recalcitrant subjects for Darwin and for an incipient Darwinism. They troubled, for instance, the already famously troublesome "analogy" between natural and artificial selection.[7] Darwin's discussion of dogs, like other domesticated animals, foregrounds the ancient origins of breeds and the gradual changes introduced by human beings. The evolution of dogs was not the work of nature alone: as Darwin argued, though we do not know the history of *any* of our domestic breeds, "Who can believe that animals closely resembling the Italian greyhound, the bloodhound, the bull-dog, or Blenheim spaniel, &c.—so unlike all wild Canidae—ever existed freely in a state of nature?"[8] Theirs was a matter of long-term, "unconscious" selection, aimed at maintaining the quality of stock rather than the creation of sub-breeds with particular traits. As with other domesticates, the process of breeding what were judged (for humans' purposes) to be the best animals led in time to dramatic changes and unanticipated "improvement," such changes paradoxically effected with the overriding intention of staying the same.[9] Darwin's discussion of this kind of artificial selection begins, significantly, with the breeding of dogs[10]: "For our purpose, a kind of Selection, which may be called Unconscious, and which results from every one trying to possess and breed from the best individual animals, is more important. Thus, a man who intends keeping pointers naturally tries to get as good dogs as he can, and afterwards breeds from his own best dogs, but he has no wish or expectation of permanently altering the breed."[11] In meeting the obvious objection that "Man selects for his own good; Nature only for that of the being which she tends," Darwin argues that such dogs, left at times to struggle for their own subsistence, and circumstanced in different environments, would also be subject to a parallel process of natural selection.[12] It is thus possible to conceive of artificial and natural selection working hand-in-hand, the same principles being at work, over the longest time-scales. This is a view with which contemporary commentators are content.[13]

Turning to dog *breeding* to explain evolution was not without its problems, however. For a start, "artificial" selection is clearly carried out not only for "man's use" or his "wants" but also for his "fancies."[14] The more *methodical* selection that we find operating on the shorter time-scales of selective breeding is clearly difficult to align with natural selection, save as loose and potentially misleading metaphor. In his discussion of the principle of diversification in the struggle for life, for instance, Darwin compares the work of nature to the actions of pigeon fanciers who by their very nature prefer *extremes*, with the modifications introduced by breeders clearly not conferring any real advantages for the animals themselves in the struggle for life. The same is true for the fancy dogs bred for whim rather than for utility.[15] In these cases it is hard to argue that anything more than a limited, heuristic analogy is in play.

More worryingly, in revisiting the classic example of artificial selection, Bert Theunissen has shown that the deficiency of Darwin's understanding of pigeon breeding was matched only by a very selective use of the evidence at his disposal.[16] Effectively, the theory of natural selection determined Darwin's understanding, or at least his presentation, of artificial selection. This was classic analogical reasoning, but the wrong way round entirely, natural selection being used as the key to understanding the artificial. And if there are problems with the famous pigeons, the development of the domestic dog was hardly more promising. For while one advantage of pigeons was the fact that relatively well differentiated breeds had been in existence since the eighteenth century, the same could not be said of dogs. Around the time of Darwin's birth there were perhaps only fifteen or so designated "breeds," and it was only from the mid-nineteenth century onward that the majority of modern fancy breeds became established.[17] The dog was thus the most *ancient* of domestic animals—the earliest known domesticate—but at the same time one of the very *youngest* in terms of the vigorously modified breed groups that the dog fancy was busy calling into existence. Since Darwin was primarily concerned with slow changes in domesticated dogs, natural selection blurring into the artificial over the very long term, these *fancy* animals were at best awkward subjects for the evolutionist.

Moreover, stress on the *antiquity* of dog breeds typically led naturalists to detect the work of providence, or else to foreground some degree of Lamarckian direct adaptation to the environment. Darwin himself struggled with assessing the balance between the two types of selection, and the role of adaptation, as is evident from his acceptance of the view that domestic dogs were derived from multiple canid ancestors, including wolves and jackals, rather than from a single species radiating out from its birthplace.[18] Darwin admits, in *The Variation of Animals under Domestication*, that "certain constitutional and climatal differences," derived from the various wild species such as the jackal, wolves, and others, must have been at play, and while he maintains that variation under domestication will have increased the total number of breeds and their great modification, there is a revealing admixture of assertion and tentativeness in his argument:

> But we cannot explain by crossing the origin of such extreme forms as thoroughbred greyhounds, bloodhounds, bulldogs, Blenheim spaniels, terriers, pugs, etc., unless we believe that forms equally or more strongly characterised in these different respects once existed in nature. But hardly any one has been bold enough to suppose that such unnatural forms ever did or could exist in a wild state. When compared with all known members of the family of Canidae they betray a distinct and abnormal origin. No instance is on record of such dogs as bloodhounds, spaniels, true greyhounds having been kept by savages: they are the product of long-continued civilisation.[19]

Darwin's language in this passage — the repetition of "but," the contrast of "in nature" and "unnatural" — betrays his struggle to acknowledge *some* role for "inheritance from distinct wild stocks, that is to changes effected under nature before domestication," while affirming the "predominant power of selection."[20]

There was, lastly, an unavoidable ambiguity in the concept of "breed" itself, which might be taken to be natural or artificial, or some Gordian knotting of the two. In a strict sense, "breed" is no more than a synonym for variety or sub-variety, and of course for Darwin a variety, even a sub-variety, was merely a species-in-waiting; taxons like breed, variety, and species are simply that—they have no fixed nature. Darwin argued that various "breeds" existed in ancient times, but he is rightly cautious about identifying them with modern sub-varieties. As George Levine puts it, "A 'dog' can be conceived in ideal doggy permanence only by giving language an ideal and atemporal relation to reality. 'Dog,' for Darwin, has to be a merely pragmatic label for an organism genealogically related to other transient forms and itself only temporarily what it is. Definition thus becomes arbitrary and inadequate."[21] This view contrasts sharply, however, with the naturalizing and essentializing of breeds that was being vigorously promoted in Darwin's own lifetime. Darwin may have looked forward to the day that even species were to be treated as "artificial combinations made for convenience," and when classifications would be replaced by genealogies, but Victorian taxonomies tended instead to reify breed differentiation, and to promote them as enduringly "natural."[22] Martin Wallen has emphasized the importance of popular breed histories in portraying the pedigree dog as a creature of both antiquity and nature, perhaps even design, but not, contra Darwin, of either artifice or accident:

> The creation and multiplication of dog breeds, beginning with the foxhound, made Enlightenment taxonomies seem to be codices of mute nature, the grammar revealing that nature had all along constituted a linguistic coherence recognizable through the logic of metaphor to the sensible human understanding. If dogs existed as breeds—especially if they had always existed as breeds that humans had only just begun to recognize the organization of—then the variability of animal nature could be read teleologically, reflecting the intention of "some hypothetical author" who structured the variability into a meaningful text waiting to be comprehended by man.[23]

These narrative histories of dog breeds do not seem to have been much disturbed by the Darwinian revolution, and are wholly incompatible with natural selection. Teleology and theology are reinstalled: breeding was visioned as a way of bringing back order, hierarchy, direction, human mastery, and anthropocentrism.[24] Any helpful *analogy* between artificial and natural selection is lost in these spurious canine *genealogies*. Dogs, in all their varieties, became naturalized, placed in the landscapes, regions, and climates that were supposed to have authored them. Evolution in the Darwinian sense hardly got a look in.

Given the difficulties involved, it is reasonable to ask why Darwin repeatedly turns to dogs to make the evolutionary argument. There are two viable answers to this question. The first is provided by David Feller, who has recently drawn attention to Darwin's background and upbringing in the Shropshire sporting set, and to the role of the dog as the huntsman's companion.[25] In the first place, a field sports background was the common denominator of English natural science, so that "the field became a sort of laboratory for the natural historian."[26] Furthermore, a common set of observational and analytical skills (Feller terms this "the hunter's gaze") was involved in this participation of naturalists in the dog-and-gun world of the English gentry. Lastly, because dogs were the inseparable companions of the sportsman, Feller recognizes that they were centrally involved in the history of natural science. In sum, a "continuity of thought about dogs and hunting" allowed and prompted Darwin to formulate his ideas about natural selection.[27] That said, hunting in its various forms was, and remains, a complex cultural practice that should hardly be taken at its own word with regard to its supposed "naturalness," its immersion in and unique respect for the environment.[28] The construction of the countryside as something "unified" by hunting, establishing relations between humans, between humans and animals, and between humans and the landscape, is a persistent but problematic mythos.[29] Emphasizing Darwin's embeddedness within the rural culture of field sports goes only so far, I think, in explaining why Darwin foregrounded the dog in his narrative of natural selection.

A second argument for the importance of dogs to the theory of natural selection may thus be more significant. Darwin's references to dogs, particularly to pet dogs, are in this view part of a rhetorical strategy for making the potentially disturbing message of evolution more accessible and acceptable, by routing it through the everyday and the familiar. We can note that whilst Darwin recognized that argument by analogy was problematic, he saw that it had the advantage of being a commonplace and familiar method, used "in judging of the common events of life."[30] Furthermore, if we define analogical inference as the *placing* of the familiar next to the unfamiliar, then we can see that the latter—the real, extraordinary and unsettling force of Darwin's argument—is brought out, justified, and made palatable by placing it alongside the mundane, the domestic, and the homely.[31] The literary critic George Levine expresses this point when he writes that "Darwin's prose brings it home to our bodies and our gardens and our zoos and wherever in our ordinary lives we encounter forms of life."[32] Many other commentators have remarked on the fact that domesticated animals provided "reassuringly homely" examples.[33] There is therefore something to be taken from Richard Richards' otherwise unpersuasive revisionism: namely the distinction between the rhetorical and the substantial elements in this "analogy." The illustrative benefits of the analogy between natural and artificial selection may be taken as distinct from its inferential and analytical accuracy: "It seems we are more likely to affirm the conclusion of an argument that has familiar ideas and imagery associated with it, even if this association is purely heuristic. In 19th-century England, where raising pigeons and keeping gardens were familiar pastimes, the association of evolution with domestic breeding might predispose opinion, even if, as analogical evidence, the association is counterproductive."[34]

It is likely not *just* a matter of strategy, of what Ritvo called Darwinism's "public relations."[35] Following the likes of George Levine and Gillian Beer, who have explored the ways in which Darwin needed to creatively imagine before he could inductively prove, we might take domestication and the domestic as not just tropes but cultural themes that played a proactive role in the formulation of the theory of natural selection, and which expressed themselves more generally in Victorian culture.[36] But even if we do not accept this, shall we call it, "unconscious" contribution, we may still see this recourse to the domestic as "methodical." It is closely linked to Darwin's famously "plain" style of speaking directly to the reader, which Darwin himself talked of as throwing "eloquence to the dogs," the long argument put across as something resembling a leisurely, domestic conversation.[37] Darwin's cautious and modest rhetoric spoke "directly to the Victorian turn toward domesticity," so that although his rhetorical strategy is first to *defamiliarize* he may be said subsequently to *refamiliarize:* to break down what we think we know, only to build it up again using domestic observations and homely examples.[38] This is, in its rhetorical presentation at least, a domestic and a domesticated pursuit of natural science.[39]

It is important to be clear here that this is not to claim that the *practice* of Darwin's science is domestic. Darwin may have settled in to work from his study at Down House, but he was dependent on a network of animal breeders and other correspondents, agents who have been described as effectively "a legion of freelance, sloppy laboratory technicians."[40] Darwin's study functioned on a minor scale as something like what has been called, in science studies, a "center of calculation."[41] Despite Darwin's network of information, and his reliance on theory as much as upon observation, however, he is at pains to present his work through a series of domestic observations. It is as if the domestic setting allowed Darwin to take analogical tiptoes or sidesteps rather than relying on the reader to make leaps of faith. Metaphor's unfamiliar comparisons are countered and complemented by the intimate and reassuring associations of metonymy. In this way the vast and the wonderful could be demonstrated in the domestic and the ordinary, "the great family" of life and the immensity of time and space in the little family of the home and in the here and now.[42] All this was still unsettling and always potentially uncanny in its vital materialism: Levine notes that "All the stable elements of our gardens, our domestic animals, our own bodies are mysteriously active, aberrant, plastic."[43] The first edition of the *Origin* also confronted the reader with a horrifying "struggle for existence" in a dog-eat-dog world: "Two canine animals in a time of dearth, may be truly said to struggle with each other which shall get food and live."[44] But to circumvent the nihilistic implications, Darwin turned not to "man" alone, as Gillian Beer suggests, but also to his (or her) companion animals.[45] Here, the references to domestic as opposed to wild dogs are transparently consoling. As Emma Townshend has recognized, "Familiarising and domesticating this strange new theory, he grounded the whole story at home, ensuring it was clearly accessible for the general Victorian reader and making the bitter pill easier to swallow. Darwin's dogs brought evolutionary theory right to the hearth rug of the Victorian home."[46] Townshend's recent book *Darwin's Dogs* has exhaustively considered the dogs in Darwin's personal life, and anticipated my arguments here, but it is worth reaffirming that Darwin's principal aid in the enterprise of domesticating evolution was the humble dog. Darwin's writing appeals directly to readers' own experiences of the animals closest to them, rather than, say, to animals in the wild or in the laboratory, invoking his readers' curiosity and *common sense* about the animals close to hand: "*Every one knows* how liable animals are to furious rage, and how plainly they show it," for instance, or again, "As *every one knows*, dogs understand many words and sentences."[47]

The Origin of Species has been judged "a surprisingly personal and domestic book" as a result, but it is *The Descent of Man* and (even more so) *The Expression of the Emotions in Man and Animals* that best illustrate this use of dogs to domesticate the evolutionary argument.[48] This is hardly surprising, since in both books, published only a year apart, Darwin's avowed purpose is to demonstrate that humans differ from animals merely by degree. Darwin declares that dogs share with us, for instance, a sense of property, the power of self-command, and (most important of all) the power of reasoning.[49] The anecdote that Darwin gives for this developed sense of intelligence is drawn from his own experience, and that of Polly, his dog:

> When I say to my terrier, in an eager voice (and I have made the trial many times), "Hi, hi, where is it?" she at once takes it as a sign that something is to be hunted, and generally first looks quickly all around, and then rushes into the nearest thicket, to scent for any game, but finding nothing, she looks up into any neighbouring tree for a squirrel. Now do not these actions clearly shew that she had in her mind a general idea or concept that some animal is to be discovered and hunted?[50]

Darwin also wants to demonstrate that many animals share not only our anatomy and mentation but also complex emotional states. Indeed, we are only able to understand them because their ability to express emotions derives from the same source. For Darwin, comparative psychology begins at home, and especially with dogs, whose entanglement with humans makes them, in the geneticist Steve Jones's words, a "gigantic experiment on the biology of sentiment."[51] Darwin insists to his readers that they take a close interest in the animals nearest to them, for "to understand, as far as is possible, the source or origin of the various expressions which may be hourly seen on the faces of the men around us, not to mention our domesticated animals, ought to possess much interest for us."[52] Here is Darwin, practicing what he preaches, describing himself out walking his retriever cross, Bob:

> I formerly possessed a large dog, who, like every other dog, was much pleased to go out walking. He showed his pleasure by trotting gravely before me with high steps, head much raised, moderately erected ears, and tail carried aloft but not stiffly. Not far from my house a path branches off to the right, leading to the hot-house, which I used often to visit for a few moments to look at my experimental plants. This was always a

great disappointment to the dog, as he did not know whether I
should continue my walk; and the instantaneous and complete
change of expression which came over him, as soon as my
body swerved in the least towards the path (and I sometimes
tried this as an experiment) was laughable. His look of dejec-
tion was known to every member of the family, and was called
his *hot-house face*. This consisted in the head drooping much,
the whole body sinking a little and remaining motionless; the
ears and tail falling suddenly down, but the tail was by no
means wagged.[53]

Beyond such relatively uncontentious observations, however, Darwin feels able to determine that domestic dogs have, inter alia, a sense
of shame, a sense of humor, and "something very like a conscience."[54]
Indeed, Darwin claims that all the senses, intuitions, emotions, and fac-
ulties that the human being possesses — "love, memory, attention, curiosity, imitation, reason, &c." — may be found, at the very least in simple
or incipient form, among the "lower animals."[55] Famously, Darwin is
even willing to consider the evolution of moral and religious consciousness from an observation of his dog growling at a parasol moved by the
breeze, apparently convinced of some invisible power at work.[56] With
examples like these, it is easy to see why Darwin's theorizing (particularly in the *Expression*) is considered amateurish and unsatisfactory.[57]
This is an overly harsh judgment, though: given Darwin's consistent appeal to the domesticated and the domestic, even an apparently marginal
and, to some, "non-Darwinian" book like the *Expression* makes a little
more sense within the long argument for descent through modification.
      The problem remains though that the *Expression*'s focus is on the uni-
versal, innate, and biologically determined, and its borderline Lamarckian focus on habit and imitation has little obvious consideration of the
role of domestication in changing animals' behavior, and little explicit
consideration of natural selection either. But if Darwin did not quite
make a full case for natural selection, his friend George Romanes did.
Romanes — now virtually forgotten, but once perhaps the most preeminent "neo-Darwinist" — saw himself mapping out animal psychology
according to the theory of descent, continuing his master's research on
emotions and instinct, and drawing on Darwin's copious notes as well
as his published work.[58] In every respect Romanes was Darwin's heir,
including his reliance on homely observations and enthusiastic anthro-

pomorphism. Like Darwin, Romanes does not quite escape from the lure of Lamarckian adaptation, but his emphasis on domestication shows him considering the intertwining of artificial and natural selection, much as Darwin instructed. Dogs were again the great exemplars: in *Animal Intelligence* (1882), Romanes argues that while the dog inherited high natural *intelligence* from the wolf and the jackal, its *emotions* have been uniquely developed by "prolonged companionship with man."[59] Domestication also developed the intellectual as well as the emotional capacities of dogs, as they learned to move from the logic of feelings to the logic of signs, to communicate with each other and with their human masters. By implication, the expression of emotions was crucial to the welfare of groups and the regulation of social interactions, and Romanes was thus in no doubt as to "the improving influences of hereditary domestication": "The definite proof which we thus have afforded of the transforming and creating influence exerted upon the mental character and instincts of species by long and persistent training, coupled with artificial selection, furnishes the strongest possible corroboration of the theory which assigns psychological development in general to the joint operation of individual experience coupled with natural selection."[60]

This work on shared emotions—continued so directly by George Romanes—was particularly important in domesticating the evolutionary narrative and linking it to emergent structures of feeling.[61] Jed Mayer has argued that "by representing evolutionary theory in these familiar domestic terms, stressing the common links that forge emotional as well as biological bonds between people and their companion animals, Darwin placed his otherwise unsettling theories of descent within an evolving culture of compassion toward nonhuman animals."[62] In this reading of Darwin and Darwinism, a close connection is drawn between science and sentiment, making the findings of evolutionary biology congruent with humanitarian politics, extending to the advocacy of animal rights. Acknowledging that animals have feelings, and showing that human beings are emotionally connected to animals, raised questions for instance about the treatment of animals in laboratories, zoos, and slaughterhouses. Darwin's own squeamishness toward the infliction of pain, and his antipathy toward animal cruelty, are well known, and of a piece with his fondness for dogs and other animals.[63] Noting that compassion and anti-cruelty ran in the family, Adrian Desmond and James Moore remark that Darwin shared the values of the Society for the Prevention of Cruelty to Animals.[64] As they further emphasize, abolitionism and animal welfare were related passions: from an early age Darwin apparently linked "horrible cruelty to animals" to "the great Sin of slavery."[65] It seems a series of small steps from Darwin's personal response to animal suffering, to the demonstration that humans share emotional expression with animals, to an endorsement of the aims of the Victorian humane movement. Very like Dickens, in fact, Darwin's personal sympathies are parlayed into a more general humanitarianism and pro-animal sentiment.[66] Indeed, it can be argued that a book like *Expression* reproduces Dickens's commitment to inducing sensation and sympathy in the reader and encouraging a communion of fellow feeling for animals as well as people.[67] Gillian Beer has noted that "the need to *please* his readers as well as to unsettle and disturb them is as vital to Darwin as it was to Dickens," and nothing could be more pleasing or consoling than, say, his images of puppies happily playing together, showing fellow feeling by licking a sick cat, or simply curling up to sleep on the carpet.[68] We are back in the comforting and consoling world of "happy families."

Just as for Dickens, however, there are necessary qualifications to this "philozoic," thoroughly domesticated, pleasingly progressive, Darwin.[69] Even such a "homely" book as the *Expression* has passages that are violently jarring to any contemporary reader persuaded that Darwin was soppy and sentimental about dogs. To wit: "A female terrier of mine lately had her puppies destroyed, and though at all times a very affectionate creature, I was much struck with the manner in which she then tried to satisfy her instinctive maternal love by extending it on me; and her desire to lick my hands rose to an insatiable passion."[70] Or this observation of reflex action, which immediately follows a charming recollection of an old cat pleasurably pounding the air with its paws when having its back scratched: "if a finger moistened with milk is placed in the mouth of a puppy, the front part of whose brain has been removed . . ."[71] Indeed, most obviously troubling to our sense of his homeliness and "humanitarianism," no matter our views on animal experiments, is Darwin's support for vivisection.[72] This cannot be shirked by insisting on Darwin's *personal* love of animals: Feller argues that labeling Darwin "a mere soldier in the army of science" when it came to vivisection contradicts what we know of Darwin as naturalist and dog lover, but he assumes that someone could not be a dog lover *and* a supporter of vivisection.[73] Darwin could easily position himself, in the context of nineteenth-century Britain, as an animal enthusiast and a proponent of animal welfare, at the same time that he could support, in however qualified a fashion, the physiological study of living beings. Paul White writes that Darwin was able to "move between his role as an observer of animals, dissecting their behaviour with his gaze, and his role as their companion and friend."[74] Rather than see love for dogs as irreconcilable with the belief that animals might be experimented upon for the good of humanity, it is necessary to consider instead how the politics of vivisection posed a direct *challenge* to what I have suggested as a Darwinian synthesis of domesticity and science.

That Darwin was maneuvered into expressing his backing for the practice of experimentation, in the teeth of an antivivisectionist movement that threatened to ban or heavily regulate emerging forms of animal experimentation and thus derail the professionalization of biomedical science, is well appreciated. In private, and eventually in public, Darwin defended vivisection against the charge that scientists inflicted appalling and unnecessary cruelty upon their animal "victims." Darwin may have blanched at the destruction of animals in the name of science, and was half-appalled at his own treatment of pigeons and puppies, but he believed that vivisection was an unfortunate necessity, that it could be properly regulated without threatening scientific progress, and that, in any case, British experimenters were gentlemen who could be entrusted with animal welfare, even if some of their European continental cousins could not. Darwin accepted the value of the knowledge obtained by those who could steel themselves, as he could not, to such unpleasant but necessary labor. The knowledge gained simply absolved the vivisectionist from the charge of unnecessary cruelty: "In the agony of death a dog has been known to caress his master, and every one has heard of the dog suffering under vivisection, who licked the hand of the operator; this man, unless the operation was fully justified by an increase of our knowledge, or unless he had a heart of stone, must have felt remorse to the last hour of his life."[75] When it came to vivisection, Darwin returned or retreated to the anthropocentric fold.[76] In the end, science, knowledge, and humanity were judged to have the greater claims. As Rod Preece puts it, "Animals mattered. Knowledge mattered far more."[77]

In the opposing argument, by contrast, vivisection was represented as the "Savage Science," the very antithesis of domestic values.[78] In the melodramatic narratives of the movement, the family pet was vulnerable to being transformed into an entirely novel phenomenon, the experimental animal, so that the vivisector became associated with the dog stealer as a threat to the sanctity and security of the home. The growing demand for laboratory animals created a market for animals naturally classed as "domestic," even if they happened to be strays and street dogs, or even lost pets.[79] And though the nation's medical schools rarely resorted to such a source of supply, the public was notoriously sensitive on the issue; as we have seen, the Battersea Dogs' Home was forced to reassure the general public that their animals would not be sold on to a painful fate at the hands of the vivisector. When the Royal Commission on Vivisection sat in 1874, the editor of the *Spectator*, R. H. Hutton, suggested that dogs and cats be specially exempted because they were eminently household pets, bred and trained up for companionship; moreover, "the tendency of any measure which recognized more explicitly the claims of family dependants to be especially guarded from anything like hostile treatment, would have a generally humanizing influence on social manners."[80] It was abundantly clear that vivisecting a dog and a frog, say, were different orders of crime. The dog, like the other "higher bred lower animals," was a fellow sufferer from the "hyper-aesthesia" attendant on civilization, so that its degree of suffering even approached that of the human.[81]

Furthermore, Darwinism's questioning of species boundaries suggested to some that "inferior" humans would not be safe from the experiments that were carried out on animals' bodies, and that perhaps above all it would be *women* that would find themselves the objects of a science that was interested more in abstract knowledge than in therapy. Since "the stereotyping of women as domestic animals was deeply entrenched in Victorian culture," vivisection cut to the very heart of the household.[82] Even Darwin cautioned that vivisection not be discussed in front of the family, for fear that it would upset the women of the house; this with good reason, since Darwin's daughter Henrietta was a notable convert to the antivivisection cause.[83] Women were to be protected from the methods and the knowledge that vivisection relied upon and produced. The gendering of emotion within medical science—something that Darwin actively propagated in his denigration of foolish and sentimental critics such as Hutton and Frances Power Cobbe—inevitably portrayed antivivisection as a woman's movement.[84] Evelleen Richards has argued that a direct identification was made between women's sexuality and nature and that of dogs and other domestic animals in the discourse of breeding.[85] Dogs were subservient, their nature malleable to the caprice of breeders; and though the propagation of animals was subject to a range of euphemisms designed to shield women from the brutishness of sexuality, radicalized women drew their own conclusions about their place in a patriarchal society.[86] The equation between wife and pet, which we have met before, made vivisection a crime against women as much as against nature, with a "fertile analogy between mutilated animals and tyrannized wives."[87] As Coral Lansbury and others have argued, women were readily identified in feminist campaigns with the domestic animals that were victimized by men's intrusive quest for knowledge.[88]

All of this made vivisection a distinctive threat to the Victorian home. The iconic locus of this sacrilegiously anti-domestic science was the household laboratory wherein heartless scientists were portrayed as carrying on their unholy work at the expense of their familial relations. In Sarah Grand's didactic novel *The Beth Book* (1897), for instance, the titular heroine is eventually enlightened and liberated from the dominance of her husband, who is not only a keen amateur vivisectionist but also a Lock Hospital surgeon under the infamous Contagious Diseases Acts for good measure. The great, gothic moment of discovery is reached when the laboratory-study, hitherto an inviolable masculine space in the heart of the house, is revealed as a chamber of horrors.[89] Consider too H. G. Wells's more famous *Island of Doctor Moreau* (1896), where the vivisector Moreau is "howled out of the country," his grotesque Darwinism displaced to an exotic and uncanny "biological station," tellingly located in the vicinity of the Galapagos.[90] Arguments like this made the case for the absolute incompatibility of vivisection and domesticity. In such representations the homely ethos of Darwinian science is wholly negated.

It was not only antivivisection propaganda that called into question the domesticated ethos of early Darwinism, however. In a kind of pincer movement, the politics of vivisection were accompanied by the rapid progress of experimental science.[91] For the work of the gentleman amateur scientist, operating from his study and reliant on his own observations and those of his correspondents, was increasingly anachronistic. The professional laboratory, with its array of specialized instruments, was fast becoming the authorized site of knowledge production. A further element of comforting domesticity was lost as British scientists were increasingly recognized as lagging far behind their Continental colleagues who could draw on decades of laboratory experience. Soraya de Chadarevian has shown that while Darwin remained lionized in Britain, the German plant physiologist Julius Sachs belittled him, and his son Francis, as no more than "literary rascals," along with the rest of the "amateur" botanists ignorant of the demands of modern experimental techniques.[92] For men like Sachs, "Only the laboratory offered the institutional and social space in which it was meaningful to speak about skills. Experimental skill was not located simply in the dexterous hands of an operator but depended on a much larger context: it was located in particular rooms, that is, in the laboratory."[93] The move away from the field and the domestic study entailed an undermining of empiricism, as the older traditions of observation gave way to a more rigorously disciplined "scientific" gaze practiced in new spaces such as the laboratory and the clinic.[94] From this point on, the observer became "a kind of power broker, or a tyrant," effecting "the fullest possible distance from his subjects compatible with the closest possible scrutiny of them."[95] Ed Cohen has noted specifically how the practice of vivisection in the experimental laboratory introduced a new model of biomedical science, one in which the notion of the organism's relation to its environment, its milieu, was decisively rejected as quaint and old-fashioned.[96]

The modern laboratory—in this period still a relatively recent innovation in Britain—remained for some time an alien phenomenon, vulnerable to being portrayed as unholy as well as unhomely.[97] Though we can argue that its creature, the laboratory animal, could only become a tool of science by undergoing yet another process of domestication, eventually even to be press-ganged as a "partner in research," the difference between such "denizens of the lab" and Darwin's animal companions is clear enough.[98] Moreover, such suspect instrumentalism could be passed on to human beings who might feel that they too were not so much therapeutic subjects but merely the vehicles for clinical discoveries and techniques; as Ian Miller writes, "The patient, like the laboratory animal, perceived him or herself to be increasingly at risk from the experimental gaze of the medical professional, and as vulnerable to becoming an object of enquiry rather than a target of therapy."[99] This growing focus on clinical research undermined the kind of empathetic observation that we find in Darwin's synthesis: the place of the nonhuman animal in scientific research became ever more vexed, as a result of "the growing divide between otherwise parallel advances in scientific knowledge and the progressive culture of compassion."[100]

Darwin was dead by 1882, and for this reason he avoided much of the obloquy that was directed at the scientific profession by the antivivisectionists.[101] With laboratory science still in its infancy, Darwin did not have to witness the dismantling of his domestic version of scientific inquiry either. There was one man who did live through this revolution, however, and who may be counted the greatest casualty in the unmak-

ing of Darwin's homely naturalism. This was George Romanes. Romanes was deeply entangled in the defense of vivisection and the demise
of the tradition of gentlemanly science, as Rob Boddice has shown.[102]
His scientific career carried on the Darwinian tradition, along with its
resort to homely anecdote and anthropomorphic enthusiasm. But this
was sharp-edged as well as soft-hearted: *unlike* Darwin, Romanes carried out vivisection in his own laboratory in his family house, combining
vivisection with the vernacular.[103] Romanes was profoundly convinced
that there was no inconsistency between pet keeping and vivisection, a
conviction that he demonstrated by offering up his own dog, Major, to
the vivisector's knife. Having his own pet vivisected seems quite extraordinary to us, but as Boddice argues, Romanes wanted to emphasize the
humanitarian generosity of the scientist, as well as avoiding any charge
of hypocrisy in exempting domestic pets from a painless fate that would
advance the cause of knowledge. It is worth quoting Boddice's sympathetic summary at some length:

> Romanes genuinely thought that having him vivisected was
> the most useful, and therefore the most moral, thing he could
> do with him. Then, as now, some would point to this as an act
> of remarkable callousness—a proof of the hardness of heart
> wrought by too frequent exposure to the spilling of blood. But
> Romanes would certainly have palled at charges of insensi-
> tivity. His was one of the more active, more acutely sensitive
> consciences in Victorian society. He simply could not see the
> cruelty in vivisection, for if he could not entirely guarantee
> its painlessness thanks to anesthesia he could at least point to
> the subjects' likely lack of sensitivity or, at worst, justify any
> pain they felt as necessary for the greater good. He understood
> vivisection as humanism, carried out with the highest moral
> intentions. Romanes may have felt a touch of sadness. He cer-
> tainly did not deny that animal pain was real, but when it was
> put into the balance with human pain there was no contest.[104]

There is an additional element of poignancy in Romanes's story, however. The sacrifice of poor Major may have been made for the good of
science, but it was increasingly a type of science that was passing men
like Romanes by. The kind of inquiry exemplified by Darwin's *Expression* and Romanes's *Animal Intelligence* was subject to increasing criticism

from a new breed of scientists, fully acquainted with modern laboratory and scientific methods, who found the reliance on anecdote and anthropomorphism wholly inadequate. Romanes's own work was destined to be taken apart by the biologist and philosopher C. Lloyd Morgan. In Morgan's *Animal Life and Intelligence* (1891), Romanes is faintly praised for his "adequate knowledge and training," only for his conclusions to be subject to withering skepticism.[105] Morgan is thoroughly unimpressed by the host of anecdotes marshaled to prove that, like us, animals might have a sense of justice, of guilt, of humor. For Morgan, while animals have intelligence, only humans have the faculty of *reason*. There is simply no continuum: "man" is a creature of ideas, ideals, and morals, and natural selection no longer has significant purchase on the progress of humanity. Even a "higher" animal like the dog lacks the human ability to use mental constructs that is fundamental to reasoning. As for the progress of the dog under domestication, Morgan has a notably lower opinion than did Romanes, or indeed Darwin: "Pet dogs are . . . a pampered, degenerate, and for the most part unhealthy race, often deteriorated by continued in-breeding."[106] Given that modern ethology would not come into being for decades, the study of animal behavior was to be removed from the home and from the province of the "amateur" naturalist. John Homans writes simply that, "After Morgan, the laboratory became the place to study animal behavior."[107] For Darwin and Romanes, science had begun at home, but from this point on, the home and the laboratory parted company: "What had once been done by gentlemen in their libraries was now done by men in special coats in the bowels of impressive new university buildings. Scientists were a new kind of priesthood, an elect, who insisted on the primacy of their own values against the soft morality of ordinary people. They were suspiciously remote from the cozy home-and-hearth notions so comforting to the Victorians."[108]

It is tempting to take the sad fate of Major, and that of Romanes, as exemplary of the *undomestication* of Darwinism. For the Darwinian attempt to cross the domestic and the scientific would ultimately prove sterile. Although the humble dog provided Darwin's principal example of domestication and descent, the unheralded arrival of the experimental animal was just too *unheimlich* to be easily domesticated. I have suggested here that vivisection was the rock upon which this project of making Darwinism homely foundered, with the antivivisectionists decrying the excesses of scientific materialism at the same time as biomedical science

increasingly removed itself from the home to the professional laboratory. Darwinism was further undomesticated in this move from a reassuringly *British* tradition of gentlemen-naturalists to a scientific tradition
imported from the Continent, still regarded with suspicion. In this way,
the good offices of what Steve Jones calls Darwin's "domestic works"
were undone by a combination of antivivisectionist propaganda and a
burgeoning biomedical profession.[109] In practice, the dichotomy was far
from absolute, but nevertheless these *extremes* helped develop a cloven
culture where science and sentiment, the rational and the noumenal, science and romanticism, were increasingly pitted against each other.

There are parallels here with what John Tosh has called the flight
from domesticity. For Tosh, the weakening bonds between masculinity
and domesticity can be observed in late Victorian sexual politics, patterns of socialization, the spatial dynamics of the home, and also popular culture, where we see for instance the rise of boys-only adventure
fiction, particularly of the colonial variety.[110] Racial and colonial discourses, linked with the new imperialism and the ideals of "Greater Britain," posed a clear challenge to a domesticated "Little England." The
connection with science may seem less obvious, but the spatial dimension of these discourses impacted upon the imagination of the relationship of the human to the animal, with the focus on anthropology as well
as zoology. It is in this context, for instance, that we can trace the rise of
the *ape* to preeminence in both evolutionary theorizing and in the popular understanding of Darwinian evolution. Throughout the nineteenth
century, the dog and the ape had contested the title of most highly developed animal, their respective champions trading the ape's innate intelligence against the dog's evident emotional sophistication. Romanes had
considerably placed the two contenders in equal first place among the
nonhuman animals, at the scale of 28 in his 50-step ladder of intellectual
development, but his generous appreciation of the dog's complex psychology suggested where his sympathies really lay.[111] This development
was inseparable from the animal's long history of human companionship,
so that domestication meant physical and geographical as well as intellectual closeness. Homans rightly notes that the close-at-hand dog was a
much more comfortable cousin than the ape: "For the Victorians, as for
ourselves, dogs brought up simple associations of home and hearth and
the ties that bind, an antidote to the tensions of the city."[112] Jennifer Mason has similarly observed that in the nineteenth century, "beliefs about
dogs and other companion animals did as much if not more than studies

of nonhuman primates to facilitate acceptance of the theory of evolution."[113] Moreover, while the dog was *everywhere*, the ape (to those in the West) was *elsewhere:* "The dog, like his master, is a citizen of the world, and can be acclimatised everywhere. But the ape is chained to the tropics."[114] The dog signified a certain comforting closeness, no challenge to the notion of a stable human-animal boundary. The ape, by contrast, was the locus of what Virginia Richter calls "anthropological anxiety," the twin fears of simianization and assimilation that stemmed from the ape's simultaneous likeness and otherness.[115] That the ape, for all these disadvantages, became the very icon of evolution, testifies to the disintegration of Darwin's domestic science, and its ability, through analogy and metaphor, "to inhabit contradictory experience without moralising it."[116] A particularly plaintive note is sounded by the naturalist and scientific popularizer F. O. Morris, who countered forlornly that "there never yet has been, and never can be, any friendship or communication between man and ape such as there is with the dog, or even the wolf."[117]

This growing fascination with the *exotic* also suggests the development of a sense in which animality itself was abjected.[118] After all, wild animals like the apes "were assigned to a more primitive and violent past and were thus ascribed to a space against which the domestic, both on the level of the home and the nation, could be defined."[119] But even the domestic realm was revealed to be subject to the violence that, after Darwin, nature came to embody. The domestic could not be wholly secured from this vision of violent animality. Martin Danahay has shown, for instance, how the viciousness of domestic animals was linked with the violence of the working classes: "Mongrel as opposed to 'pure bred' dogs thus could be used to reinscribe Victorian social divisions onto the natural world, and present social distinctions as arising spontaneously from the natural order."[120] A distinct class and racial consciousness is apparent, for instance, even in the otherwise homely Romanes. Applying principles of evolution to the phenomena of mind, Romanes put the stress more on nurture than on nature, developing the theme of canine plasticity to such an extent that even the human consciousness of class and caste might be transferred to the dog:

> Pride, sense of dignity, and self-respect are very conspicuously exhibited by well-treated dogs. As with man, so with the friend of man, it is only those whose lines of fortune have fallen in pleasant places, and whose feelings may therefore be said to

have profited by the refining influences of culture, that display in any conspicuous measure the emotions in question. "Curs of low degree," and even many dogs of better social position, have never enjoyed those conditions essential to moral refinement, which alone can engender a true sense of self-respect and dignity. A "low-life" dog may not like to have his tail pulled, any more than a gutter child may like to have his ears boxed; but here it is physical pain rather than wounded pride that causes the smart. Among "high-life" dogs, however, the case is different. Here wounded sensibilities and loss of esteem are capable of producing much keener suffering than is mere physical pain; so that among such dogs a whipping produces quite a different and a much more lasting effect than in the case of their rougher brethren, who, as soon as it is over, give themselves a shake and think no more about it.[121]

Here, the familiar division between the civilized, respectable dog and the low-born cur is reintroduced, this time authorized by comparative psychology. This vision of the mental evolution of the domestic dog considers the influence of human mastery to work hand-in-hand with natural selection in effecting the dog's "improvement." Romanes ends up portraying dogs as so plastic as to be imbued with the consciousness of "good breeding."[122] Proper human companionship raises the moral qualities to such an extent that the dog can be said to be "bourgeoisified" by evolution.[123] But the distinction between the two types of selection becomes increasingly confused, as breeding becomes an analogy that can be utilized in discussing the natural selection of human beings. For just as there are animals capable of moral refinement, so there are human beings with little but brute nature in them—such as the "degraded" English women quarreling violently in the streets, or the brawling Irishwomen put forward by Darwin as examples of the "lower members of the Order to which Man belongs."[124] Domestication becomes here a measure of breeding defined as both a cultural *and* a natural category.

So it is not entirely correct to say that Darwinism was undomesticated. We may see a focus on domestication and breeding returning in the form of eugenics—"the biologisation of political discourse" endorsed by social Darwinism—in the program of race improvement designed to counter physical and moral degeneration.[125] While the biopolitical tradition constituted in principle "a breach in the anthropocentric prejudice of man's absolute superiority," racial anthropology and eugenics turned the insights of Darwin inside out. With social Darwinism, the animal became "a point of division within humanity, between species of people who were separated by their relation to life—and thus to death, since the easy life of some turned out to be directly proportional to the forced death of others."[126] Danahay claims that by imagining humans as domestic animals, eugenics opened up a space for such a form of biopower, a space in which "human bodies were increasingly subject to techno-scientific manipulation in the name of the 'animal.'"[127] As Darwin himself put it, "The weak members of civilised societies propagate their kind. No one who has attended to the breeding of domestic animals will doubt that this must be highly injurious to the race of man. It is surprising how soon a want of care, or care wrongly directed, leads to the degeneration of a domestic race; but, excepting in the case of man himself, hardly anyone is so ignorant to allow his worst animals to breed."[128]

Such a variant of Darwinism was certainly focused on the domestic, but it just as certainly was the opposite of homely. If we return, finally, to where we started, the disputed analogy between artificial and natural selection, we can see that the this is even more troubling and confusing when turned back on the question of the *human*. Edward Beasley has recently rejected the falsely comforting view of Darwin propounded by Adrian Desmond and James Moore, focusing instead on the Darwin who in the *Descent of Man* oscillated between rejection of race as a meaningful way of grouping individuals and the uncritical employment of just such thinking, particularly when he conceives of a struggle between the more "civilized" and the more "savage" races.[129] To explain this, Beasley posits that Darwin, via Walter Bagehot, came to accept an equation of culture with race, with acquired cultural characteristics leading in a Lamarckian manner to physical differentiation. Bagehot, whom Beasley portrays as the English Gobineau, makes the comparison with animal breeds quite explicit: "There are breeds in the animal man just as in the animal dog. When you hunt with greyhounds and course with beagles, then, and not till then, may you expect the inbred habits of a thousand years to pass away, that Hindoos can be free, or that Englishmen will be slaves."[130]

In the *Descent of Man*, Darwin famously places the embryo of the dog and the embryo of the human being side by side, to show that they are indistinguishable, to show that "man" is after all "only" an animal.[131] But the views on race that he seems to have developed led in the rather less amenable direction of equating "breeds" with "races," so that the argument for "higher" and "lower" animals may be transposed very straightforwardly into "higher" and "lower" races, at home or abroad.[132] And if "breeds" exist only through the elimination of "curs," as Martin Wallen recognizes, this acceptance of hierarchy shades into something evidently more uncomfortable and sinister. There are no "curs" in nature, any more than there are pure and permanent "breeds," and any rational understanding recognizes the many advantages of the "mongrel" over the "purebred"; but from the viewpoint of the newly vitalized racism of the later nineteenth century, the scientific understanding of variation and selection could be taken to imply that some "races," like the intermediate and inadequate "curs" abjured by dog breeders, were destined only for extinction. Darwinism, then, ultimately helped to shore up an anthropocentric vision of the world—and, by simultaneously anthropomorphizing the "lower" orders, endorsed some of the worst inferences of scientific racism. The animal is no longer, like the companion dog, placed side by side with the human, but is instead relegated, like the ape, to the lower rungs of the ladder of civilization, paradoxically taking some of the human species with him.

CHAPTER 5

A Place for the Animal Dead
Animal Souls, Pet Cemeteries, and the Heavenly Home

*I*N THE previous chapter, I argued that the un-domestication of
Darwinism was bound up with an apparent conflict between science
and sentiment in the assessment of the claims of nonhuman animals.
In truth, too stark a distinction is misleading: animal welfarists could
recommend an unsentimental rationalism, while the most anthropocentric of scientists necessarily traded in emotion. As Oscar Wilde put it, in
reference to the higher calling that the artistic "vivisection" of human life
represented, what was really wonderful was the mixing of "the curious
hard logic of passion and the emotional coloured life of the intellect."[1]
Antivivisectionists such as Frances Power Cobbe advised, from the one
camp, that activists needed a cool head as well as warm blood, caution-
ing against the dangers of being associated with "womanish" sentimentality; antivivisectionists also laid claim to the scientific mainstream,
arguing that vivisectionism was simply bad science.[2] The opposing party,
by contrast, appealed to sensibility as well as to sense: thus T. H. Huxley
claimed that the vivisector, in his quest for knowledge that would allevi-
ate human suffering, was truly "humane" and feeling, while for his op-
ponent it was a matter of "Let Art & Science, Men & Women die / But let
no tear suffuse a lap dog's eye!"[3] All the same, the fact that the work of
the vivisector was presented by supporters as necessitating the *mastery*
of emotions, even to the extent of inculcating something like a military
discipline in approaching the "struggle" with nature in the laboratory,
or alternatively steeling oneself to becoming a well-tuned "instrument"
of science, indicates how the terms of the debate could become increasingly polarized: "heart," on the one hand, "science" on the other, to bor-

row Wilkie Collins's dichotomy.[4] Sentimentality, once so prized, was fast becoming the enemy of scientific inquiry, while the "smooth cool men of science" found themselves increasingly labeled as mere heartless materialists.[5]

Antipathy toward scientific "materialism" keyed into a wider strain of hostility toward "modernity" and "positivism," involving a distinctive critique of individualism, secularism, capitalism, bourgeois materialism, and a number of other distinctively modern evils.[6] These complaints, as we have seen, found a ready villain in the vivisectionist, while sentimental attitudes toward animals, in the form of pet keeping, figured as an antidote to these ills of civilization: as Kathleen Kete puts it, "The image of the evil scientist appeared alongside the construct of the pet."[7] Sentimental attachment to individual animals came to be a measure of the highest worth—care, compassion, and "mercy" being valued above scientific knowledge or even "progress." This was also a profoundly *gendered* movement and moment, for the scientific abuse of animals was represented quite characteristically as a specimen of an inherently *male* violence: toward animals, toward nature, but also toward women and the home life that was considered their province.[8] If domesticity is defined as "a mode of utopian opposition to the fallenness of the wider bourgeois society," then women were allotted a special role as its principal defenders.[9] We have seen already that dog stealing was interpreted in this characteristically gendered way, but here I want to explore further the ways in which resistance to the perceived abuse of animals was a preeminently female—indeed, a *feminist*—issue.

In this chapter, I examine how middle-class women challenged anthropocentric attitudes in late Victorian Britain, not head-on, as in the well-known antivivisectionist cause—rather, indirectly, through the deeply felt desire to memorialize dead pets, to dignify their passing, and to believe that they might be reunited with them in the afterlife. This chapter touches, therefore, on the ancient question of animal souls, on philosophy, religion, and spirituality, and on the imaginative geography of heaven itself. But there is a material as well as an abstract geography at stake here: the development of the pet cemetery as a memorial landscape in the Victorian city.[10] I argue that, odd as these eccentric and ex-centric emanations of grief and hope may appear, they amount to a distinctive late Victorian "structure of feeling," arising in opposition to what were taken to be the blandishments of scientific, religious, and cultural orthodoxy. This may at first glance not look much like an act

of resistance—perhaps at best a reactive resentment of what passed for
rationalism—but resistance I think it was. As Karen Raber has noted,
grief and mourning for pets is a demonstration of the attribution of personhood to animals, companion species being transformed into second
selves.[11] Moreover, since "animals' lack of religious belief, and their presumed exclusion from the life of the spirit that survives death, had tradi-
tionally been a criterion of distinction between them and mankind," any
challenge to this orthodoxy had profound implications for how people
saw themselves in relation to their animals.[12]

Let me begin with the place of the dog in the Victorian imagination of
death. The notion of canine fidelity, which reached its apogee in the
Victorian years, is a familiar enough theme, but it should be considered
rather as a threnody given that it was principally organized around the
issue of death or dying. The exemplary fidelity of the dog triumphed,
in Victorian sentimental culture, even over death, and we may see this
exemplified in the popularity of the innumerable reproductions of Landseer's *The Shepherd's Last Mourner* (c. 1837) and its siblings—Landseer's
own *Faithful Hound* (1830) and *The Shepherd's Grave* (1884), or Archer's
The Empty Cradle (date unknown), for instance—on the walls of the
households of every class and status. Perhaps of greater power still was
the heartwarming saga of the greatest of Victorian mourning dogs, Greyfriars Bobby, banished from his master's grave by church and civil authority, but in his continuing vigil an emblem of faithfulness in a faithless
world.[13] Great sentimental and popular favorites, these animal figures
were reminders of a love that lasted beyond the grave, a reassurance of
the loving heart's dominion over both the living and the dead. Dogs, as
John Morley has noted in his social history of Victorian death, were in
this way given "a firm place in the Victorian language of grief."[14]

This discursive place for animals was intimately related to, over-
determined by, the material and imaginative geographies of the bourgeois household and Victorian domestic ideology respectively. As dogs
were installed as the domestic pet par excellence, so they were metonymically associated with the institutions of the family and the household,
the ascribed virtues of which the Victorian middle class held so dear.
Dogs were readily subsumed under the ideal of domesticity that exerted
so powerful an influence in nineteenth-century Britain, and this should
be considered as "not just a pattern of residence or a web of obligations,
but a profound attachment: a state of mind as well as a physical orienta-

tion."[15] The humble dog, with its characteristic virtues of constancy and companionship, trust and trustworthiness, came to exemplify all that the respectable Victorian world associated with family life, so much so that by the end of the Victorian age we can say with John Gillis that pets had become "sovereign masters of domestic space" symbolizing those qualities that families often found wanting in themselves.[16] Idealized for their quasi-familial virtues, and inseparable from the imaginative landscape of the family, the domestic dog was firmly installed at the heart of the respectable Victorian household, a kind of household god.

The domestic destiny of pet dogs clearly lies behind the profound grief of their owners at their passing. Pet dogs were necessarily prominent as living and breathing memento mori. The dog's short life, its devoted affection and loyalty, and above all its cherished status as a dependent pet and undeniable member of the family, all made it a specially convenient emblem of the loss of all loved ones: "The friendships formed and the associations made for such a period are not easily effaced, and can never be replaced. That, indeed, is the saddest feature of the whole question of pets. They are short-lived. One has scarcely time to grow fond of them, to find them entwined in our hearts, before they are rudely wrenched away from us by the cruel hand of Death."[17] In literature there are any number of instances of memorials to a favorite dog.[18] But such sentiments attained material form with the elaborate memorials that owners, from Lord Byron and Queen Victoria downward, constructed for their favorite pets. The domestic dog was thus loved, mourned, and memorialized in a manner that cuts to the heart of Victorian middle-class family sentiment.

Now, there are good reasons for considering that these cultural commentaries on, and commemorations of, animal death were, in large part, suffused with anthropocentric values, and thus ultimately reinforcing of the divide between animals and humans. Diana Donald has commented, about pictures such as *The Shepherd's Last Mourner,* that while transparently consolatory, they also focus on the inability of the dog to understand death: "We are moved and heart-warmed by the idea of a dog's unshakeable fidelity, and this aspect of the image must explain its enduring popularity. At the same time, the spectacle of an animal helpless in its suffering prompts peculiarly strong impulses of sympathy. . . . Here, the dog's presumed bewilderment in the face of death plays a part."[19] Perhaps most forcefully, Teresa Mangum has insisted that the need to incorporate animal deaths into a human culture of grief, mourning, and memorialization only reinforces the anthropocentric priorities of Victorian pet owners. Mangum thus speculates that "surprised by the intensity of grief, many animal owners sought to reconcile cultural confidence in human superiority with personal feelings of bereavement that sometimes dealt a stronger blow than grief for departed human companions."[20] Mangum sees the mourning of pets as only encouraging "the avoidance of responsibility towards 'animals' as a whole," since there was a clear separation between beloved "pets" and the rest of the animal world.[21] For her, even the pet cemetery, set apart as it is from the rest of society, is a marker only of indifference toward animals "as a whole": "By literally or metaphorically burying animals, pet owners joined this social ambition to hide animals and their suffering from public view and hence, from public responsibility."[22] Looking specifically at one of the earliest pet cemeteries in the world, adjoining London's Hyde Park, I want to take issue with what is, I think, a perverse reading, one that does not adequately recognize the elements of a culture of grief and memorialization that were not simply reconciled with general attitudes of human superiority and indifference to the treatment of animals. Chief among these elements were the question of animal souls and the nature of the life to come: a complementary *imaginative geography* that challenged Victorian orthodoxies.

There is perhaps no more fitting memorial to the sentimental attachments between Victorian pets and pet owners than the small dogs' cemetery that occupies an obscure corner of London's Hyde Park (figure 12). A short distance from the busy Bayswater Road lies the last resting place of a few hundred dogs—and the odd cat, canary, and maybe a monkey too—the vast majority of which have uniform headstones and loving inscriptions from their bereaved masters and mistresses. Dating from 1880, this is the oldest pet cemetery in Britain, though Gillis notes that such cemeteries could be found in France from the 1870s, and the "graceful and harmless custom" of burying pet dogs was said by the *Strand* magazine in 1893 to have been by that time common in Germany.[23] The origin of the Hyde Park dogs' cemetery, like its nearest American counterpart, in Hartsdale, New York, was purely accidental, when a dog belonging to a family that often visited the park and its gatekeeper at Victoria Lodge, a Mr. Winbridge, was granted a burial there. This dog, a Maltese terrier called Cherry, apparently fond of appearing in drawing-room entertainments in the guise of "a soldier" or "a sick

baby," was buried "in the spot he had loved so well in his life": "So intelligent and so amiable a dog assuredly deserved a Christian burial," as the
Strand charmingly put it.[24] Mr. Winbridge allowed ever more of his lodge
garden to be used for burials, so that in time the entire garden became
a veritable "canine necropolis," its space filled in its entirety with the
pleasingly uniform headstones and boundary tiles. The carriageways of
Hyde Park were responsible for many of the dogs that came to the burial
ground in the ensuing years, and E. A. Brayley Hodgetts in the *Strand*
suggested rather significantly that the very domestication and dependency of pet dogs' nature had unfitted them for the Darwinian struggle
for life outside the protection of the domestic hearth:

> It would appear . . . that the very tenderness and care that
> are lavished upon them unfit them for the rude and heartless
> world, and make them unable to look out for themselves. They
> have got so used to be taken care of that they become as help-
> less as children, and are flurried and lose their head when out
> of doors or exposed to an unexpected danger. Pet-dogs do
> not possess that most important knack of "getting out of the
> way," which is one of the first lessons which animals as well as
> human beings have to learn to fit them for the stern battle of
> life.[25]

Whatever the cause, however, the dogs' cemetery was soon more or less
full, and with a few exceptions closed to new interments.

We must first recognize that the notion that such cemeteries effect a
segregation of human and animal worlds is misleading. Far from hiding
animal death in its own space, animal cemeteries are, as Hilda Kean has
argued, "places of overlapping, if not competing, geographies in which
human and animal are blurred in various ways."[26] Nor is such "blurring"
simply a matter of anthropomorphism, the inevitability of commemora-
tion of animals' lives in human language and representation:

> The place, the physical landscape of the cemetery, is itself a
> celebration of a particular personal cross-species relationship.
> Justification is not needed; nor are measures to convince the
> unsympathetic of the existence of the sentience of animals.
> Animals do not need to "speak" from beyond the grave to
> convince particular humans that they have consciousness—in

Figure 12. The Dogs' Cemetery, Hyde Park, London. (Photography by David Beckingham, courtesy of David Beckingham)

this context it is a given. Although an animal "voice" is absent, many traces of the animal's activities and sense of agency are present.[27]

Just as important, however, is the substantive argument made by these memorials, either implicitly or explicitly. Of course, the dominant strain is one of grief and loss. The memorials in the Hyde Park cemetery, which date from around 1881, leave no doubt as to the depth of their owners' affection and sense of bereavement. The language of many is effusive and elaborate, not to say gushing: "The most intelligent, faithful, gentle, sweet tempered & affectionate dog that ever lived: & adored by his devoted and sorrowing friend Sir H. Seton Gordon, Bart." Others are more straightforwardly addressed, but no less sentimental: "Dear little 'Smut,'" "In tender memory of sweet little 'Tiny,'" "In loving memory of my little Dorrit." These inscriptions testify, however, to something more than just grief. What is most striking about several memorials in this dogs' cemetery—and it is a sentiment I think implicit in many, arguably

all, of the others—is the hope exhibited that owner and pet might meet
again in the hereafter. The family, of which the pet dog was so much a
part, would not perhaps be sundered by death. Perhaps even more than
the sentimental sincerity of these inscriptions, this is what today's observer will find most distancing as well as distracting.

This hope is very clearly expressed in several memorials. In addition
to the arguably ambiguous address of "au revoir," there are the explicit
inscriptions for beloved pets such as "darling 'Tiddy'" (figure 13), b.
1895, d. 1901:

> Shall He whose name is love
> Deny our loving friends a home above?
> Nay, He who orders all things for the best
> In paradise will surely give them rest

Or that in memory of a "Wee Bobbit" (figure 14), d. 1901:

> When our lonely lives are o'er
> And our spirits from this earth shall roam
> We hope he'll be there waiting
> To give us a welcome home

The fact that such sentiments point to both the cherished hope for
future reunion, and a clearly expressed emphasis on the heavenly home
that awaits both animal and man, is the matter at the heart of this chapter. Towards the end of the nineteenth century, many Victorians were
not shy of reviving the old question of the immortality of animals' souls,
and devoted considerable emotional and cultural energies toward imagining a spiritual home that was analogous to the middle-class household.
The depth of these Victorians' investment in domestic ideology was so
great, we may say, that even death itself was potentially domesticable,
and the lives and deaths of animals played a small but significant role in
that process.

Brayley Hodgetts, writing in 1893, had concluded by stating that "as a
pretty custom and graceful tribute to the memory of the affectionate and
faithful 'friend of man' no objection can be raised to the burial of dogs."[28]
In earlier years, however, few commentators would have been quite so
sanguine. Dogs, like all animals, could not of course be buried in conse-

Figure 13. "Our Darling 'Tiddy,'" the Dogs' Cemetery, Hyde Park, London. (Photography by author)

Figure 14. "Wee Bobbit," the Dogs' Cemetery, Hyde Park, London. (Photography by author)

crated ground, though clandestine funerals were not unknown. The inadmissibility of animals into sacred space was only one expression of the distance that orthodox Christianity insisted should prevail between man and beast, a gap that had narrowed with the influence of humanists, secularists, and skeptics, but that had certainly not disappeared. Orthodox theology was thoroughly anthropocentric, and its doctrinal construction of the moral community can here be seen to take clear geographical form in the proscription of animal burials.

The alternatives for the disposal of the remains of pet dogs were therefore bleak: while a lucky few would have the honor of an interment at the bottom of their owners' garden, most others would have been disposed of via the river or the dustheap. For much of the period, the disposal of dogs was generally regarded in fact as more of a sanitary than a spiritual concern. We can certainly place the interest in the burial of pets within the same moral and spiritual framework as the reformed practice of interment, and the parallel growth of sanitary suburban cemeteries.[29] The burial/cremation controversy of late Victorian times, concerning the proper disposal of human remains, was marked by the invocation of scientific and religious, rational and moral, arguments, but we should note that this was not free of associations with the treatment of animals. The argument against interment could be interpreted by some as bringing the treatment of human beings down to the strictly sanitary level of disposal of animals' organic remains. And from the countervailing camp, a leader writer on the disposal question noted in 1885 that a rationalist "sanitarian" had kept a dead dog, covered with earth, in an open box in the center of his sitting room, and that within a few weeks the dog had resolved itself into carbolic acid and watery vapor without offense: proof that human burial was equally sanitary.[30] Pat Jalland has noted the work of advocates of interment in promoting a reformed practice; and the burial of dogs was again said to be equally inoffensive, given that the "earth-to-earth" system was invariably practiced, rather than the lead coffins which were available to their human cousins.[31]

To treat dead dogs as simply "waste," however, was also to introduce a concern for the dignity of animals that paralleled that which animated discussions about "lower-class" humans. Pauper funerals, and interment in the public grave, were widely regarded as a sign of failure compared to the private plot that conferred cultural membership and respectability. There was an enduring association between common graves for paupers and rubbish tips and wasteland.[32] Furthermore, the question of the disposal of dead dogs also reflects the uncomfortable fact that many pauper corpses found their way to the dissection table as well as the common grave.[33] If the dignity of paupers was haunted by the specter of anatomization, perhaps too did attention to the proper interment of animals affront the culture of vivisection.[34] In this way, the disposal of dogs was infused with some of the characteristic elements of the concern for the disposal of human beings: dogs, lower in evolutionary estimation, were invariably subject to greater indignities, but their fate could not be kept wholly separate from that of their human counterparts.

The disposal of nonhuman animal remains formed part of a wider debate that pitted scientific rationalism against religious and spiritual moralism. From the 1860s to the end of the century and beyond, the antagonism between science and faith, between naturalism and supernaturalism, reached an extraordinary intensity, with both orthodox religion and rationalist science emerging, for many, the losers. Men and women dissatisfied with the limitations of both mainstream Christianity and scientific naturalism, and "intensely preoccupied with questions of death and immortality," looked to a new spirituality not entirely divorced from science and religion but clearly heterodox to both.[35] Bourgeois women were in the vanguard of this movement, and as we shall see, the spiritual or theological question of the future life for animals was bound up with the argument against vivisection and with the vision of a domestic heaven, in the elaboration of both of which women were specially prominent. As Coral Lansbury pointed out, identification with animals was a classed and gendered response, with certain groups within society—such as women of the privileged classes—identifying emotionally with the suffering of animals and willing to critique materialism, science, and patriarchy in equal measure.[36] Kathleen Kete has similarly demonstrated that for many women, concerns with animal welfare were "an escape from a dangerous and masculine scientific world."[37] Kete usefully adds that "by the late 1860s and 1870s the affective behavior of canines offered dramatic contrast to an increasingly cruel bourgeois and urban world, male, alienating, and relentlessly unsentimental. The pet became the countericon of the scientific, and dehumanized, age."[38] That the majority of pet owners burying their dogs in Hyde Park were women— "With a few exceptions, the dogs whose remains are interred there have belonged to ladies residing in the neighbourhood"—is suggestive rather than conclusive, for sure, but the burial of pets does seem to have resonated especially strongly with those groups most prominent in the antivivisection and animal welfare movement.[39]

Nor would it be unreasonable to surmise that the late-nineteenth-century interest, especially among middle-class women, in spiritualism and unorthodox faith played some kind of part in the burial of pets. Dogs' cemeteries like Hyde Park's are arguably infused with such spiritual(ist) associations. Sharon Marcus has written of the suburban cemetery as a kind of "controlled haunting," the only place where the domesticated, family-based ideal of Victorian ideology could be made a reality, and in the dogs' cemetery we find a very close parallel.[40] Domestic pets here inhabited a "family plot" that commemorated their conjoined lives with human beings, under the aegis of the family—the central mystery of Victorian culture—and expressing in material form the hope that that family may be reunited, in its entirety, after death. We can infer that the appearance of pet cemeteries in the later nineteenth century was a reaction to the kinds of grosser materialism and blind faith in progress that were to be associated with the scientific movement, with dissection, cremation, and vivisection. Pet cemeteries should not be seen as simply an extension of middle-class humanitarian concerns, up to and well past the line of anthropomorphic whimsy, therefore; rather, we should note that their proponents were attempting to redraw the boundaries of the moral community, by raising the treatment of dead pets to something that approximated the (proper) treatment of dead people. And in so doing, they necessarily came into direct conflict with the anthropocentric moral geography of orthodox Christianity.

It is important here that we put the stress on *orthodox* Christianity. Religion has regularly been castigated as perhaps the predominant source of anthropocentric attitudes, authorizing a blatantly instrumentalist view of animals designed for the service of human beings, with Judaism and Christianity singled out for opprobrium.[41] But religions are rich and diverse traditions, rather than static sources of doctrine, as Chien-Hui Li notes with Christianity in mind.[42] Christianity and Christian themes were major resources for the incipient animal protection movement, though we should quickly add that the treatment of Lewis Gompertz by the SPCA shows this Christianity at its exclusive and presumptuous worst.[43] All the same, faith was rather more obviously a source of changing attitudes to animals than the secular Darwinism examined in the previous chapter.[44]

The question of death and the afterlife, and the animal soul, was the key theme here in this resistance to theological orthodoxy. The animal rights advocate Henry Salt recognized that "the denial of immortality to animals (unless, of course, it be also denied to men) tends strongly to lessen their chance of being justly and considerately treated."[45] And the novelist and animal activist Annie Thomas had this to say about "dog-nature," expressing what she believed, and, sarcastically, what she ought to believe: "It is something above us, and something beyond us, though it *is* soulless (we are told), and we are the greatest of created things."[46] This was certainly heterodox. Taking the long view, Augustine and Aquinas were quite canonical: animals did not possess souls; ergo, they did not share in the afterlife. Ecclesiastical authorities, as Zeb Tortorici has noted for Bourbon Mexico, were adamant about keeping the sacraments undefiled by animals, reserving burial for humans, and following "a sacred geography that was determined by the Church's rules about orthodoxy, heresy, and the uniqueness of the human soul."[47] However, although the Church denied spiritual existence to animals, popular culture throughout the ages was more ambivalent, with a carnivalesque culture that on the one hand affirmed the human-animal boundary, but on the other left room for affection for privileged pets, confounding the authoritarian "theological colonization" of the animal question.[48] So for all the stress on orthodoxy, there was a recurrent questioning of the uniqueness of humans. Tague has noted that for eighteenth-century Britain, "the belief that animals did not have immortal souls could lead to conflicts between the desire to mourn and a sense that such mourning might be inappropriate," and that such tensions stimulated thinking about the connections, rather than the differences, between humans and animals.[49] By the later nineteenth century, whatever earlier burlesque and satirical strains there may have been seem to have given way to the entirely sincere belief in animal souls shared by many Victorian pet owners.

Unlike the burial of humans, interment of animals lacked what Julie-Marie Strange calls a "cultural script."[50] But there were nevertheless resources in Christianity, at least, that offered pet owners a basis for resisting a mainstream culture that refused pet owners consolation. The hope that animals' souls might live on after death when their material forms had perished is evident in the Hyde Park cemetery, and it is made most explicit by the invocation of scriptural authority. On headstones in the cemetery we find this characteristic recourse to the Bible: the assertion in Luke 12:6 that "not one of them is forgotten before God" is bolstered by that of Psalms 50:10 that "every beast of the forest is mine." More subtly, readers are directed to Romans 8:21 — "the creature itself also shall be delivered from the bondage of corruption into the glorious liberty of the children of God." It is clear from these quotations that Christianity, despite its hegemonic anthropocentrism, provided cultural resources enough to allow pet owners to entertain the hope for a spiritual reunion. Opponents could of course marshal the same resources to prove a contrary point—most obviously with references to "the beasts that perish" (Psalms 49:12, 20) — but scriptural authority was ambiguous enough on the question, as proponents of the immortality of animal souls were quick to point out. For instance, the well-known science popularizer the Reverend J. G. Wood, in his two-volume work *Man and Beast: Here and Hereafter* (1874), argued that the Old Testament was typically misinterpreted, and that there was, at the very least, nothing conclusive about the temporal chains of the animal kingdom.[51] Animals' spiritual existence remained an open question, with the links to contemporary animal welfare concerns being obvious to the likes of the reviewer for the *Pall Mall Gazette*, who commented that "cruelty to animals and thoughtlessness about their wants are so rife that we almost wish the Woodists were likely to be a large sect."[52]

That such a belief or suggestion could be a powerful consoling force is amply demonstrated by the letters that Wood received from correspondents reacting to his broaching the subject in an earlier treatise. While some readers responded with sarcasm and invective, objecting (in characteristic anthropocentric fashion) "to sharing immortality with a cheese-mite," many others were reassured by an idea "which they had long held in their hearts, but had been afraid to express."[53] One such correspondent asked for just such reassurance in these words: "I should like to know if you think that in the next stage of existence our animals will know us individually as they do now in a measure by smell, and scent, and voice. I am anxious to see your work on the proofs of immortality in animals. I do so hope that, when I pass beyond the veil, I shall know and be recognized by a dear old pet dog, 'Beppo,' a most devoted animal, who lived and died by us."[54] Another, a lawyer whose derogation of humanity it is tempting to ascribe to his profession, railed more confidently against those who would deny a heaven to his lost retriever and its kin: "Upon the whole, I think that he was a much more exemplary character than many men and women whom I have known, and I should be very happy to meet him again in some other sphere. I would rather hunt with him on a planetoid, or a ring of Saturn, than spend my time in a narrow heaven which some zealots would arrogate to themselves and their small sect, if they could."[55] But perhaps most evocative of the pain felt on the death of a treasured pet, and a need for reassurance that flew in the face of orthodox religion, is the case provided by Jane Welsh Carlyle in response to the death of her dog Nero in 1860. Nero, a Cuban or Maltese mix, was finally put down with a dose of prussic acid, having lingered in pain after an accident a few months previously when he had been run over by a butcher's cart. His throat crushed by the wheels of the cart, Nero suffered on as an asthmatic invalid for the remaining months of his life, before a medical friend of the Carlyles, a Dr. Barnes, was at last called in to administer the fatal dose. This was a bitter blow even for that arch-stoic and critic of unmanly sentimentality Thomas Carlyle; for his wife, whose limited domestic happiness was metonymically and symbolically inseparable from her pet, the death of poor Nero struck even harder. What made matters worse, she complained, was to be held to be indulging inappropriate feelings for her pet. As she later wrote to Dr. Barnes, "I wouldn't be at home for visitors to criticise my swollen eyes,

and smile at grief 'about a dog.'"[56] Jane Carlyle's sensitivity on this point
extended to the emotions she felt about the value of Nero's life, and the
hope she expressed for its future:

> What is become of that little beautiful, graceful Life, so full of
> love and loyalty and sense of duty, up to the last moment that
> it animated the body of that little dog? Is it to be extinguished,
> abolished, annihilated in an instant, while the brutalized, two-
> legged, so-called human creature who dies in a ditch, after
> having outraged all duties, and caused nothing but pain and
> disgust to all concerned with him, — he to live forever? It is
> impossible for me to believe that! I couldn't help saying so
> in writing to my Aunt Grace, and expected a terrible lecture
> for it. But not so! Grace, who had been fond of my little dog,
> couldn't find in her heart to speak unkindly on this subject,
> nay, actually gave me a reference to certain verses in Romans
> which seemed to warrant my belief in the immortality of ani-
> mal life as well as human. One thing is sure, anyhow: my little
> dog is buried at the top of our Garden; and I grieve for him as
> if he had been my little human child.[57]

Jane Carlyle's attachment to her lost dog, and the hopes she expressed
here, have an interest beyond the biographical. For one thing, the social
pressure in Victorian society to suppress such feelings of grief, and to
deny the elevation of an animal to the level of even the worst of humans,
is noted in the bitterest terms. But it is the hope for a future life for the
closest of animal companions that is again most striking, and Jane Carlyle's sympathetic aunt suggests the willingness of many to countenance
such yearning.

   Despite our reaction to this speculation on the future life of animals,
which perhaps is more or less in line with Victorian orthodoxy on this
point, a moment's reflection confirms that it is the idea that we do *not*
share the next life with other creatures that counts, in the context of
human history and culture, as the aberrant belief.[58] We may reasonably
ask why, if we assent to an afterlife, we should strain at this particular
gnat. Virtually all societies outside of the modern West have considered
the life to come as inclusive of the animal kingdom, as the widespread
concern for animal memorialization attests. In the high Victorian period
there was, for all its unorthodoxy, a nagging undercurrent of specula-

tion about animal immortality. In her review of "the consciousness of dogs," for example, the campaigning feminist and philanthropist Frances Power Cobbe raises, in an intellectual argument, more or less the exact question raised so emotionally by Jane Carlyle:

> One point only remains to be touched, and that with great
> hesitation. Must our tenderness for our humble friends end
> at the hour when their brief lives come to a close? Is there no
> hope that something in the dog, as well as something in man,
> may survive the dissolution of the fleshly frame? Undoubtedly
> many of the firmer grounds for human faith in immortality are
> wanting in the case of the creature who, so far as we discern,
> has no consciousness of such a destiny—no moral freedom,
> whose high purpose (so often failing here) must have fulfil-
> ment hereafter—no sense of that Divine communion which
> gives to the saint the assurance that "God will not leave his
> soul in Hades, nor suffer His holy one to see corruption."
> On the other hand, the unmerited sufferings of brutes lends
> warrant to the hope that perfect Justice will not leave them
> unrequited; while the veil which hangs over the "how" and the
> "whither" of the exodus of the human soul from the dissolving
> body, allows us at least room to speculate whether a similar
> law may not prevail with regard to the "spirit of the beast,"
> when divided from its physical form.[59]

This intellectual undercurrent—strong enough to be labeled a tradi-tion—had its roots in an earlier age.[60] Although, as Jane Carlyle's letter suggests, the Bible offered certain resources that encouraged specu-lation, the authority most cited in defense of this view was that of the venerable Bishop Butler, with the physical theology of his influential *Analogies of Religion*.[61] This was closely followed by the great John Wes-ley, whose suggestion that in the afterlife the animal kingdom might be elevated in the sphere of creation, to occupy the place that human be-ings would vacate as they attained the status of angels, was especially cherished; and to this could be added the arguments of Richard Dean's *Essay on the Future Life of Brute Creatures* (1728) and others. In 1836 Isaac Taylor had essayed this theme of the afterlife treated as a branch of the physiology of the species, and readily confessed that the argument, "if pushed to its consequences, would go near to imply the immortality of birds, beasts, and fishes, insects and zoophytes!"[62] It was for him a theoretical and moral "embarrassment" to acknowledge "a brotherhood of mind, such as shall include the polypus, the sea jelly, and the animacule of a stagnant pool," so that ultimately Taylor strenuously rejected this troubling reductio ad absurdum of the physical theory of a future life.[63] Toward the end of the century, however, the absurdity of this position was to many less and less patent, and speculative writers returned to Butler and the Bible, and the ancients, to question the exclusion of animals from the life to come.

The naturalist and divine F. O. Morris provides a helpfully full review of the various authorities concerning the probability of animals' future life.[64] Morris, a vehement antivivisectionist, entertained the prospects that animals might have an immortal soul largely as a spur to anticruelty attitudes: no one, he believed, would be cruel to an animal if that creature were believed to exist after death. The antivivisectionist James Macaulay also wrote, "If, as some wise and good men have supposed, there may be a place for lower creatures than man in a future world, we should feel the responsibility of our relation to them now all the greater."[65] Richard French, the historian of Victorian antivivisection, is therefore right to emphasize the dependence of such thinking on the vivisection question.[66] Morris, not unusually, links the question of vivisection and cruelty firmly to the materialist and mechanistic understanding of nature he believed was ushered in by the "preposterous and idle vagaries" of Darwin, and propagated by Huxley and others. For Morris, it was Huxley's portrayal of animals as conscious but not intelligent machines that justified the "atrocious, cold-blooded, and cowardly cruelties practised by the experimenters on living animals," and he invited Huxley, as a believer in human kinship with the animals, to try himself the test of animal sensation under the vivisector's knife.[67]

Morris, again quite characteristically, adds to the authority of Butler and others evidence from observation and reflection of animals' mental capacities, reasoning from the premise that the destruction of anything not material is simply incompatible with Christian doctrine:

> No one can watch without any emotion the eye glazing in
> death of a faithful dog or horse, the mild look of a dying bird,
> or the expiring throb of a wounded animal. Who can avoid
> the thought that something is going away which he cannot
> bring back, nor any power of his then stay, even for awhile,

the departure of? And if it be some long known and favourite
companion, conspicuous perhaps for fidelity, affection and
sagacity, whose bodily life is ebbing away, — who is there who
can resist the thought, that he is not parting with the dying
creature for ever, but that the same CREATOR who gave the
spirit, and now commands it to "return," will one day restore
it, and bid it live again?[68]

The "mild hope," therefore, could be buttressed not only by anecdote
and reflection but by strenuous theological reasoning. We should note
that the characteristic eclecticism of the case put forward for the immortality of animal souls — the scriptural authority and theological prec-
edents, the argument by analogy between man and beast, the anecdotes
of sagacity and higher powers, the doctrine of compensation for present
suffering — served to throw doubt upon the authority of orthodox religious and ethical thinking. The message is that there is no convincing
proof that animals are excluded from heaven, and much to suggest —
emotionally, intellectually, empirically, ethically — that they are not.[69] For
French, this literature on the future life of animals consists merely of
"quotation, tortuous biblical exegesis, and emotional exhortation," that
should be interpreted merely as an outgrowth of attitudes toward pets,
"rather than as the preexistent and wholly rational intellectual substruc-
ture of the [antivivisection] movement."[70] In sum, "this theological and
ethical discussion was less a fundamental underpinning for the antivivisection movement as a whole than a by-product of psychological and
intellectual forces manifested by the movement, for which animals became symbolic."[71] While there is much truth in this, and certainly in the
importance of pets, it is surely a mistake to dismiss the reasoning behind
such speculation as entirely dependent on these external "psychological and intellectual forces." Nor indeed should the emotional structure
of pet keeping be considered antithetical to the abstract theological and
philosophical speculation that I have demonstrated. Secondary it may
well have been to the heart of the antivivisection movement, but the
question as to whether animals have a future life remained, for many
like Jane Carlyle, an emotional and intellectual investment of the first
order. Elizabeth Barrett Browning likewise seems to have seriously considered the question of the "Souls of Dogs."[72] It certainly does not seem
appropriate to dismiss these responses in psychic or reactionary terms.
The question of an afterlife for animals can serve as a reminder not so

much of high Victorian sentimentality or anthropomorphic excess, as of the late Victorians' profound spiritual imagination. No small part of this creative faculty, as the next section will demonstrate, was an inclusive eschatological geography that welcomed both humans and other animals. This "eschatopography," to indulge in an ugly but useful neologism, tells us something important about Victorian thinking on spiritual destiny and the hopes for an afterlife, but it also indicates the expanded sense of moral community that some individuals were able to conceive or perceive.

Curiously, such speculation, while insistent about the indestructibility of that which partook of the spirit, as opposed to the perishability of the material, quite happily complemented and coexisted with a strong belief in the physicality and materiality of the afterlife. Though Isaac Taylor did not in the end endorse the belief in animal immortality, his stress on the *physical* nature of the afterlife was influentially insistent on the importance of place; rather than the nowhere of a disembodied spirit, Taylor substituted what he called "the acquirement of locality."[73] Speculation about the future existence of pets, if not the animal and natural kingdom in its entirety, could tap into this concern for physicality and materiality. More to the point, this social heaven was an analogue of the earthly middle-class home—"a home with a great and happy and loving family in it"—so that the dominance of the family in the respectable Victorian moral imagination was carried over to the afterlife wholesale.[74] As the historian of the family John Gillis has perceptively noted, the house or the home, from being merely a way station, took on aspects once reserved only for the heavenly destination.[75] Not only was a heavenly bliss possible within the walls of the loving family home, heaven itself was to be considered literally as a home: the idea in this sense referring, as Dickens's Nicholas Nickleby replies to the family-less Smike, as "the place where, in default of a better, those I love are gathered together."[76] If "the Victorian ideal bypasses repentance and death, makes heaven itself a home, and promises thereby an enclosure that includes eternity," Dickens played a role in replacing a faded faith with the notion that one would arrive in heaven "to find it was already home."[77] As the author of the popular and self-explanatorily titled *Heaven Our Home* (1861) puts it, "Mourners in Zion! your present separation from these once dear friends of yours is not for ever! Soon you will meet them again in an eternal home of love, and recognise them, and speak with them in the language of heaven, and walk with them in white through its courts of glory!"[78]

Colleen McDannell and Bernhard Lang have traced the emergence of this "modern heaven" from its beginnings with Swedenborg in the eighteenth century, through its golden age in the nineteenth, to its status as a minority belief in our own day. In this developing conceptualization of heaven, the nearness and similarity of the other world to our own is emphasized, as is the eternal and transcendent nature of love, family, progress, and work. More precisely, Pat Jalland has insisted on the importance of the later nineteenth century, at which time this belief became more explicit and less conditional, and became the primary consolation for many mourners.[79] Though evangelicalism was "the religion of the home as well as of the heart," the heaven-home formula was increasingly apparent from the 1860s on, that is, with the decline of evangelicalism and the reduced emphasis on Hell, and also in reaction to insecurities provoked by the rise of science, biblical criticism, and agnostic Darwinianism.[80] Jalland departs from McDannell and Lang's claim that the 1860s witnessed the displacement of a theocentric version of Heaven by twin anthropocentric models, those of a progressive heaven of growth and useful activity, and one based on the family in the home. But we only need here to note that these could be in practice reconciled with the model of family reunion dominating the model of a social heaven. It may be better to conclude that heaven-as-home theology could certainly be theocentric, with its emphasis on rest and comfort, but that active pursuits such as amusement and recreation were also envisaged, so that the distinctions are not so easily drawn. And whatever the case, pets were potentially a part of this newly *domesticated* heaven: "Even pets exist in the other world. Not only do they play and give pleasure to the souls, but they encourage loving sensitivity. . . . Pets, sports, and amusement parks all keep the soul busy while at the same time developing its emotional sophistication."[81]

The importance of this "modern" conception of heaven is thus that pets, explicitly, are envisaged as sharing the afterlife, as part of the heavenly home. This was welcome news to many of the Victorian animal activists. Frances Power Cobbe, speaking through her animal amanuensis, Hajjin, makes this appeal: "Surely it would not make people less enjoy any good place that it would be full of loving and happy animals! I should think it would be dull (I am sure my mistress would find it so) in a garden of Eden without birds and beasts."[82] Of the philozoic writer Edward Bruce Hamley, it was said that he was similarly "inclined to cherish the hope that he might meet his four-footed friends in a future state of existence. In any case, it is difficult to conceive him as perfectly happy in a Paradise where the cats and the dogs were literally cast out."[83] This desire is nowhere better exemplified, however, than in the work of the American author Elizabeth Stuart Phelps, whose influential didactic novel, *The Gates Ajar* (1868), a best seller on both sides of the Atlantic, portrayed a solid and tangible vision of the life to come. Drawing straightforwardly on Bishop Butler's physical theory of another life, Phelps insists on a reassuringly familiar afterlife. With its "heavenly society consisting of Victorian families," *The Gates Ajar* impresses the domestic and familial heaven on its readers, insisting that "a happy home is the happiest thing in the world. I do not see why it should not be in any world."[84] This faith is exemplified in an all too laughably sentimental passage describing how the heroine, having come to master her grief in the consolation of a real and familial heaven, could no longer speak to a child with the cold anthropocentrism of orthodox theology:

> "There was that poor little fellow whose guinea-pig died, — do you remember?"
>
> "Only half; what was it?"
>
> "'O mamma,' he sobbed out, behind his handkerchief, 'don't great big elephants have souls?'
>
> "'No, my son.'
>
> "'Nor camels, mamma?'
>
> "'Nor bears, nor alligators, nor chickens?'
>
> "'O no, dear.'
>
> "'O mamma mamma! Don't little CLEAN — *white* — *guinea-pigs* have souls?'
>
> "I never should have had the heart to say no to that; especially as we have no positive proof to the contrary."[85]

What this conversation shows in the novel is that the heroine, Mary, has internalized the lessons of her mentor, and of Phelps herself. From now on, she understands that we must imagine heaven in and on our own terms — in just the way a mother must speak to her child in language that she can readily understand. Since we cannot know what heaven is really like, we must set aside doctrine and dogma for a hopeful faith in a world that we will urgently welcome. And while we cannot presume to know and to fully understand the mysteries of God, so that it is better to keep an open mind on questions such as the future life of animals, which doctrine simply cannot resolve, we should not dismiss our own hopes for a life to come in which family friends, even pets, are welcome and present. Having learned this lesson, the previously death-fixated Mary becomes accepting of God's wisdom and mercy. "How spiritual-minded Mary has grown," a relative comments almost immediately after this episode. It is a measure of Mary's spiritual growth that she has come to accept the superficially unorthodox questions that fringe the belief in a physical heaven.[86]

In the sequel, *Beyond the Gates,* which involves a visit to heaven itself, Phelps is even more explicit about the place of animal friends in the life to come:

> We stopped before a small and quiet house built of curiously inlaid woods. . . . So exquisite was the carving and coloring, that on a larger scale the effect might have interfered with the solidity of the building, but so modest were the proportions of this charming house, that its dignity was only enhanced by its delicacy. It was shielded by trees, some familiar to me, others strange. There were flowers—not too many; birds; and I noticed a fine dog sunning himself upon the steps.[87]

In this comfortable and consoling vision, the dog has become, in death as in life, the first to greet us on the other side: an entirely appropriately construction given that the dog's relationship with humans "has always located it on the boundary between wildness and domesticity" and has long been associated with the doorway or threshold of the house. The belief in the dog as messenger or intermediary between this world and the next is indeed widespread and ancient—"It is an interstitial creature, neither person nor beast, forever oscillating uncomfortably between the roles of high-status animal and low-status person."[88]

That these beliefs are preeminent in an unorthodox Christian spirituality is not negligible; and their propagation in late Victorian society might profitably be linked to spiritualism and the unorthodox fringe. The special appeal of such ideas to women, in the context of women's dissatisfaction with scientific "progress," modernity, and established religion alike, and the rehabilitation of materialist arguments to naturalize the spiritual, can hardly be denied.[89] Nevertheless, Christian religious ideas allowed plenty of room for such speculation, however far they were from the mainstream. At the end of the century, Christian religiosity could become perhaps the key resource in the struggle against materialism, mechanism, scientifically authorized cruelty, and so on; and while science and secularism might once have seemed to offer a route toward breaking down the differences between men and animals—the "narrowing gap" in the early modern period that Keith Thomas has noted—by the end of the century this meant only a new kind of exploitation.[90] It was religion and spirituality, allied with a literalism and physicalism that are distinctively modern, that offered a way of preserving the entwined relationships of animals and humans, even beyond the claims and chains of the temporal world.[91]

I hope to have demonstrated that the dogs' cemetery in Hyde Park has a significance almost completely concealed by its marginality and its odd charm. It is of course a striking memorial to the place of the domestic pet in Victorian culture, but the solemn memorials and extravagant emotions on display are too easily mocked. By contrast, I have tried to treat these sentiments with seriousness and some sympathy, to show that the late Victorian moral imagination of nonhuman animals was enlarged by philosophical and spiritual speculation, taking material form in the shape of the pet cemetery but keying into, however tentatively, an alternative, less anthropocentric, ethics. Pet owners, not just in the first throes of grief but also in considered reflection, constructed a place for their pets' remains and a place for their putative souls. Some at least were willing to make the leap to imagining a future, better world in which humans and their pets might be reunited, at the last, in a familiar heaven that took on the very image of bourgeois domesticity. They were encouraged and empowered by, inter alia, unorthodox Christianity, antivivisectionism, feminism, spiritualism, anti-rationalism, and a distaste for scientific materialism.

Can we say that, in their vision of the afterlife, animal death was domesticated? This claim would go against some of what we think we know about our modern anthropocentric culture. In a version of the idea that animals are abjected in modern society, Jonathan Burt has argued that "the loss in human-animal relations in the nineteenth century is primarily the marginalization of animal death rather than animal disappearance per se."[92] This denial of death echoes Martin Heidegger's emphatic assertion that the animal is excluded from "being-towards-death," that it has no experience of death *as* death, so that we might even say that the nonhuman animal cannot even "properly" die, merely perish.[93] Such an expulsion of animals from the House of Death, so to speak, may be the very grandest and most fateful of anthropocentric gestures. One result is simply the wholesale disposal of animals, the refusal to contemplate that they might possess grievable lives. As Kari Weil puts it, "Nonhuman animals belong to *the constitutive outside of the human*, designating the boundary between what or who is and is not grievable according to what or who is or is not humanized."[94] This itself shows "how far 'domestication' has strayed from its association with the cosy hearth and sheltering enclosures of the *domus*."[95] Set apart from these ungrievable others, Teresa Mangum sees in the pet cemetery only complicity with this wholesale, anonymous, undomesticated death.[96]

Burt's statement, however, ignores the ways in which death and the afterlife, even for animals, might after all be domesticated, made homely and hospitable, for pets as well as their owners. "An impossible, illicit geography of proximity," Anne Dufourmantelle calls our "nearness" to the other who demands hospitality, including the animal other that Derrida has explored in his hyperbolic ethics.[97] It might be better to say that this geography is *incalculable* or *uncalculating*, however, for there are surely possibilities of hospitality, even toward animals in this "zoosphere," even if this is a limit case, calling into question the very boundaries that allow hospitality, even if we see this capacity for conditional hospitality towards animal others as what after all makes us "human."[98] Finding a place for the animal dead was not, or not merely, a confirmation of human privilege, a sentimental sop that authorized the indifference to the perishing of animals in their herded and hunted masses. It was also a challenge to the established boundaries of anthropocentric orthodoxy: Mangum ignores I think the genuine potential for resistance in this late Victorian culture, with its refusal of the unnecessary tyrannies of the nature-culture distinction. So the desire to domesticate animal death is to me an ethical as well as an emotional statement. We might acknowledge that in these odd projects an intertwined geography of humans and other animals was constructed, not simply in material form but beyond this in emotion and imagination, reason and reflection, grief and hope. In such "excessive" projects we might see, in William Lynn's terms, a deliberate and determined boundary transgression, a rejection of the theology and scientific ideology of extrinsic value, and an embracing of nonhuman animals in a shared moral community.[99] It is misleading to denigrate such insistent and beguiling speculation as merely the superfluity of a middle-class culture sentimentally devoted to its pets and indignant at the callous treatment and disposal of animals. Nor should sentiments be casually dismissed as a historical excess.[100] We should not recklessly ignore what mourning for pets tells us about the moral status of animals in the culture we have inherited: "Let us be aware that grief for pet animals is more than just an overflow for draining emotion. It is also a springboard for awakening our moral concern for the millions of creatures who have intrinsic value, whose lives are wasted and twisted at our hands, and yet for whom no tears are shed."[101]

CHAPTER 6

Assembling the Dog-Walking City
Rabies, Muzzling, and the Freedom to be Led

THE PREVIOUS chapter described the most audacious attempt to provide a home for animal companions—the domestication of the hereafter as a "homely" space to be shared with departed pets. This imaginative, emotional, hope-filled geography had its counterpart, as we have seen, in the material realm. There was, however, another attempt by dog owners and dog lovers to domesticate the city on behalf of animals, and this is the endeavor to defend and also develop *public* spaces as places where humans and dogs would be welcomed. These dog owners' interests resided simply in claiming the rights of responsible human guardians to take their animals out into the public city, to take them for a walk. This is such an everyday phenomenon that it is remarkably easy to overlook just how contentious the practice once was: after all, literally as well as symbolically, dogs and humans have walked together down through the ages, from the beginnings of animal domestication to the present day. It seems absurd to think of such companionship as recent, let alone worthy of investigation. We might, however, consider dog walking, in the cultural and historical geographical perspective of human-animal relations, as indeed a distinctively *modern* practice, inseparable from the phenomena of "domestication" that this book has already traced at length: a practice that has developed under particular conditions, the result of certain struggles, and installed in specific sites. If we accept the fact that walking the dog is a distinctive type of *spatial* practice, for all that it is now largely taken for granted, we may then ask how this practice became normalized. In doing so, the acknowledged modernity of the "walking city," long familiar to historians, might perhaps be expanded to include the creation of what I venture to call a "dog-walking city," one in which humans with their animal companions were allowed, accepted, and indeed eventually encouraged into social and public space.[1]

I want to proceed in this chapter by contrasting two moments in the history of animals' access to public space in Victorian and Edwardian London, which I will use to represent two kinds of approaches to the problem of the public dog. The first, the history of the call for dogs to be *muzzled* in public, particularly under the fear of rabies, I want to label as classically *disciplinary*, following Michel Foucault's famous theorization of control and surveillance. The second, for which I take the dog lead or *leash* as an emblem, I take to be by contrast a more "liberal" opening up of public spaces for dogs and their owners—we can address this in terms of *regulation* or "governmentality," to make use again of the Foucauldian terminology.[2] Both are related, of course, but while the first forwards a more overt kind of control, the medical policing of unsanitary and dangerous animals, the second more obviously involves what Foucault describes as "the conduct of conduct," operating through a model of the responsible pet owner rather than directly upon the animals themselves. In a positive spin, this is also about the provision of spaces and environments in which particular human-animal behaviors are tolerated and even celebrated. This argument and policy may be seen as "liberal," perhaps even classically so, in its focus on the creation of responsible subjects, whose rights and liberties must be entrenched and respected, the acknowledged conditions for the model of modern government itself. But this is also a liberalism that *includes* animals, as it extends from the human being to the dog at the end of the leash. We could, at the risk of belaboring the Foucauldian point, think of this as "the conduct of conduct of conduct," insofar as this involves the governmental regulation of responsible humans *and* their equally responsibilized animals. I term this positive liberalism here the freedom to be led.

This is far from an unproblematic contrast, and I want to make clear at the start that this is not a matter of control *versus* freedom, of medical muzzlers *versus* dog-loving liberals; it must be stressed that liberalism and its geographies always operated via conditional and regulated freedoms, and that the liberalism of the Victorian state was coercive, liable to suspension, at times and in places even murderously indifferent.[3] Moreover, although these may seem like theoretical niceties, it is important for my purposes here to extend and challenge the Foucauldian problematic of rule, with its anthropocentric emphases on discourse and discipline, and the larger figure of the *"dispositifs"* or "apparatuses" that connect them.[4] By contrast to this vision of order, we can conceive of the creation of a metropolis not simply by government and authority, by language and discourse, or even exclusively by humans—but rather out of practices, behaviors, and performances that coordinate the agency of animals, of humans, even of things. The familiar figure of a human being walking a companion dog with the aid of a lead is part of just such an *"assemblage,"* to use the related, but distinct, theoretical language.[5] "Assemblage," in the technical sense, describes an open set of relations, a loose and pro-visional bringing together of heterogeneous elements that nevertheless produces distinctive effects and makes up what we call social order.[6] Whether or not this particular theoretical argument is appealing, the central point is that the general thesis of the disciplining and regulation of animals in the city needs to be complemented by a story about non-human animals *playing their part* in the domestication of urban space. In time, I want to argue here, the human being and the dog, connected to each other by the lead or the leash, would become naturalized, such that most traces of the struggles over the dog-walking dyad disappear as if they had never existed. Only then might we say that a "dog-walking city" had emerged, the result of a certain compact or dispensation—be-tween humans, certainly, but also between humans and dogs, and the "public" and "social" world they have *together* helped to create.

This very brief theoretical preface out of the way, I want to return to the place of dogs in the Victorian city. The most pressing problem for the authorities throughout our period was the seemingly uncontrolled pres-ence of animals in urban space. We can readily agree with John Walton's observation that "from mid-Victorian times, and increasingly in the late nineteenth century, the uncontrolled urban dog came to be perceived as a serious problem."[7] As the *Times* expatiated, "We feel strongly that in town life dogs introduce an element, which, for their own sake, should be brought under strict control."[8] Throughout this book I have returned many times to the problem of the "stray"—the apparently ownerless or "masterless" dog wandering the public streets at will. Such an errant ani-mal was a living, mobile affront to the vaunted "improvement" and mod-ernization of the city. Indeed, the more that the streets and spaces of the capital *were* "improved," the more the presence of the unimproved and disorderly (whether beast or human) stood starkly revealed.[9] We have seen that the stray was the beastly counterpart of an already bestialized residuum, sharing in the latter's fecklessness, equally lacking any productive place in British society; both kinds of vagrants could be deemed as "waste," by definition out of place.[10]

Strays were moreover seen as "the site of danger and disease to the social body."[11] Uncontrolled animals posed a number of sanitary dangers, but what really turned this concern for the vagrant animal into a preeminent problem of biosecurity was the species-leaping disease of rabies. The Earl of Arundel essayed a familiar complaint to Home Secretary Sir George Grey in 1850 when he noted the unusual "number of dogs loose about London, apparently without owners"—worse, he felt, than any other town on the Continent "save Turkey or Greece"—but he instanced as his specific rationale for writing his encounter with a rabid dog: "I am the more alive to the nuisance at this instant inasmuch as (by good luck having a stout oak stick in my hand) I destroyed a mad dog of the sheep dog kind this morning in St. Paul's Churchyard with very considerable difficulty."[12] This fear of rabies made the stray dog not merely an embarrassment or a nuisance, but a potentially fatal vector of urban modernity.

Of course, compared to such Victorian mass killers as cholera, typhus, and typhoid, the death toll exacted by hydrophobia was negligible, but the chronic concern with rabies in the nineteenth century indicates that something more than a rational "biopolitical" calculation was at work.[13] There were several things that made rabies different from other zoonotic infections. It was a disease whose origins were very imperfectly understood—not until the end of the century, for example, did the theory of the spontaneous generation of rabies, perhaps linked to climate, to pampering, or ill-treatment, fall out of favor with medical experts. It was also a pathogen caught from domestic animals, rather than from, say, rats or fleas, and potentially not just from wandering brutes but also from beloved companions. Rabies/hydrophobia was a disease that as a result never knew its place—the cultural imagination of the disease conjured up a contagion that spread through the poorest classes to threaten the whole structure of society, invading the home as it did so. Rabies had a demonstrably appalling significance for bourgeois society and its practices of pet keeping, and for the entire ideology of domesticity and domestication, given that a beloved family pet might be reduced to the grossest animality and a potential killer of those to whom it should be closest. This was the ultimate bourgeois nightmare, then: simply put, "rabies revealed, didactically, the beastly nature of the domesticated beast."[14] Culturally, the microbial "colonization of man's-best-friend" threatened a breakdown of social and cultural order both in the streets and in the family home, a reversion to animality that revealed the fragility of civil life itself.[15] In her remarkable study of *la rage* in nineteenth-century France, Kathleen Kete notes, without exaggeration, that "the fear of rabies lies at the intersection of the organizing themes of bourgeois life and can be read as an expression of unease about modern civilization and its tolls, about the uncertain conquest of culture over nature."[16]

In Britain, this concern about the threat of rabies can be traced in comparable ways to the modernization of the metropolis, from the 1830s to the end of the century, and indeed beyond this to our own day.[17] Once again, it was never simply an epidemiological issue, for from the beginning it was regarded as a species of moral contagion, inseparable from the wider question of the condition of England and its degraded and perhaps revolutionary poor: Neil Pemberton and Michael Worboys thus note that "the main fear was less about rabies than a generalized anxiety about the moral status of the working class that was refracted through their dogs."[18] The association between rabid dogs and the lowest and the criminal classes was strongly advanced in the 1830s, when it was suggested that the dog-fighting proclivities of the lower classes uniquely contributed to the spread of the disease. As one complainant to Home Secretary Robert Peel claimed, "99 dogs out of 100 that are prowling about the public streets have either no owner or belong to paupers & thieves—The scenes about London when they congregate on Sundays for the purpose of dog fighting are a disgrace to a civilized country."[19]

As the darkest side of the undisciplined canine metropolis, the fear of rabies and hydrophobia prompted the most drastic proposals for the control of animals in the streets. For some, "the terrors of a terrible disorder" added to the conviction that no dogs should ever be allowed to run free in cities.[20] Others canvassed the short, sharp shock of a "universal quarantine for Dogs within the Kingdom," in order to bring to an end what might providentially be looked back upon as the "Era of Canine Madness."[21] Quarantine, which hearkens back to Foucault's medical model of the "plague city," is a crude, blunt, and indeed ancient biopolitical technology, a ready recourse where animal diseases are concerned.[22] But in the political climate of the 1830s, where the most stringent demands of medical policing were associated with tyranny and reaction, quarantine and its associated policy of muzzling dogs in the streets were never seriously contemplated by the British state. In the event, the incidence of rabies declined in subsequent decades, its seeming amelioration coinciding with the rise of the early Victorian animal welfare movement and its more positive view of animal companions. Although the problem of stray dogs continued periodically to attract attention, the specifically medical rationale for disciplining of animals lost some of its force in these early Victorian years.

Panics over rabies, and calls for the stringent regulation of dogs and their owners, resurfaced with a vengeance in the 1860s, however, this time in a much more propitious era for state-sponsored sanitary intervention. From this date on, rabies and hydrophobia were increasingly brought under the authority of medical science, subject to a kind of "medical takeover," although it would still be police technologies rather than medical science that would be relied upon to combat the rabies menace.[23] As Harriet Ritvo argues, "Defining rabid dogs as guilty rather than sick transformed an epizootic from a medical problem into a police problem. From this point of view the main job of disease control was intensive moral surveillance of the dog population, in order to purge it of the errant members who had deviated from standards of moral as well as physical soundness."[24] Since the most consistent focus was on the habits of the human poor, however, this was never simply about policing animals. It was also, inevitably, about policing people: "London was regarded as the Mecca of the dissolute, the lazy, the mendicant, the rough and the spendthrift. Stray or rabid dogs, like their human counterparts, epitomized this threatening presence which cried out for regulation — or destruction."[25]

The biosecurity problem of rabies was also therefore a preeminently "biopolitical" question, one involving a distinctive political anthropology — the question of how *humans* were to be governed. Most important, in the second half of the nineteenth century, the persistent association between rabies and the pauperized masses began to be accompanied by a wider questioning of the habits of dog owners, whatever their status. The rabies question was no longer *only* a problem of the stray, nor was a policing of the dog population focused exclusively on the poor and their pets. The rabies panics of the later nineteenth century also took in otherwise respectable dogs and their otherwise respectable owners. So

while the veterinarian and rabies expert George Fleming sounded a classic refrain when he complained of the canine oxygen-thieves who infest
the hovels of the poor—

> How often have we seen large numbers of such currish brutes
> in the most squalid parts of large towns, living with their own-
> ers in the miserable and badly-ventilated dwellings that com-
> pose such regions, consuming a portion of the food that their
> owners were so much in need of themselves, and contributing
> to make these dwellings still more insalubrious by absorbing
> their share of the oxygen that was already far too insufficient
> in quantity to maintain health, and largely aiding their ten-
> dency to become rabid, these parasites are a nuisance, and a
> source of waste and insalubrity.[26]

—he went on to say that the same wastefulness and parasitical nature
is just as true of the *rich* who keep dogs for pleasure. Not just so-called
masterless dogs but also properly identified pets, walking with their
owners in the streets, became the targets of an invigorated call for medical surveillance and control. The question of which animals were the
more susceptible to rabies, and the more likely to propagate it, was never
conclusively settled, but there were many who ventured to argue that
domestic pets were *more* likely than mongrels to be subject to the disease:
"It seems to be an established fact that the vagabond dogs who prowl
the streets homeless and masterless are less frequently afflicted by rabies
than any others. The majority of mad dogs it would appear therefore, are
to be found among the upper and middle classes of the dog tribe."[27] By
the time of the crucial Select Committee on rabies of 1887, this view—
which contrasts forcefully with that of the 1830s—had prominent and
powerful advocates. Sir Charles Warren, newly appointed commissioner
of the Metropolitan Police, argued for instance that there was in fact
more rabies in "pampered dogs" than in "starving curs."[28]

Indeed, pet dogs became principal targets of government intervention in this era because virtually everyone agreed on the necessity that
strays should be eliminated. Defenders of dogs before the 1887 Select
Committee did not dispute the necessity for strays to be removed from
the streets. RSPCA secretary John Colam recommended, for instance,
that the police should "take every stray dog to the Dogs' Home and have
it destroyed if a home cannot be found for it."[29] What they disputed was

merely the manner of such killing, and whether this might in fact be overkill. Thus Colam could not countenance the practice of killing suspect dogs on the spot, a responsibility that had fallen on the police since 1839.[30] Such killing was offensively public, left alarmingly to the discretion of individual constables, and in all too many cases the wholly unnecessary result of panic and hasty profiling. Colam complained that four out of every five dogs killed as mad were not rabid, the police returns thus being wholly worthless.[31] We should also note here that rural working and sporting dogs were largely exonerated from blame for rabies and exempted from any proposed regulation—despite the arguments of men like Colam.[32] Sporting dogs such as foxhounds were described as characteristically kept in a state of isolation, and always under proper control, while terriers and sheep dogs were presumed to be "always under observation."[33] Pets, by contrast, were urban animals virtually by definition, and it was the city that was clearly identified as the locus of rabies. While some witnesses advocated universal muzzling, Commissioner Warren made it clear that such a strategy was unnecessary, for "the danger only exists in crowded streets, and there is much more danger, so far as one can understand, of rabies where dogs lead such unhealthy lives as they do in towns"; the veterinarian George Fleming concurred, arguing that "rabies exists pretty well all the year round in some of our large towns" and "nearly always starts from the town as the centre and gets into the country."[34] The point therefore was how to tackle rabies in the city: certainly by getting rid of strays, but *also* by trying to control pet dogs and their owners.

For many of the expert witnesses to the Select Committee in 1887, any presumption that the city dweller should have the right to keep dogs *at all*, or at least those larger dogs that might be considered dangerous or "treacherous," was the issue at hand. In a textbook example of a leading question, the Earl of Carnarvon asked Sir Charles Warren whether, in his opinion, "quite apart from any legislative or technical reasons for muzzling or not muzzling dogs, is it not a preposterous and a monstrous thing that any one should have the power in a crowded town like this to take with him, unmuzzled, enormous dogs capable of doing irremediable mischief at a moment's notice?" Warren gratefully took the opportunity to declare his opposition to the practice of keeping such dogs: "I think it is quite beyond all reason. We start with the consideration that the streets are the playground of the children of the metropolis, and to allow unmuzzled dogs there seems quite beyond reason. Many children get so

frightened by dogs that the effect of the fright lasts through their lives."[35]
The campaign against rabies led to consideration of the policing of pets,
and threatened nothing less than the *undomestication* of the British dog:
the very status of dogs as urban animals, as pets, was at stake here.

The great difficulty was how to actually go about policing dogs in the
city. The complexity and inadequacy of the law with regard to the control of companion animals was readily acknowledged. There was a clear
medical rationale for sanitary intervention, but the law provided only
guidelines and directions, and thoroughly ambiguous ones at that. The
law was a blunt instrument, literally so when it came to the injunction
to destroy suspected dogs on the spot, but in the second half of the nineteenth century this lack of precision was further compounded by the
passing of a host of overlapping statutes, with separate authorities and
jurisdictions only adding to the confusion. The most obvious and direct
examples of biosecurity legislation were the Contagious Diseases (Animals) Acts of 1869 and 1878, but dogs were not even classed as subject
to their statutes until an 1886 amendment added rabies to the schedule
of diseases, extending the provisions from cattle, sheep, goats, and swine
to "any kind of four-footed beasts."[36] This amendment allowed the Privy
Council to pass the first of their Rabies Orders in 1886 and 1887, empowering local authorities to pass orders for the muzzling of dogs and
the seizure, detention, and disposal of strays—crucially, as a preventive
measure, even if there were no reported cases of rabies in the district under discussion. The effectiveness of this enabling legislation was limited,
however; and few local authorities actually took up the options laid before them. Moreover, while the Privy Council's powers were transferred
in 1889 to the Board of Agriculture, allowing muzzling and control to
be imposed on subjected districts, this central control lasted for only
three years.[37] Before 1889 and after 1892, localism and voluntarism remained the watchwords, weakening the state's ability to mount anything
like a systematic defense against rabies and hydrophobia. It was readily
admitted that any system of uncoordinated local action "produces the
maximum of local irritation with the minimum of general and permanent
good."[38]
    Without a committed and national program of compulsory interven-
tion, the fight against rabies relied upon the distinctly limited powers
provided by the Dogs Act of 1871, which stipulated that dogs be muzzled in "public places" by order of any local authority where a case of

rabies had been identified in a district, and that dogs should in any event be kept "under control." The Dogs Act, Commissioner Warren noted, did have the distinct advantage of "affording power to go against the owner, and not only against the dog."[39] All the same, critics observed that the fact that restrictions could be ordered only where a rabid or suspected dog was found within the district of the local authority rendered these powers of scant practical use.[40] In addition, there was some difficulty in defining "a public place" under the Act, this question being left up to the magistrates, who introduced one more element of discretion and inconsistency. London did have the additional assistance of the Metropolitan Streets Act of 1867, which stipulated that stray dogs could and should be seized—and ultimately destroyed—if they were found not in the control of any person, or unmuzzled, even if they were accompanied by their owners, whenever the police commissioners had issued a muzzling order. Other cities, under the Towns Police Clauses Act dating back to 1847, also had powers to arrest and fine dog owners if they allowed at large any unmuzzled, ferocious dog, any dog that they believed to be rabid, or any dog during the time dogs were prohibited to be at large. Once again, though, this legislation was regularly found wanting. Everyone agreed that the system of penalties under the muzzling orders of 1885 (authorized by the Metropolitan Streets Act, 1867) was hopelessly ineffective—police might seize a dog, but the owner could claim it back from the Dogs' Home if they fetched a muzzle, or indeed at once if they happened to have one on their person. Dog owners wanting to evade restrictions could simply walk around with a muzzle, while their dogs ran free. Moreover, although the Metropolitan Streets Act impelled constables to seize stray, ownerless dogs if they came in their way, there was no direction that *all* unmuzzled or unleashed dogs should be systematically apprehended. Police commitment to clearing the streets of stray dogs was often called into question, while the police themselves pleaded, as we have seen in chapter 3, that they did not have sufficient resources to carry out this demanding and demeaning work.

A final reason for failure was a matter of political geography: the Metropolitan Streets Act only applied to the County of London, and not to the much more extensive Metropolitan Police district. The result was a patchwork geography of muzzling, raising the specter of rabid dogs moving from "controlled" to "uncontrolled" districts. With Parliament unwilling to face down opposition from gentry and landowners in the countryside, there was no question of the kind of "universal" muzzling advocated by the most committed medical hygienists. There was a brief experiment by the Board of Agriculture in 1889 to extend muzzling orders beyond London to the Home Counties, but this was quickly revoked a year later. The return to the boundaries of the Metropolitan Police district, within and without "the Pale" as the *Daily Graphic* had it, simply continued to affirm the seemingly arbitrary enforcement of muzzling.[41] Dog advocates as well as committed sanitarians complained of the inconsistency and arbitrariness of the blanket restriction of all dogs in one area compared with the lack of control altogether in another. This was pointed out by the *Daily Graphic,* imagining a dialogue between a "Village Tyke" and a city-dwelling "Dachshund, Esq.": "The 'House' can't know of the state of things. Just get your guvnor to ask if they think it is a case of what is called 'British love of fair play,' to let some dogs go where they like, if they only wear a collar, while all the rest are kept caged up with muzzles."[42]

Inevitably, then, local authorities fell back upon sporadic campaigns against strays, constant calls for better control of dogs, and the entirely reactive measure of muzzling orders when and where cases of rabies were identified. The most intractable problem, however, was simply that outside of these specified situations the Dogs Act and its equivalents only required dogs to be "under proper control." But what constituted the proper control of a dog was, as magistrates found, at best a moot point. The requirements of the Dogs Act generated several controversies. Much as central government may have wanted to rely upon local authorities to decide for themselves how to use the powers conferred by the Dogs Act, magistrates repeatedly turned to the Home Office for guidance. "The difficulty putting an uniform construction on the DOGS ACT" was noted by the Oxford bench in 1877, complaining that the language of the legislation was obscure and incomplete.[43] Some regarded the muzzle as sufficient security, though others argued that this protection was illusory; proponents of the leash found themselves in confrontation with those who did not believe that it could prevent a dog from attacking and biting. This was the view of Metropolitan Commissioner Warren, who averred in 1887 that leading a dog was not of any use whatsoever when it came to the safety of strangers—indeed he thought that being led made them more liable to bite.[44] Professor Victor Horsley, the eminent surgeon (and ardent vivisectionist), concurred that the leash was not only ineffective but also cruel and counterproductive: "Personally, I would not care to lead a dog, I mean to say it is a great restraint to the dog, as you can see in the street; and therefore it makes life a burden to it. If the dog is properly muzzled there is no reason why it should be led at all. Moreover, permitting the leading of dogs is a bad practice, because it leads people to think that if they just take the dog out led that is sufficient."[45] Magistrates in Huntingdon stated to the Home Secretary that they were inclined to this stricter view that the leash was not enough: "Having a dog in a string unmuzzled who might bite persons or dogs passing is not having them 'under control.'"[46] Others felt, however, that a dog could be managed without needing to restrain it in these ways. The Home Secretary himself was asked to adjudicate whether the Ormskirk Justices of the Peace had exceeded their authority by insisting that dogs be *leashed*, a Mr. Robert Anderson of Aughton regarding this as a cruel and pointless measure: "I feel very sore on the point in question—I possess two intelligent and harmless dogs, one of them too powerful to be led by a string, and I call it nothing but downright cruelty and tyranny to deprive me of the companions of my evening walks when no sufficient cause has been shown to prevent all dogs having perfect freedom."[47] Anderson was somewhat mollified by the Home Office's reply that "intelligent and harmless" dogs taking a walk with their master would indeed be considered as under control. The local paper agreed that "dogs as a rule can be controlled by a look or a word. . . . The animal may be free to gambol about so long as it is subject to the call of its master or some responsible person."[48] On the other hand, the local magistrates, reasonably enough, wanted to know just who was to decide whether a dog was "intelligent and harmless," insisting that the only reasonable interpretation was the use of the lead: "for it is impossible to say that a dog at large no matter how short a distance it may be from the person in charge of it can be controlled."[49]

Magistrates, policemen, and park keepers came increasingly to settle on the interpretation that *either* the muzzle *or* the leash was sufficient, though dog owners continued to debate the point. In 1886 a George Roberts was brought before Highgate magistrates for allowing a dog to be at large and not under proper control in a public thoroughfare. The point was that the dog was neither muzzled nor led; it was, according to the police constable, "running first on one side and then on the other, and then back to [the] defendant." The local magistrate asked specifically about the requirement of "proper control," asking the police constable directly, "You mean to say that if a dog is walking by the side of the owner you take that?" In the end, a majority verdict accepted that the dog *was* under proper control and dismissed the summons.[50] In the same year, a Mr. Henry Laylands was charged with having an uncontrolled St. Bernard at large in the Belsize Road, South Hampstead, "without a muzzle, collar, or leader." The local police constable stated that he asked Mr. Laylands whether he was aware that the dog was not muzzled, and told him that the dog ought to be led. After several attempts the constable managed to put a string round the dog's neck and led it to the station. The defendant claimed, however, that the dog had been under his control the whole time: "He had had the animal for seven years, and it was perfectly harmless, and had never attempted to bite anybody." The magistrate was compelled to caution Mr. Laylands, but said that he was of the opinion that the dog was indeed under control, dismissing the summons, "although very reluctantly."[51]

A different result was that of a William Rogers, who was repeatedly summonsed for allowing his dog to be at large in Kensington Gardens. When instructed that he must either muzzle or lead his dog, Mr. Rogers's response was that "he should do nothing of the kind, because the animal was under proper control":

> His dog was so quiet that it went to the bathing ground among the children, and nobody was afraid of it, and it had never bitten any one. The existing order of regulation with respect to dogs was very perplexing. A man must lead or muzzle his dog when walking down the Strand, but directly he got to where Temple-bar used to be, he could let it run loose, simply because he was then in the City. Six or seven magistrates had decided in favour of his reading of the law, and a number of others held an opposite opinion, so that really no-one knew how to act.

Only a few days earlier, on a similar summons, complete with public hilarity, Rogers had responded with this retort:

> When a dog had a "lead" on it was in a state of captivity, and to use a muzzle was cruel, but when walking at the feet of its master, ready to obey his beck and call, it was then under control. . . . The control that the Act required was such as a husband had over his wife, a father had over his children, or a pedagogue had over his pupils. (Laughter.) His dog had never

bitten any one and was under perfect control. It was a small animal, but was very clever. It would fetch his letters, run for two ounces of beef, and get a shilling out of a pail of water. (Laughter.)

On both occasions it was agreed that the interpretation of the words "reasonable control" was a moot point, but Rogers was fined anyway.[52] One can only sympathize with the Middlesex magistrate who wrote to the *Times* to ask to have the question of what is "proper control" determined by a higher authority.[53]

Any attempt to discipline dogs faced a host of practical difficulties, therefore, and we should be cautious in assuming that the medical case for control—particularly the call for dogs to be muzzled—was at all efficacious in the fight against rabies. The muzzling policies that were the cornerstone of the state's fight against rabies for a generation were also deeply controversial. John Walton, Harriet Ritvo, and—more recently—Neil Pemberton and Michael Worboys have all demonstrated how debates over rabies in Britain were conducted in the context of a struggle between a medical community more or less united in prioritizing public health over the interests of private individuals and personal prejudices, and a community of dog owners and fanciers mobilized against what they portrayed as unnecessary, authoritarian, and fundamentally illiberal regulations.[54] Hilda Kean has emphasized the extent to which the control of the dog, under the impress of the rabies panics, became for the Victorians a political question of the first importance, for "dogs were part of the family and in intervening here the state was meddling in issues outside its remit."[55] The muzzling controversies clearly take their place alongside the debates over vaccination and the Contagious Diseases Acts, part of a larger struggle over the legitimacy of government intervention in the liberty of the subject.[56]

The arguments of many outraged dog owners combined objections to the muzzle both practical and principled, contending that the muzzling orders would be an infringement of their civil liberties as well as cruel to their dogs. The novelist Ouida insisted that "the muzzled dog is a dog constantly tormented and oppressed," adding for good measure that the muzzle would only further restrict the little liberty allowed to the animal: "Dogs rarely at any time get enough air and exercise; the muzzle regulation makes this little become less, for owners do not like the trouble and torment involved in putting on the muzzle, and leave the poor animal at home, or tied up, rather than take him out with this absurd append-age."[57] In the *Times*, one correspondent offered a different case against the muzzle, emphasizing its role in cultivating a climate of fear against domestic dogs:

> The appearance of dogs with their mouths in cages is beget-ting among children—especially where there is no home pet to serve as a correcting influence—a fear which not only tends to prevent the growth of an affection for these lovable and lov-ing animals, but is a source of actual danger. The familiarity with which young children are wont to treat dogs is so rarely resented by even the least socially inclined of their race that it is a question whether anything is gained by the carefulness with which some well-intentioned people caution their little ones not to touch strange animals. But, however this may be, there can be no doubt that to bring up a child to fear dogs is greatly to increase the risk of its being bitten. How muzzled dogs are turned to educational account by nurses—a bogey-loving race—may be gathered from a viva voce lesson at which I assisted a few days since. To the question of a six-year old child, "Why do dogs wear those things on their mouths?" the answer was given "Because they'd bite people and send them mad"—an answer that has no doubt been made to thousands of children by those upon whom devolves so large a part of the early culture of the rising generation.[58]

The noted theriophile and antivivisectionist Frances Power Cobbe concurred with this view that it was the public visibility of the muzzle that dehumanized and debased, but she extended the argument by char-acterizing the muzzle as not only inhumane but illiberal, symbolizing as it did a political oppression that was incompatible with British values: "My objection to muzzles is that they are teaching the British public to regard with suspicion, dread, and finally hatred animals whose attach-ment to mankind has been a source of pure and humanizing pleasure to millions, and which has formed a link (surely not undesigned by the Creator?) between our race and all other tribes of earth and air."[59] Some, like the editors of the *Ladies Kennel Gazette*, went even further, present-ing the policy as a wholesale breakdown in the British body politic: "A tyranny—resourceful, vexatious, pettifogging and unmanly—which is visibly creeping and growing in the body politic, which emasculates the public spirit and which is a far greater danger than any physical malady. To inoculate a nation with cowardice, terror and fear is to injure it more than any bubonic plague which could be imported into it."[60]

The *gendered* nature of these responses is particularly notable, and has attracted a great deal of attention, but it is not simply a womanly sentimentality—as their opponents tended to chide—that lay behind this opposition to state-sanctioned muzzling orders. Dog advocates consistently raised the theme of the state oppression of animals and their owners. The techniques and technologies associated with the later-nineteenth-century fight against rabies and hydrophobia never lost their political associations, not even with the advent of Pasteur's laboratory identification of the rabies pathogen and the breakthrough of vaccination. Pasteur's reliance on vivisection for his breakthroughs simply made things worse, and antivivisectionists and dog defenders refused to accept either the moral or the scientific authority of "Pasteurism." Muzzling was irredeemably associated by its opponents with authoritarianism and illiberalism, with scientific materialism and masculinism, and projected as alien to British culture and values. It was, in short, a thoroughly undomesticated policy.[61] The force of anti-muzzling sentiment was predicated on the argument that the muzzling restrictions were a form of political oppression of the dog, not simply cruelty. Muzzling was seen as a political imposition upon an animal who deserved a place not only as a member of the family but also as part of the British nation. It was a question of rights as well as of welfare. Precisely for this reason, the rescinding of muzzling orders was represented as an instance of "emancipation" for dogs. On the occasion of the revoking of the Board of Agriculture's muzzling order, at the beginning of the year of 1891, for instance, a small procession in Hyde Park was organized by way of celebration (fig. 15): "The demonstration was organized by a gentleman who is the happy father—we beg pardon, we mean the fortunate proprietor—of five: a black retriever, a spaniel, and three fox terriers. On the 1st January, 1891, that gentleman took his happy family for a walk. The dogs wore their muzzle no longer fastened cruelly upon their mouths, but dangling freely from their collars; while the retriever wore, also, suspended at his throat, a ticket bearing the significant superscription 'Emancipation Day.'"[62]

The combination of muzzling with national quarantine measures has still been seen as ultimately successful, with Britain being declared rabies-

Figure 15. "The Repeal of the Muzzling Order: Collars and Addresses—An Incident of 'Emancipation Day,'" *Daily Graphic* 5 January, 1891, 4. (Reproduced by kind permission of the Syndics of Cambridge University Library)

free in the early years of the twentieth century. The victory over rabies could in this way be presented as a defeat of the undisciplined dog. Hilda Kean has argued that British rabies legislation approved "a dangerously vague form of control" that could be brought to bear indiscriminately upon the canine population, respectable or unrespectable.[63] However, while muzzling appears to represent one of the most stringent and successful attempts to restrict the movements and the actions of dogs in public space, the muzzle was in all likelihood ineffective as a means of combatting rabies. As we have seen, muzzling orders were only sporadically enforced even in the metropolis—allowed to lapse, revoked, and revised several times before all muzzling restrictions were finally lifted in 1899, after the seeming eradication of rabies in the capital. Even the proponents of the muzzle admitted that it would not work as a direct prophylactic device. In their recent authoritative account, Pemberton and Worboys have noted that many defenders of the muzzle felt that it acted instead as "a badge, indicating a well-cared-for dog and responsible owner, allowing the police to concentrate on the unmuzzled strays of thoughtless owners."[64] In their considered view, "The power of muzzling was less a direct method of preventing rabid dogs biting than a reassuring symbol of administrative control of the problem, and distinguishing animals that were disciplined and ordered from those that were not."[65]

Many of the witnesses before the 1897 Royal Commission on vivisection conceded this point. A Dr. Brunton, for instance, although firmly in favor of the muzzle, agreed that it really worked principally as a signal of potential danger: "If muzzles were invariably worn by dogs that were not rabid, the mere fact of a dog having a muzzle on would show that it was safe, and the fact of a dog having the muzzle off would be at once an indication that the dog was to be shunned."[66] In the scopic or ocular economy of the city, it was important that signs of danger were clear, unambiguous, and universal, a requirement that the technology of the muzzle apparently met far more successfully than merely a label on an animal's collar: "The mere fact of the dog having a label on would not indicate to anyone, and to children especially, the danger of the dog, whereas if adults and children were taught that every dog without a muzzle was a dangerous animal and was to be avoided, I think that that would tend considerably to prevent the spread of hydrophobia."[67] The muzzle was particularly commended by its advocates as readily observable by the *police*, who could instantly be assured that a dog belonged to a responsible owner, and who could then dispose of unwanted strays. As veterinary surgeon Fleming put it, "I look upon muzzles not so much as a preventive against biting, but as an indication that the dog has an owner."[68] Muzzling orders thus represented a call for a discipline of owners as much as their dogs, suggesting that the history of the muzzle was always more about the image of order than the efficacy of medical control: "Muzzling demonstrated the power of governmental authorities to interfere in ordinary life and the violence deemed necessary to suppress some kind of threatening behaviour. Urban streets full of muzzled dogs suggested not only the docility of both canines and humans, but also the omnipresence of regulation, which restricted the freedom of owners as well as that of their animals."[69]

In effect, the muzzle worked not as a means of preventing the transmission of rabies, but as a way of distinguishing "owned" from "ownerless" dogs in the public sphere. There is a sense in which such a technology can be seen to produce disciplined "subjects"—not just human subjects, but canine ones too, and just as important, pairing them up in a mutually reinforcing relationship of care and responsibility.[70] The *Morning Post*, reflecting on the status of the public animal, best captured this normalized, disciplined relationship between human and animal:

> A dog without a master is an anomaly, an incomplete creature. He is as much out of place as a knocker without a door. Cast upon his own resources he lives what has long been emphatically styled a dog's life. Every man's hand, and still more every boy's hand, is against him. He is put to miserable shifts to get a bare livelihood. His native sense of rectitude quickly gives way, and he falls into habits of petty, timorous pilfering. He loses the courage to bite, and his very bark has a sound of fear in it. A respectable well-fed dog, trotting at his master's side with the grand consciousness that his license is paid for, and that his muzzle is of the newest regulation pattern, disdains even to notice the loafing cur that belongs to nobody. Your stray dog has no hold on society—unless, indeed, in despair at his isolation, he attaches himself to the State for a brief space, through the medium of the postman's or the milkman's leg. He can give no surety for his good behaviour. Here is where he is at a hopeless disadvantage as compared with the dog that can show an owner. The man belongs to the dog just as much as the dog to the man.[71]

The muzzle, which seems with hindsight to be such a straightforward and practical response to a biotic threat, turns out to be little more than a symbol of control, marking out the respectable dog owner from his unrespectable equivalents, whether human or beast. The reduction in the incidence of rabies—and the ultimate victory over the disease—was likely not the result of muzzling per se but that of a range of factors, including the promotion in this way of more disciplined pet owners: "The government was helped by the relentless campaigns to clear the streets of stray dogs and the promotion of responsible ownership by animal welfare organisations, the new pet supply industries, and popular images of the loyal, affectionate domestic pet."[72]

We may argue the point further. For the muzzle was typically seen as cruel and unnecessary, with many within the most pragmatic wing of the dog lobby turning to the license and the dog lead as a perfectly viable alternative. Not everyone approved of the collar and the lead, on security or animal welfare grounds, yet the dog lobby could promote it as a technology that was at least as effective as the muzzle in distinguishing the responsible owner and the disciplined dog, with the advantage of being less cruel to the dog, and less frightening to the public. In terms of licensing, a system of registration was widely canvassed as an effective and humane, and largely unobjectionable, system of ensuring the responsibility of dog owners: in response to the president of the Board of Agriculture's support for muzzling orders, one letter writer argued, "If he will take up the question of a systematic licensing and registration of dogs and their owners, he will be doing far more towards the control of hydrophobia than can ever be accomplished by the present vexatious regulations."[73] The point once more was that attention and supervision were clearly directed at the owners of dogs, rather than coercion being imposed on the dogs themselves. For sure, not everyone saw this as liberal — "Better the muzzle for six months than this miserable foreign plan, with its attendant degrading police *espionage*," argued one dog lover.[74] Many owners continued to believe that dogs could be under control without having to resort to any imposition on their animals' freedom. But these measures were, in essence, liberal alternatives to the disciplinary coercion represented by the muzzle, predicated on the encouragement of dog owners to take greater responsibility for their animals. As E. D. Vesey, the secretary of the newly formed Dog-Owners' Protection Association put it, "What we want is effective personal supervision of their dogs by dog owners, and any measure which is calculated to bring home responsibility to the owner of a dog is at least worthy of being discussed."[75]

Dog owners also demonstrated their responsibility by fully accepting the necessity to put down the unfortunately "masterless" dog. The 1887 Select Committee conclusions accepted the views of opponents against the muzzle while recording their animus against the stray: "It must be admitted, however, that there are very many who do not consider that the muzzle itself was the effective instrument of checking rabies; but that the seizure, detention, and destruction of stray dogs, and the unusual care which dog owners exercised under pressure, were of no little avail in bringing about the diminution of the disorder."[76] John Colam of the RSPCA affirmed the position that "slaughtering stray dogs taken out of the streets . . . is a very effective means of reducing rabies."[77] Again we come back to the responsibilization of dog owners rather than to the direct restriction of their animals: the construction of dog-owning citizens in a liberal city. Thus the historian Patrick Joyce has written that "the vitalisation of the city . . . involved the conscription of the animal world, so that this world was humanised and involved in similar disciplinary routines to the human one. . . . The undisciplined subject had an undisciplined dog, the disciplined one a pet. The pet was social, the dog remained in the natural world."[78] The lead—and the collar and the license too—should therefore be interpreted as the technologies of a liberal alternative to more intrusive systems of discipline and control. We have here something like the normalization of the dog/walker pairing, and its representation as the sign of the respectable and responsible pet-owning citizen. These technologies of the "disciplined dog" played a key part in "the performance of respectable middle-class identities."[79] It is possible, therefore, without disagreeing with the general conclusions of previous accounts, to argue for a stronger narrative of inclusion and even empowerment of animals and their owners in the public space of the late Victorian city. Instead of seeing muzzling, and quarantine, as technical victories, sternly enforced in the face of sentimental opposition, it is the compromises with the dog lobby that are more likely to have contributed to the eradication of epidemic rabies from the geo-body of the nation. We should see technologies like the muzzle, the collar, the lead, and the license alike as attempts, not to discipline animals directly, but rather to represent and regulate the conduct of their human companions. Following Patrick Joyce, whose earlier comment on the disciplining of pets we may thus follow through to its conclusion, we may argue that these policies owe a great deal more to the "governmentality" of the liberal city than to any more direct, coercive, and disciplinary form of intervention.[80]

From the muzzle to the leash, then. From muzzling, direct discipline, and exclusion, to leashing, regulatory governance, and inclusion. Rather than think of these elements in an undifferentiated story about the restriction of the animal in the modern city, perhaps we can think of these as two distinct series, distinctive in their understanding of the place of dogs and their owners in public space. In any case, I have argued ultimately against any suggestion that moral and medical policing were victorious in their positioning of the dog as a public menace. I would venture to argue that it is the self-professed "dog lover" who emerges largely victorious in this struggle. What we have here, moreover, is something like the domestication of public space. Just as animals were welcomed into the private space of the home, in the form of the "pet," so too were animals allowed to be properly public in a newly domesticated public sphere. Animals could have their identity asserted as "pets"—albeit so long as they had the collar and the leash and were accepted as under proper control. It was perhaps the police who ultimately ended up, as it were, muzzled. The animals themselves were free to be led in the "liberal" spaces of the modern city.

We may go one step further still, however, and make a space for the dog not just as a sort of quasi-enfranchised, liberal political subject, conditionally allowed into public space, but also as an agent in its own right, operating within a distinctive urban "assemblage." In terms of agency, Jason Hribal has recently complained of the dominant strains in the history of animals: "The animals are not seen as agents. They are not active, as labourers, prisoners, or resistors. Rather, the animals are presented as static characters that have, over time, been used, displayed, and abused by humans. They emerge as objects—empty of any real substance."[81] This may be too harsh a judgment on an emergent discipline with diverse methodologies, but it is still a useful reminder that we should acknowledge dogs as having their own interests, their own capacities, their own agency. Understanding the simple practice of walking the dog certainly means accepting that dogs are "competent, skillful, playful, and often infinitely patient companions."[82] We should readily recognize too that this agency is acknowledged by all narratives of discipline: if we grant the "permanent provocation" of a recalcitrant animality, we see that pets can never be completely under control. Anand Pandian writes, in a different context, that this "stubborn and irredeemable animal nature was the moral condition that demanded a close and continuous regime of supervision and control."[83] It is true too that human beings become disciplined at the same time, with the "shepherd game" of Foucault's pastoral power a means by which we discipline ourselves: "We imagine ourselves as sovereign individuals who train the lesser animals. In fact when we 'train' dogs, we ourselves are being trained to be dog trainers and owners."[84] But there is an unmistakable condescension in the tendency to criticize the action of disciplinary technologies for producing "domesticated" people as well as subordinated animals.[85] The training of animals—their domestication if you will—is not only about discipline in this sense of controlling animals' agency, or that of humans, for that matter.

"Domestication" surely works on animals and humans not so much *alike* as *together*, and it involves practices of communication, care and mutual trust, as much as it does control and coercion. Such "training" is also a form of management or government that serves to establish domestic animals "as moral beings capable of being endowed with certain rights and duties."[86] What we do when we walk the dog is not simply to reduce it to a disciplined object; rather, we engage with it, or rather with *him* or *her*, as a subject, "bonded in significant otherness," accepting that we are domesticated and interpellated by them as well as the other way round.[87] Emma Mason has written recently in this vein that "dog training in this context becomes paramount, an act of love that makes the world in which the companion species resides a liveable one, wherein humans and dogs respond obediently to each other, with respect and with love."[88]

Such "training" is not simply about the actions of humans. It also recognizes the agency of the animals being socialized, even their *political* agency, for as Sue Donaldson and Will Kymlicka have observed, dogs by their sheer presence may be advocates and agents of change; using the example of dogs being exercised in the public realm, they note, "It becomes much harder to cling to ideas about the dangers of dogs in public spaces when you regularly witness the opposite."[89] The normalization of dog walking in the scopic economy of the late Victorian city indicates exactly this kind of "political participation"—the animals themselves, with their distinctive needs, projects, and interests, helping to domesticate the city.

We need to stress that these animals' agency and that of their humans were bound together, entangled with a complex array of forces. In technical, theoretical terms, we would be better off considering the agency of animals and humans as "emergent capacities" within an "assemblage" of heterogeneous components and relations. That means that we ought to see animal agency as contingently enabled, and produced in relation to that of other components, such as the rabies virus, human beings, political cultures and traditions, and objects and technologies such as the humble leash. All of these elements contributed to the assemblage that I am calling here the "dog-walking city." At the risk of inviting further skepticism from the uncommitted, the recently floated concept of "hudography" serves a useful purpose in support of the proposition that dog walking be acknowledged as a specific kind of modern practice. Unwieldy as it is, "hudography" is a helpful concept in gesturing to the entangled spatialities of dogs and humans and the hybrid social world to whose creation both species may be said to have contributed. The work of Donna Haraway and others on the relationship between —

what she calls the "knotting" of—human beings and companion species is a central resource here.[90] By focusing on what exactly happens when (and where) species meet, by directing attention away from the tropes of human disciplining of animals and towards stories of "co-habitation, co-evolution, and embodied cross-species sociality," Haraway crucially argues for the local, site-specific, contingent, and material reproduction of what is "animal," "natural," "human," and "cultural."[91] Instead of starting with abstractions like "nature" and "culture," therefore, attention to the messy modalities of a life shared with other species invites an awareness of our own contingent and situated "animality." Discipline—not as shorthand for "social control," but in the more complex sense of "training" or "domestication"—is an important modality of such entanglement. And if we accept this view of the human-animal urban assemblage in the era of rabies panics in late Victorian Britain, we are better placed to consider the defense of a dog-walking city as a historical phenomenon whose emergence is worthy of note.[92] The geography that I have narrated here, paradoxically concerning the "humanizing" or domestication of the city for dogs and their walkers, depends upon this recognition of our cohabitation and cross-species sociality with animal others, and on the positive encouragement of these others in the heart of the modern metropolis that has resulted. This is a form of domestication that acts on animals, but also on human beings, and still further on the built environment of the modern city. By the end of the nineteenth century, rabies was officially eradicated in Britain, but it could also be claimed that dogs and their companions were more fully domesticated as well.

Conclusion

O SAY that dogs were fully domesticated by the end of our period is to claim far too much, of course. For one thing, dogs were never wholly scoured from the streets, safely privatized and made respectable in the confinements of proper middle-class homes. Only much more recently have stray dogs more or less disappeared from British streets. Nor is it true to say that dogs have ever become universally accepted, in Britain or elsewhere. For large numbers of people, dogs remain merely nuisances and hazards, treated with aversion or outright hostility. For all too many, only when dogs become "pets" and companions are they considered rightful recipients of compassion and empathy. Alternatively, only where they are "useful," in other ways, as workers or experimental subjects, say, are dogs granted some value. But the gears of the "anthropological machine" grind away relentlessly, all but guaranteeing the precedence of the interests of human beings, however urgent, however trivial.[1] Even in the qualified form of "pets," dogs find their natures curtailed, their needs and desires unmet, and are unceremoniously deemed surplus to requirements if they fail to fulfill the conditions of a domestic social contract to which they never agreed in the first place.

This is manifestly a species of a more general moral schizophrenia toward nonhuman animals, but it takes particularly acute form when "man's best friend"—his "first friend," as Rudyard Kipling memorably has it—is considered, and these paradoxes are best exemplified in the Victorian age, when many of these issues were newly minted.[2] I have characterized this structure of feeling as a kind of ruthless sentimental-

ity, with care and killing, love and indifference, high principle and low
pragmatism, seemingly inseparable. It is worth reiterating that this condition describes the many who *loved* their domestic dogs as much as those
who had little time for animal welfare. The growth of a concern for dogs
characteristically ignored the "necessary" cruelty meted out to animals
used for food, manufacturing, transport, entertainment, and scientific research, inter alia; but it also practiced an "economy of affection" in relation to other, less fortunate canines.[3] Inevitably, it was the unloved "cur"
and the unredeemable "stray" who found themselves being removed and
destroyed, in the name of "improvement," hygiene, public safety, and in
the name of "humanity" too. The paradoxes were not lost on Victorian
animal rights campaigners. Thus Henry Salt—the greatest animal advocate of the age—welcomed the appearance of homes for lost and starving
dogs, but he instanced this as proof of the "general indifferentism which
can allow the most familiar domestic animals to become homeless."[4]

Ruthless sentimentality was enabled rather than merely informed
by a moral geography that strictly demarcated the street dog from the
domestic "pet." This distinction, rooted as it was in the imaginative geographies of public and private and the idealization of the home, was
central to the Victorian domestication of the dog. This book has set out
to explain how this happened and to trace its consequences. Such a domestication opened up opportunities for dog stealers to prey upon the
supposedly secure hearth, for instance; it presided over the development of rescue homes and the associated fate of animals thus rendered
"homeless"; a kind of domestication was instanced in the development
of a domestic form of scientific praxis and exemplification, and, in the
failure of this enterprise, the demotion of the dog from scientific companion to experimental animal; partly by way of response, dog owners
were inspired to question theological orthodoxy and imagine a future
life for their animals in a heavenly home; and, lastly, we have explored
the problem of the walking of dogs, the struggle over how they might
be considered properly under control, and how the public spaces of the
modern metropolis might be domesticated. The protean inconsisten-
cies involved and revealed meant that this "domestication" was always a
strained metaphor, so much so that it borders upon catachresis. But the
very paradoxes of this cultural geography provided the motive force for
this distinctively Victorian version of the "anthropological machine."

And the most euphemistically domesticating gesture of all, to return
to my preamble, was the notion that British dogs were granted a *national*

home. Taken uncritically, the "nation of dog lovers" tag that emerged in the early twentieth century *obscures* this contentious history and geography, investing as it does in a fiction of uniform national sentiment toward an homogeneous class of compliant and obligated canines. It stirs into the mix of ruthless sentiment and blatant inconsistency a further ingredient of cultural self-congratulation of a particularly egregious kind. We have already seen how Percy Fitzgerald's paean to the nineteenth-century "emancipation" of the British dog belies or betrays its complacencies by recurrently separating the respectable from the rough, the "civilized" from the "barbaric," the good dog from the bad. Again and again we have seen this disingenuous dualism, even, or perhaps especially, among those who saw themselves as the friends of dogs. Surely no other single species has been subject to this deadly distinction between pets and pests.

The idea that Britain became a nation of dog lovers nevertheless registers the prospect that these animals might, in some way, be included within the political community. We may take Fitzgerald's vision of canine enfranchisement, premature and prejudiced as it is, as a starting point for considering in conclusion the *political* status of dogs in Victorian Britain. The idea moots the possibility that domestication can be understood not just in providing homes for (a few) deserving animals, but in granting a sort of *homeland* too, however compromised. A political reading of what domestication means (or once again what it might mean) involves more than a call for the conditional right of animals to inhabit public space, for it presumes that dogs be recognized as worthy of more than merely toleration or paternalistic care. In the vision of a contemporary political theory that challenges anthropocentrism, for instance, dogs may be considered as participants in the public sphere, as political subjects, even perhaps as co-citizens.[5] Although animal rights theorists have considered the vast range of nonhuman animals, and are often, understandably, averse to drawing invidious distinctions or endorsing ameliorism or gradualism, it is surely dogs that have the greatest potential to be proposed as potential fellow citizens in this way. I am reminded of Italo Calvino's marvelous observation that the city of cats and the city of men lie one within the other, but are not the same city.[6] The city of dogs, by contrast, can hardly be distinguished from that in which most of us live. Dogs, above all creatures, partake of the dense bonds of interdependence, the shared spaces, the complex social and political relationships that we share with other animals.[7] Dogs are *close* to us—geographically if not genealogically. They might be considered, if not kin, then certainly "kith," in the real sense that dogs have not been strangers for thousands and thousands of years, even if we do not truly treat them as family.[8] Henry Salt recognized this special relationship between human beings and all of the "domestic" animals, but his words lead us to the situation of the dog in particular: "Apart from the universal rights they possess in common with all intelligent beings, domestic animals have a special claim on man's courtesy and sense of fairness, inasmuch as they are not his fellow-creatures only, but his fellow workers, his dependents, and in many cases the familiar associates and trusted inmates of his home."[9] Because of this unique history and geography, dogs have the prior claim to a *political* relationship with human beings.

How far was this relationship acknowledged in the Victorian age? To what extent might we argue that dogs became a part of the British polity? These may seem strange and awkward questions, though they stop far short of suggesting that animals were recognized as citizens in anything like the ideals of contemporary critical theory. As if in answer to Percy Fitzgerald, Ouida's Puck, in his captivity, refuses to countenance any bromides about "emancipation": "You think you have no slaves in England! Why, half the races in creation moan, and strive, and suffer, daily and hourly, under your merciless tyrannies! . . . I pray you, not to brag aloud that you keep no slaves, not to bawl from the housetops of your reverence for freedom."[10] It would be hard to argue with Ouida's assessment of the realities of life, and death, for dogs and other animals in Britain, then or now. Talk of citizenship in this sense strikes us as laughable. Still, we may forward the limited claim that the British state, by the end of the nineteenth century, *did* come to take political account of dogs as inhabitants of these isles. We can argue, specifically, that as dogs became part of political debate and discussion, as they acquired advocates and representatives, and as they came to be recognized through government regulation, so they were interpellated as political subjects of a particular kind.

First, as we have seen, the much-touted domestic destiny of household pets did not shield or prevent them from this public and political career. One of the paradoxes of domestic ideology's investment in the separation of public and private was the fact that domestic relations became matters of public, political moment.[11] To take a parallel case of creatures often unable to reason or to speak for themselves, as child welfare become a matter of moment, so did children become political subjects, proleptically recognized as citizens. A similar thing happens, I would argue, with the Victorian "dog question": as participants in these public debates, dogs became political actors. I mean this to be a strong claim: as has been noted in the previous chapter, by their presence and their actions in public space, dogs exercised some form of political agency.[12] They were no less political subjects than, say, infants, who were equally incapable of representing themselves, at least in the language of the politically exclusive public sphere that derives from the anthropocentric "modern constitution."[13] The philosopher Jane Bennett, following John Dewey and others, has considered the constitution of more-than-human publics from more-than-human problems, with politics reimagined as a form of ecology, and we may see dogs and other animals as political actors in just this way.[14] Dogs were not merely political objects, then, and it is important to stress that the dog question was a political and not just a human-defined *biopolitical* concern.[15]

Of course, dogs were inevitably dependent upon self-appointed representatives in the machinery of political advocacy, and the formation of a dog lobby toward the end of the nineteenth century is a notable accomplishment, albeit by no means an unambiguous one. There had been dog "fanciers" for generations, and the later Victorian development of dog shows and pedigree associations was ultimately to be dominated by the Kennel Club, founded in 1873, its mission being "to promote the general improvement of dogs."[16] Less remarked upon is the fact that the "fancy" quite quickly turned into a "lobby," concerned with animal welfare and the rights of dog owners as well as with various forms of canine "improvement." The rabies scares of the later nineteenth century, in particular, impelled dog owners and breeders to protect their interests, including the "right" to have animal companions, but also what they considered to be the "rights" of their dogs. Dogs also became public and political animals as a result of this political activism by dog breeders and owners. It should be noted here that contention within the dog lobby, including the de facto leadership of the Kennel Club, is another sign of the politicization of what came, only half-jokingly, to be called "dogdom."[17]

Finally, we can suggest that dogs were constituted as political subjects because they were increasingly recognized by the state as beings to be *governed*, to be addressed via the arts and practices of a more-than-human "governmentality." Dogs, with a few other nonhuman animals, became politically *countable*, and their owners similarly *accountable* to the state, via mundane technologies such as the dog license. Regulatory regimes like these confirmed the indispensability of the modern dog, enlarged as well as disciplined dog ownership, and enhanced dogs' legal status to boot.[18] Dogs were conferred with something like a civic personality, demanding of recognition; they were thus "practically citizens," in Kimberly Smith's words—though it should be quickly pointed out that this extension of citizenship does not preclude practices that would be unthinkable for their human counterparts.[19] We can give some sense of the number of these canine quasi-"citizens." Toward the end of the century, in England, Wales, and Scotland, there were over one and a half million dogs, either licensed or granted exemptions, roughly one dog for every twenty human beings.[20] Though the number of wholly unlicensed dogs can only be guessed at, there were perhaps at least as many again for the whole of Britain.[21] But the important point is that these one and a half million dogs were *politically authorized*, having some state recognition of their legitimate existence. We do not have to accept Henry Salt's argument that such "legislative recognition" by the state, such as the laws on animal welfare, implies the rights of animals themselves.[22] That position has been ridiculed by the philosopher John Passmore, who argued that many things are protected by law that do not have "rights" (in the restricted sense of the word), and that the growth of animal welfare should be seen merely as the *constriction* of the rights of *humans*.[23] But Passmore misses the fact that technologies such as the dog license acknowledge at the very least the rights of dog owners and, albeit indirectly, the claims of dogs themselves to legitimate existence.

In these historically specific ways, some animals—domestic dogs—were included in some kind of wider political reckoning. It was not just a matter of extending the moral franchise: by the end of the Victorian age, there was an established place in the British polity for domestic dogs.[24] We should be careful not to give this argument too positive a spin, for sure. There are all too many reasons to concede that this political inclusion of dogs remained selective and conditional. The attempt to make dogs *private* beings resulted in the very public "dog question," but at the same time, the attempt to make dogs *public*—to confer upon them some kind of civic recognition, some civil status, even quasi-citizenship—was paradoxically dependent upon making them *private*, via the idealization of the domesticated animal. The more that dogs were regulated, the more that they were accepted as domestic animals and good "citizens," so their legal status was enhanced, but this came only at the expense of becoming *property*.[25] Since it was always more difficult for the poor to

Figure 16. "Waiting for the Verdict — Scene at a Glasgow Police Station during a Campaign against Stray Dogs," *Graphic,* 28 July 1877, 85. (Reproduced by kind permission of the Syndics of Cambridge University Library)

keep dogs, the rights of dog owners were also unequally compromised rather than universally constricted, in Passmore's sense.[26] Meanwhile, the unlicensed, unregulated, unrecognized dog became a kind of "anti-citizen," caught in a legal limbo, an object of police and suspicion, and always in dread of the verdict of a black-capped human arbiter (fig. 16).

Few spoke up for his or her rights. Even the dog lobby tended to call for the destruction of the stray and the mongrel, making a claim for responsibility and a bid for respectability. Many of these other dogs were sacrificed in order that pets, particularly pedigreed ones, could be endowed with whatever civic privileges were on offer. And even so, the political status of dogs in Britain was ambiguous and fragile, vulnerable to revocation in times of crisis, such as happened in the First World War when demand for food put people first and furthermore questioned pet owners' patriotism.[27] We can speak with Edward Tenner of "national dogs" and "citizen canines," therefore, but we need to acknowledge, as he does, that dogs are only ever "conditional citizens"—"perpetual new-comers," never fully "naturalized," forced to accommodate themselves to their hosts' political culture and ever-suspicious surveillance.[28]

All the same, even to take into account the narrow political boundaries of canine citizenship, in the Victorian age or for that matter in ours, is to recognize that dogs have become in the intervening years political beings of a sort. That we should work toward extending their rights, toward genuinely treating domestic animals as some kind of *citizens,* I have no doubt, and although this is not a book of advocacy, I hope to have made a contribution to thinking about how we might live with animals, start-ing (and absolutely not ending) with our closest animal companions.[29] By revisiting the "dog question" in Victorian Britain, considering it from a number of perspectives and approaches, I have all along wanted to bring out the complexities and the paradoxes in our own relationship with dogs, and to try to learn from how the Victorians grappled, practi-cally and emotionally, with the fact that they shared space with these nonhuman others. There is far more at stake here than a narrative of sentimental attachment and developing sensitivity to suffering can ever encompass. This itself is salutary, for as Donna Haraway admonishes, "Dog people need to learn how to inherit difficult histories in order to shape more vital multi-species futures."[30] Difficult histories: and difficult geographies too, I would add. Like her, I also want to change the minds of those who react instinctively against the supposedly empty sentimen-tality inherent in companionship with animals. By showing how (some)

Victorians valued "the homely, ordinary, daily, affectional lives of animals," and how they, and their companions, challenged the constraints of a ferociously anthropocentric culture, we might better be able to change the narrative, redraw the map, in positive and progressive ways.[31] If it is true that the Victorians "invented" the modern dog, perhaps we might concede that they also invented what the dog might one day become.

Notes

Introduction

1. Ritvo, "Animals in Nineteenth-Century Britain," considers the competing narratives. It is difficult to separate the idea of the British love of animals from the country's enduring passion for field sports, as when Sarah Tytler saw, in Landseer's animal art, "evidence of the kindly satisfaction with which a matter of fact and plain-spoken race recognise in their four-footed allies attributes which constitute them far more than useful dependants—privileged and cherished comrades" (*Landseer's Dogs*, 11).

2. As an exemplary account of the British love for animals, arguing that humanitarian feeling culminated in the eighteenth century, see Harwood, *Love for Animals*.

3. See, for instance, in the context of antivivisectionism, Massey, *Natural Genesis*, 501.

4. Leighton, *Dogs and All about Them*, iii.

5. I have found examples no earlier than the late nineteenth century, such as the *Newcastle Weekly Courant*, 8 February 1896, or *Speaker*, 5 February 1898, 186.

6. Fitzgerald, "Dogs in Britain," 553.

7. Pemberton and Worboys, *Mad Dogs and Englishmen*, 6–7.

8. See Howell, "Dog Fancy at War."

9. *Times*, 10 March 1866, 7. See also the editorial in the *Times*, 12 March 1866, 8, which, in arguing that dog lovers were likely a majority in the countryside, and dog haters in the towns, similarly suggests how far the companion dog was from cultural acceptance.

10. *British Fancier*, 9 September 1892, 169.

11. Homans, *What's a Dog For?*, 1.

12. See Fudge, "Left-Handed Blow," 4–5. See also Ritvo, *Noble Cows and Hybrid Zebras*, 1–11, for reflections on the growth of animal studies.

13. Salt, *Animals' Rights*, 4.

14. Briggs, *Victorian Things*, 67.

15. Ritvo, *Animal Estate*. For pioneering work, see Harrison, "Animals and the State," and Walton, "Mad Dogs and Englishmen."

16. Thomas, *Man and the Natural World*. For discussion of the Victorian birth of environmentalism, see Ritvo, *Dawn of Green*, and Winter, *Secure from Rash Assault*.

17. Ritvo, *Animal Estate*, 2. For a sketching in of the current agenda within Victorian studies, see McKechnie and Miller, "Victorian Animals," and for

Ritvo's own reflections, see her *Noble Cows and Hybrid Zebras*. For a polemical riposte on the lack of animal agency in the history of animals, see Hribal, "Animals, Agency, and Class." See also Pearson and Weismantel, "Does 'The Animal' Exist?," 27.

18. Briggs, *Victorian Things*, 41.

19. For good introductions see Fudge, *Animal*, and Weil, *Thinking Animals*, as well as Kalof and Fitzgerald, *Animals Reader*. For the philosophical question of animals and animality, an excellent recent overview is supplied by Oliver, *Animal Lessons*. For recent work on animal history, informed by the animal turn, see Benson, "Animal Writes"; Brantz, *Beastly Natures*; Ham and Senior, *Animal Acts*; Kalof and Resl, *Cultural History of Animals*.

20. For the place of animals in political theory, see, to pick only a sample of recent work, Donaldson and Kymlicka, *Zoopolis*; Francione, *Introduction to Animal Rights*; Garner, *Theory of Justice for Animals*; Smith, *Governing Animals*.

21. In the Nietzschean strain, exercising the power of domesticating animals typically results in the domesticating and disciplining of humans and/or humanity: "Zarathustra shall not become the shepherd and dog of a herd" (Nietzsche, *Thus Spoke Zarathustra*, 23). See also the discussion in Deleuze and Guattari, *Thousand Plateaus*, 265–66, with its memorable if surely tongue-in-cheek observation that *"anyone who likes cats or dogs is a fool"* (265, emphasis in original).

22. See Linzey and Cohn, "Terms of Discourse," for a discussion of the issue of language. The decision to use conventional terms in this book derives also from the fact that much of this book necessarily has to engage with the language of past thought, here Victorian terms and terminology, including those that Linzey and Cohn and others would regard as inherently derogatory toward nonhuman animals, and the fact that the idealism inherent in contemporary terminology, such as replacing "pet" with "companion animal," necessarily neglects the axis of dominance and subordination that existed and exists in practice (see Peggs, *Animals and Sociology*, 76). My use of conventional terms is not meant to imply endorsement of derogation or domination.

23. For introductions, see Philo and Wilbert, *Animal Spaces, Beastly Places*; Urbanik, *Placing Animals*; Wolch, "Anima Urbis;" Wolch and Emel, *Animal Geographies*.

24. Pearson and Weismantel, "Does 'The Animal' Exist?," 22.

25. Philo and Wilbert, *Animal Spaces, Beastly Places*, 5.

26. Peggs, *Animals and Sociology*, 88. See Jerolmack, "How Pigeons Became Rats," for an example of this "cultural-spatial logic."

27. Anderson, "Animals, Science, and Spectacle in the City," 30. On the long history of anthropocentrism in Western philosophy, see Steiner, *Anthropocentrism and Its Discontents*. I have also found particularly helpful the arguments of Erica Fudge on the conjoining of an anxious anthropocentrism and an ambiguous an-

thropomorphism in the "Age of Reason," which she has developed in *Perceiving Animals* and *Brutal Reasoning.*

28. Scholtmeijer, *Animal Victims in Modern Fiction,* 145.

29. Donald, "Beastly Sights"; Philo, "Animals, Geography, and the City."

30. Emel and Wolch, "Witnessing the Animal Moment," 22.

31. Anderson, "Animals, Science, and Spectacle in the City." For zoos, see also Anderson, "Walk on the Wild Side"; Baratay and Hardouin Fugier, *Zoo;* Brantz, "Domestication of Empire," 88–90; Braverman, *Zooland;* Malamud, *Reading Zoos.*

32. Derrida, *The Animal That Therefore I Am,* 34, emphasis in original.

33. Berger, *Why Look at Animals?* These essays were originally published in 1977 in *New Society.* For Berger's discussion of the peasant's world, see *Pig Earth.*

34. Baker, *Postmodern Animal,* 21–22. See also Lippit, *Electric Animal,* 2–3: "Modernity can be defined by the disappearance of wildlife from humanity's habitat and by the reappearance of the same in humanity's reflections on itself."

35. Coetzee, *Lives of Animals,* 101.

36. Van Sittert and Swart, "*Canis Familiaris,*" 139. See also Van Sittert, "Class and Canicide," 210.

37. Watts, "Afterword: Enclosure," 292, emphasis in original.

38. For example, see Griffin, "Animal Maiming."

39. Crucially, even now, "human cities teem with non-domesticated animals," as well as domesticated ones (Donaldson and Kymlicka, *Zoopolis,* 8).

40. Atkins, introduction to *Animal Cities,* 2.

41. Mason, *Civilized Creatures,* 2. See also Hardy, "Pioneers in the Victorian Provinces," 373–74, and Flanders, *Victorian City,* 207–8.

42. McShane and Tarr, *Horse in the City.* For a discussion of horses' visibility, but at the same time a suffering that was *not* immediately visible, and which called for an empathetic and imaginative approach from observers, see Miele, "Horse-Sense."

43. See, for instance, Burt, *Rat,* and Shipstone, *Becoming-Rat.*

44. See Jones, "'Sight of Creatures Strange to Our Clime,'" and Simons, *Tiger That Swallowed the Boy* and *Rossetti's Wombat.*

45. Thomas, *Man and the Natural World.* Arthur MacGregor's recent large-scale survey, *Animal Encounters,* which refuses to focus on practices such as pet keeping, repeats this narrative of distancing and alienation from the animal world.

46. Boddice, *History of Attitudes and Behaviours toward Animals,* 84.

47. See Hardy, "Pioneers in the Victorian Provinces," noting the particular difficulties encountered in the metropolis.

48. Alternatively, the social anthropologist Edmund Leach preferred to discriminate social space via the sequence of self, pet, livestock, game, wild ani-

mal: "Animal Categories and Verbal Abuse," cited by Baker, *Postmodern Animal*, 166–67.

49. For abjection, see Kristeva, *Powers of Horror*. Jacques Derrida also spoke of the purification of the animal in man: see Wolfe, *Before the Law*, 9. For Latour, see *We Have Never Been Modern*, 10–12.

50. Creaney, "Paralytic Animation," 18–19.

51. Latour, *We Have Never Been Modern*. Moreover, we can point to the "asinity" (in Derrida's terms) of the concept of "animal," and the inadequacy of the view that this is simply the abjected "other" of the human; domesticated animals in particular—and I would add domestic animals even more so—complicate the distinction between *bios* and *zoe* that has been argued as fundamental to the notion of humanity: see Wolfe, *Before the Law*, 54–55.

52. Ritvo, *Noble Cows and Hybrid Zebras*, 11. For the ethical implications today, see Palmer, "Placing Animals."

53. Shaler, *Domesticated Animals*, 18.

54. Hollingshead, "Two Dog Shows," 493.

55. For an overview and discussion, see Nast, "Critical Pet Studies." An early, important statement is Shell, "Family Pet."

56. Deleuze and Guattari tellingly refer to "Oedipal animals" (*Thousand Plateaus*, 265). See Thrift, *Knowing Capitalism*, 210. For a notably carceral example of recent writing about the treatment of animals, and humans, see Thierman, "Apparatuses of Animality."

57. Anderson, "Animal Domestication"; Hochadel, "Darwin in the Monkey Cage" and "Watching Exotic Animals Next Door." See also Salt, *Animals' Rights*, 36.

58. Sloterdijk, "Rules for the Human Zoo," 21. Notoriously, the Nazis attempted to undo and overcome such "domestication": see Sax, *Animals in the Third Reich*.

59. Wolch and Emel, preface to *Animal Geographies*, xiii.

60. See, especially, Hinchliffe, *Geographies of Nature*, and Whatmore, *Hybrid Geographies*.

61. Tomlinson, *Animal Crossings*, 39–40.

62. Weil, *Thinking Animals*, 16.

63. Raber, "From Sheep to Meat," provides a recent summary, arguing that the early modern histories of animal husbandry and pet keeping are inseparable. This follows Keith Thomas in seeing pet keeping as a melancholy replacement for an alienated rural nature, but rather more sharply traces the "personhood of pets" as emerging in distinction to the "calculus of cattle."

64. Rubin, *Impressionist Cats and Dogs*, 57.

65. Brown, *Homeless Dogs*, 20. Tague, "Dead Pets," asserts the eighteenth-century origins of pets but notes that widespread usage of the term had to wait until the nineteenth century; moreover, it is the associated problematizing of

public animals in the nineteenth century, a focus of this book, that is equally important and that suggests that the nineteenth century was the more formative period.

66. Clutton-Brock, "Unnatural World," 26. See also Morey, *Dogs, Domestication.*

67. See Cassidy, "Introduction: Domestication Reconsidered," and Hodder, *Entangled,* 78–80, on dependence and dependency between humans and nonhuman animals.

68. Ritvo, *Platypus and the Mermaid,* 39–40.

69. This followed with "Pease's Act" of 1835. The Society for the Prevention of Cruelty to Animals gained its royal suffix in 1840.

70. Scholtmeijer, *Animal Victims,* 81.

71. Brantz, "Domestication of Empire," 93.

72. Anderson, "A Walk on the Wild Side" and "Animal Domestication in Geographic Perspective."

73. Power, "Domestication and the Dog," 371.

74. Power, "Domestication and the Dog," 373. The reference is to Haraway, *When Species Meet.*

75. Salt, *Animals' Rights,* 32.

76. Cassidy, "Introduction: Domestication Reconsidered," 5. Cassidy is drawing here on Bulliet's developmental narrative of domestication: *Herders, Hunters, and Hamburgers.* However, while Bulliet asserts pet keeping as iconic of a "postdomestic" society, I want to stress the continuing importance of domestication in the literal, geographical sense of animals becoming "acclimated to a home" (46).

77. Joyce, *State of Freedom,* 334.

78. For an agenda, see Blunt and Varley, "Geographies of Home," and the subsequent papers in this special issue of *Cultural Geographies.*

79. Blunt and Dowling, *Home,* 22.

80. Bachelard, *Poetics of Space;* Rybczynski, *Home.*

81. Quoted by Behlmer, *Friends of the Family,* 28.

82. Douglas, "Idea of Home," 290. Note too Norbert Elias's discussion of the role of space in separating humanity and animality, in *Civilizing Process.*

83. Blunt and Dowling, *Home,* 2.

84. Donald, "Tranquil Havens?"

85. See Gleadle, *Borderline Citizens,* 5. Flanders, *The Victorian House,* also usefully combines the prescriptive and the descriptive.

86. Classic work includes Armstrong, *Desire and Domestic Fiction;* Davidoff and Hall, *Family Fortunes;* and Poovey, *Uneven Developments.*

87. Cohen, *Professional Domesticity,* 10. The most cited critique has been Vickery, "Golden Age to Separate Spheres?" Two anniversary reflections provide welcome distance from the immediate debates, however: Gleadle, "Revisiting *Family Fortunes,*" and Steinbach, "Can We Still Use 'Separate Spheres'?"

88. For example, Gleadle, *Borderline Citizens*; Langland, *Nobody's Angels*; Marcus, *Apartment Stories*; Tange, *Architectural Identities*; and Tosh, *Man's Place*.

89. Gilbert, *Citizen's Body*.

90. Blunt and Dowling, *Home*, 27.

91. Mayhew, *London Labour and the London Poor*, 2012 edition, 293. In his introduction, xxxii, Robert Douglas-Fairhurst observes that this is both a model for Mayhew's writing and "a utopian dream of city life."

92. Behlmer, *Friends of the Family*, 21.

93. Hitchings, "At Home with Someone Nonhuman," 183.

94. Dixon, "Domestic Pets," 248.

95. *Beeton's Book of Poultry and Domestic Animals*, iv.

96. *Cassell's Household Guide*, 2.

97. Thus the maidservant Hannah Cullwick notes, for 14 July 1860, that she washed the dog, between cleaning the privy and the scullery floor and washing out the sinks; see Flanders, *Victorian House*, 109–10. In her diaries, Cullwick compares herself to a dog several times and occasionally wore a dog collar under her clothes for the delight of her "Massa," Arthur Munby.

98. *Beeton's Book of Poultry and Domestic Animals*, 545.

99. Excellent introductions can be found in Franklin, *Animals and Modern Cultures*, 84–104, and Fudge, *Pets*.

100. Douglas, "Idea of a Home," 306.

101. "In the world of prisons, as in the world of dogs . . . the vertical is not one of the dimensions of space, it is the dimension of power" (Foucault, "Force of Flight," 170).

102. Tuan, *Dominance and Affection*.

103. Bennett, *Enchantment of Modern Life*, 52.

104. Pearson, *Rights of the Defenseless*, 21, 29.

105. Mason, *Civilized Creatures*, 14.

106. See *Children's Household Pets*.

107. Grier, "Childhood Socialization," 95.

108. Mason, *Civilized Creatures*, 43.

109. Shaler, *Domesticated Animals*, 11.

110. See Bachelard, *Poetics of Space*, 91, on the fire in the hearth as the image of refuge.

111. "Magenta," *Treatment of Our Domesticated Dogs*, 6–7. Note, however, that *Cassell's Household Guide* seems content, at least in the edition I have consulted, for dogs to be kenneled.

112. For the contemporary world, see Power, "Furry Families."

113. Mangum, "Dog Years, Human Fears," 36. The thesis of *embourgeoisement* is explored most impressively in Kete, *Beast in the Boudoir*.

114. McKenzie, "Dogs and the Public Sphere," 236.

115. Shaler, *Domesticated Animals*, 38–39. Shaler was a full-time racist and

apologist for slavery: it is perhaps not too glib to note that Shaler conceived of black people as dominated, and increasingly so, by their "animal" natures, and thus similarly requiring what he calls the "stronger mastering hand" (Shaler, "Negro Problem," 698).

116. Kete, *"La Rage* and the Bourgeoisie," 102.

117. Brantz, "Domestication of Empire," 79–80.

118. See Thompson, *Public and Private Lives of Animals,* and Chase and Levenson, *Spectacle of Intimacy.*

119. Chase and Levenson, *Spectacle of Intimacy,* 5, 6, 13.

120. See Leach, "Anthropological Aspects of Language."

121. For discussion of animals as objects in the Victorian and Edwardian home, see Briggs, *Victorian Things,* and Cheang, "Women, Pets, and Imperialism." This work may be aligned with Daniel Miller's work on the material geographies of home: see Miller, "Why Some Things Matter." The reference here is again to Elias, *Civilizing Process.*

122. McKenzie, "Dogs and the Public Sphere," 249.

123. Behlmer, *Friends of the Family,* 2, on the "deification of the domestic."

124. Brown, *Homeless Dogs,* 69–70.

1. Dogs in Dickensland

1. Forster, *Life of Charles Dickens,* 218, n. 226.

2. See Mamie Dickens, *My Father as I Recall Him,* 79–87, 94–95.

3. Ward, *Charles Dickens,* 106. See also Hamley, *Our Poor Relations,* 58, and Fields, "Some Memories of Charles Dickens."

4. Fitzgerald, "Dickens's Dogs." The article is unsigned, but the attribution is confirmed in Fitzgerald's *Memories of Charles Dickens,* 10. For Fitzgerald, Landseer, and Dickens, see Gray, "Dickens and Dogs," an article to which I am much indebted.

5. Fitzgerald, "Dickens's Dogs," 48.

6. Nash, *Rights of Nature.*

7. *Times,* 18 October 1860, 8.

8. Fitzgerald, "Dickens's Dogs," 50.

9. In fairness, Landseer too was praised for moving from type to genera to species to variety, all the way to the individual dogs and their distinct personalities; see Tytler, *Landseer's Dogs,* 7.

10. Fitzgerald, "Dickens's Dogs," 50.

11. Waters, *Dickens and the Politics of the Family,* 204–5.

12. Fitzgerald, "Dickens's Dogs," 50.

13. See Mamie Dickens, *My Father,* 11–12.

14. Chesterton, *Charles Dickens,* 78. "Bozland" is the appealing alternative: see *Graphic,* 25 July 1896, 120.

15. Li, "Mobilizing Literature," 37.

16. Lansbury, *Old Brown Dog*, 175; Li, "Mobilizing Literature," 46. For Dickens and animal welfare, see Harrison, "Animals and the State," 812. On Dickens's giving evidence against an omnibus driver, see Enkvist, "Charles Dickens in the Witness Box," cited in Richardson, *Dickens and the Workhouse*, 339, n. 57. On Dickens's antivivisection credentials, see "Charles Dickens and Vivisection," *Animals Defender and Zoophilist*. Note, however, that Richard Ryder, *Animal Revolution*, 100, claims that Dickens, while opposed to vivisection, was never actively involved with the RSPCA.

17. Richardson, *Dickens and the Workhouse*, 138–39, 205. See Dickens, *Oliver Twist*, ch. 3.

18. Hollingshead, "Two Dog Shows," 497.

19. Smiley, *Charles Dickens*, 54.

20. Curran, "Pets," 192.

21. Hartley, *Dickens and the House of Fallen Women*, 38.

22. Chase and Levenson, *Spectacle of Intimacy*, 101.

23. Moore, "Beastly Criminals and Criminal Beasts." For the history of Urania Cottage, see Hartley, *Dickens and the House of Fallen Women*.

24. Dickens, *Bleak House*, ch. 11. See Plotkin, "Home-Made Savages," for the propaedeutic and practical links between "home" and "Homeland."

25. Dickens, *Barnaby Rudge*, ch. 46; cited in Armstrong, *Dickens and the Concept of Home*, 75–76.

26. See Schwarzbach, *Dickens and the City*, 114–42.

27. Dennis Walder, introduction to Dickens, *Sketches by Boz*, xxv.

28. Dickens, *Dombey and Son*, ch. 6; Tambling, *Going Astray*, 109.

29. Dickens, *Martin Chuzzlewit*, ch. 5, 124.

30. Dickens, *Oliver Twist*, ch. 21. See Mee, *Cambridge Introduction to Charles Dickens*, 58.

31. See Donald, "'Beastly Sights,'" 66.

32. Philo, "Animals, Geography, and the City," 63–64.

33. Bowen, *Other Dickens*, 90–91. Chesterton refers to Dickens's childhood in the blacking factory as a "bestial nightmare," his frustrations those of "a wild beast in a cage" (*Charles Dickens*, 18, 20).

34. Tambling, *Dickens and London*.

35. See, for instance, Kreilkamp, "Dying like a Dog," and Moore, "Beastly Criminals and Criminal Beasts."

36. For Dickens's *eidometropolis*, see Tambling, *Going Astray*.

37. Dickens, "Shy Neighbourhoods," 211, *All the Year Round*, 26 May 1860, reprinted in Dickens, *Selected Journalism*, 211.

38. Dickens, "Shy Neighbourhoods," 207.

39. Dickens, "Shy Neighbourhoods," 208–10.

40. Loudon, *Domestic Pets*, 7.

41. See Driver, "Moral Geographies."

42. Dickens, *Martin Chuzzlewit*, ch. 13.

43. Dickens, *Bleak House*, ch. 1.

44. For the great treatment of this theme, see Miller, *The Novel and the Police*.

45. *Hand-Book about Our Domestic Pets*, 46.

46. Cited by Douglas-Fairhurst, *Becoming Dickens*, 20–21.

47. Dickens, *Bleak House*, ch. 31.

48. Dickens, *Bleak House*, ch. 16. On this theme, see Wylie, *Caught between Two Spheres*.

49. Douglas-Fairhurst, *Becoming Dickens*, 24.

50. Kreilkamp, "Dying like a Dog," 82, 84. See *Martin Chuzzlewit*, ch. 30, on the hard life of a dog.

51. Dickens, *Barnaby Rudge*, ch. 18; *Great Expectations*, ch. 39.

52. Munich, "Domesticity," 129.

53. Armstrong, *Dickens and the Concept of Home*, 124; Donald, *Picturing Animals in Britain*, 139.

54. Pearson, *Rights of the Defenseless*, 37, 45.

55. Pearson, *Rights of the Defenseless*, 54.

56. Dickens, *Our Mutual Friend*, ch. 13. See Munich, *Queen Victoria's Secrets*, 131.

57. Dickens, *Little Dorrit*, ch. 27.

58. Armstrong, *Dickens and the Concept of Home*, 143.

59. Dickens, *Christmas Carol*, stave 3, 60.

60. Bodenheimer, *Knowing Dickens*, 139.

61. Armstrong, *Desire and Domestic Fiction*, 184.

62. For perhaps the strongest presentation of the disciplinary function of domestic ideology in Dickens, though demonstrating in his work a resistance to the closure this implies, see Waters, *Dickens and the Politics of the Family*.

63. Mee, *Cambridge Introduction to Charles Dickens*, 67.

64. Other attributions to Dickens: Curran, "Pets," 192, and Kean, *Animal Rights*, 90.

65. Gray, in her review of Garry Jenkins, *A Home of Their Own*, 152, writes, "While it is to Dickens's credit that he published the article, and though he was astutely observant of street dogs, it wasn't his habit to write sentimentally about their plight." See Hollingshead, *My Lifetime*, 20–21, for confirmation of authorship.

66. The same argument raised by Gray goes for Dickens's putative authorship of the antivivisection article "Inhumane Humanity," *All the Year Round*, 17 March 1866, 238–41. This is uncritically accepted by French, *Antivivisectionism*, 34; Preece, *Brute Souls*, 416; and Ryder, *Animal Revolution*, 100.

67. Mee, "Dickens, Gender, and Domesticity," 74. See also Waters, *Dickens and the Politics of the Family*.

68. Rose, "Flogging and Fascination," 519–20. See also Macdonald, "Red-Headed Animal."

69. Armstrong, *Dickens and the Concept of Home*, 63.

70. Dickens, *The Cricket on the Hearth*, Chirp the First.

71. Dickens, "Mr. Minns and His Cousin," in *Sketches by Boz*.

72. Dickens, "Mr. Minns and His Cousin," in *Sketches by Boz*.

73. Douglas-Fairhurst, *Becoming Dickens*, 112.

74. Bodenheimer, *Knowing Dickens*, 142.

75. Dickens, "Sentiment," in *Sketches by Boz*, 376.

76. Chesterton, *Charles Dickens*, 14.

77. Cited in Bodenheimer, *Knowing Dickens*, 190.

78. House and Storey, *Letters of Charles Dickens*, 1:555.

79. Forster, *Life of Charles Dickens*, 218, n. 226; Mamie Dickens, *My Father as I Recall Him*, 79–80.

80. Forster, *Life of Charles Dickens*, 63; Dickens, *David Copperfield*, ch. 11.

81. Charles Collins, "Charles Dickens's Study," *The Graphic*, Christmas number, 1870, cited by Slater, *Charles Dickens*, 256; Slater thinks this is possibly a "dog thief."

82. Cited by Slater, *Charles Dickens*, 265.

83. See Mr. George's self-description, *Bleak House*, ch. 63.

84. Cited in Veyne, *Foucault*, 74. For "world without interiority," see Clark, "Dickens through Blanchot."

85. From at least the time of Chesterton, *Charles Dickens*. See also Tambling, *Going Astray*, 223; Hatten, *End of Domesticity*, 34; Sadrin, *Parentage and Inheritance*, 18.

86. Chesterton, *Charles Dickens*, 27.

87. Bodenheimer, *Knowing Dickens*, 126–69.

88. Dickens, *Old Curiosity Shop*, ch. 18.

89. Fitzgerald, "Dickens's Dogs," 50.

90. Fitzgerald, *Memories of Charles Dickens*, 10, 11.

91. On dogs and animal acts, see Schlicke, *Dickens and Popular Entertainment*, 103–20.

92. In her revision to our understanding of melodrama, Juliet John, *Dickens's Villains*, foregrounds melodrama over pantomime's protean approach to the self, but she disputes the Foucauldian association of privacy with carceral interiority, on the grounds of its neglect of melodrama's populism and cultural inclusivity. For George Levine, there is a Darwinian/anti-Darwinian differentiation between romantic uniformitarianism and stage melodrama (*Darwin and the Novelists*, 134).

93. Douglas-Fairhurst, *Becoming Dickens*, 83.

94. Moody, *Illegitimate Theatre*, 91–93.

95. Moody, *Illegitimate Theatre*, 213.

96. *Memoirs of Joseph Grimaldi*, 156.

97. Moody, *Illegitimate Theatre*, 210. See Buckmaster, "'We Are All Actors in the Pantomime of Life,'" and "'A Man of Great Feeling and Sensibility.'" See

also Stott, *Pantomime Life of Joseph Grimaldi,* and Douglas-Fairhurst, *Becoming Dickens,* 112.

98. Dickens, "A Christmas Tree," in *Christmas Stories,* 1850, cited by Waters, *Dickens and the Politics of the Family,* 67.

99. Moody, *Illegitimate Theatre,* 224. Dickens's satire on America casts its people as the sons of nature, descendants of Orson, but no more capable of feeling than the swine in the streets (*Martin Chuzzlewit,* ch. 22).

100. Cited by Toru Sasaki, in his introduction to Chesterton, *Charles Dickens,* xvii. For a similarly enchanting vision of "vital materialism," see Bennett, *Vibrant Matter.*

101. Dickens, *Martin Chuzzlewit,* ch. 4.

102. Levine, *Darwin and the Novelists,* 137. Chesterton similarly notes that Dickens "produced monsters with a kind of carelessness, like enormous by-products; life producing the rhinocerous, and art Mr Bunsby" (*Charles Dickens,* 10.)

103. Buckmaster, in "'A Man of Great Feeling and Sensibility,'" draws attention to the contrivance of everyday life in London, not merely on the stage.

104. Dickens, *Martin Chuzzlewit,* ch. 53.

105. See Trotter, *Cooking with Mud,* and Moody, *Illegitimate Theatre,* 218.

106. Dickens may have been horrified by the mature Maria Beadnell, but he must have been amused by the fact that her pet dog, his old rival for her (now no longer wanted) affections, ended up as a stuffed ornament in the hallway; see Douglas-Fairhurst, *Becoming Dickens,* 106.

107. Moody, *Illegitimate Theatre,* 225; Baumgarten, "Fictions of the City," 114.

108. Croker, "Canine Chapter," 326.

109. Francione, *Introduction to Animal Rights.*

110. Fitzgerald, "Dickens's Dogs," 49.

111. Fitzgerald, "Dickens's Dogs," 49.

112. Fairholme and Pain, *Century of Work for Animals,* 45.

113. Trollope, *American Senator,* 504.

114. Flint, "Origins, Species and *Great Expectations.*"

115. Chesterton, *Charles Dickens,* 138.

116. Dickens, *Bleak House,* ch. 16.

117. See Gray, "Dickens and Dogs," 18–19.

118. Dickens, *Old Curiosity Shop,* ch. 62.

119. Dickens to Percy Fitzgerald, 6 November 1866, in Storey, *Letters of Charles Dickens,* 11:264. Sultan met his end sometime in early September.

120. Dickens to W. W. F. De Cerjat, 1 January 1867, in Storey, *Letters of Charles Dickens,* 11:291.

121. Slater, *Charles Dickens,* 555. For the erasure of the animal by language, culture, and literature, see Lippit, *Electric Animal.*

122. See Arluke, "Managing Emotions."

123. Callow, *Charles Dickens*, 306.

124. Douglas-Fairhurst, *Becoming Dickens*, 36. Douglas-Fairhurst follows this with the excellent image of Dickens "observing them with the cool eye of a farmer sizing up his livestock."

125. Fenton, "Portrait of a Victorian Painter," 164.

126. Cohen, *Professional Domesticity*, 106, in the context of the construction of what she calls "home effects."

2. Flush and the Banditti

1. Karlin, *Robert Browning and Elizabeth Barrett*, 306.

2. This episode is related in Elizabeth Barrett's correspondence, and from this source in numerous biographies; see, for instance, Markus, *Dared and Done*, 58–64. See also Adams, *Shaggy Muses*, 26–29, 36–38.

3. Woolf, *Flush*, 78–80. Compare Elizabeth Barrett's reaction to the denizens of Whitechapel—"The faces of those men!" (Karlin, *Robert Browning and Elizabeth Barrett*, 311).

4. See King, *Virginia Woolf*, 473–74; Lee, *Virginia Woolf*, 620–21. Nonhuman narrators contribute to "it-narratives" that might include objects as well as animals: see Bellamy, "It-Narrators." Brown, *Homeless Dogs*, 23, notes the rise of the itinerant dog narrator, which she sees as a direct creation of the bourgeois phenomenon of pet keeping. Note the development of the genre from this animal satire to talking animal protagonists as the vehicle of domestic sentiment, and an emphasis on empathy and sympathy with animals rather than satire.

5. Ouida, *Puck*, 82.

6. The best short introduction to the book and its themes is by Kate Flint, for the Oxford University Press edition of Woolf, *Flush*. Flint is especially strong and perceptive on the personal and societal contexts for Woolf's sustained concern for the connections between humans and animals. As she notes, *Flush* has not received much critical attention, but see nevertheless Szladits, "Flush the Spaniel"; DeSalvo, *Virginia Woolf*, 285–288; and, especially, Squier, *Virginia Woolf and London*.

7. An early review, by Burra in the *Nineteenth Century*, noted that Woolf used Flush "almost as Swift used the Houyhnhnms, but without anger, rather with the gentlest irony, weaving together the lives of beast and man" (see Majumdar and McLaurin, *Virginia Woolf*, 321).

8. Brown, *Homeless Dogs*, 116, 133. It is worth noting that dognapping features at least as early as Mary Elliott's *Confidential Memoirs, or, Adventures of a Parrot, a Greyhound, a Cat, and a Monkey* (London, William Darton, 1821). See Brown, *Homeless Dogs*, 134.

9. Wolch and Emel, "Bringing the Animals Back In," 632–36; Munich, "Domesticity," 127. Kevin Morrison argues that Barrett, as much as Woolf, ar-

ticulates a serious rethinking of human and nonhuman animal relations, in his sympathetic, psychologically acute account of Flush's "significant otherness" for Elizabeth Barrett (see Morrison, "Elizabeth Barrett Browning's Dog Days").

10. Squier, *Virginia Woolf and London*, 127.

11. Woolf, *Flush*, 76.

12. Ritvo, *Animal Estate*.

13. British Parliamentary Papers (hereafter BPP) 1844 (549), iv.

14. Mayhew, *London's Underworld*, 232.

15. *Town* 51 (19 May 1838): 1.

16. *Town* 51 (19 May 1838): 1. The article refers to "the Greens" as London's premier dog stealers, that family having taken the palm from the "Hankeys," one of whom ended his days as an executed felon a quarter of a century previously. Old Bailey records (http://www.oldbaileyonline.org) suggest that the latter is thirty-year-old George *Handley*, convicted of breaking and entering and sentenced to death in 1817.

17. Mayhew, *London Labour*, 1968 ed., 52, emphasis in original.

18. The *Report*, BPP 1844 (549), gives the addresses of the dog stealers as follows: Whetstone Park, Lincoln's Inn Fields; Chapel Mews, Foley Place; Keppel Mews South and Woburn Mews, Russell Square; Kensal New Town, Paddington; New Road, St. Pancras; Hammersmith; Shepherdess Walk City Road; Bateman Street, Spitalfields; and Cottage Place, Goswell Road. The *Town* 51 (19 May 1838: 1) refers to Battle-bridge, toward Maiden Lane, as notorious at that time for both nippers and receivers.

19. Mayhew, *London Labour*, 1968 ed., 41–42.

20. Mayhew, *London Labour*, 1968 ed., 50.

21. *Morning Post*, 7 May 1844, 6; Karlin, *Robert Browning and Elizabeth Barrett*, 303. Judith Flanders accepts the representation of professionalism, though she doubts the profitability of dog stealing as a criminal industry: see her *Victorian City*, 379.

22. Robert Browning to Elizabeth Barrett, 4 September 1846, cited by Karlin, *Robert Browning and Elizabeth Barrett*, 308.

23. *London Review*, quoted in the *Times*, 7 October 1861, 9. "Such is the system adopted by this class of depredators, that they elude the utmost vigilance, and we seldom or never hear of their being brought to the bar of offended justice," lamented the *Town* (51 [19 May 1838]: 1).

24. *Morning Post*, 7 May 1844, 6.

25. Karlin, *Robert Browning and Elizabeth Barrett*, 304; BPP 1844 (549), 26.

26. In this regard, note the reaction of the *Times* (2 August 1844, 4) to the evidence of William Bishop at the Select Committee, acknowledging that "the mode in which the feelings of the fair sex are played upon forms one of the most instructive points of his evidence."

27. As part of her argument that Woolf's *Flush* is as much a commentary on

the 1930s as the 1840s, Snaith sees in the presentation of Whitechapel an acknowledgment of complicity but also a direct challenge to the rise of anti-alienism and anti-Semitism in Britain; see Snaith, "Fanciers, Footnotes, and Fascism." In this regard, note that Ouida's premier dog stealer is named Bill Jacobs.

28. Turner, *Reckoning with the Beast*, 78.

29. Munich, "Domesticity," 140.

30. *Times*, 2 August 1844, 4.

31. As Kimberly Smith notes, property theory even now is not very well developed when it comes to animals (*Governing Animals*, 73).

32. BPP 1844 (549), 3.

33. *Times*, 12 June 1845, 3.

34. Ironically, while such a spaniel might derive its value from its distinguishing marks, or "properties," it did not necessarily qualify as *legal* property.

35. Ritvo, *Animal Estate*, 2.

36. Seipp, "Concept of Property," 85.

37. Milsom, *Historical Foundations of the Common Law*, 426.

38. Baker, *Reports of Sir John Spelman*, 318.

39. These distinctions were all reassessed by the Criminal Code Commissioners of 1879, who simplified the law on theft by making all tame living creatures (except pigeons, if not in a dovecote or on their owners' land) equally capable of being stolen; see Stephen, *History of the Criminal Law of England*, 163.

40. BPP 1844 (549), 3.

41. *Times*, 26 June 1845, 3.

42. *Hansard* 81 (1845): 1185–86. Other opponents of the dog-stealing bill insisted, rather less scrupulously, that dogs were simply a great nuisance, "generally speaking, of the most degenerated species, and, like Indian idols, they were prized on account of their ugliness. . . . There were more instances of human beings dying through hydrophobia from the bite of dogs of the pet class than from the bite of any other" (*Times*, 26 June 1845, 3).

43. *Times*, 12 June 1845, 3.

44. *Times*, 25 March 1845, 7.

45. BPP 1844 (549), iv.

46. *Hansard* 81 (1845): 385.

47. *Hansard* 81 (1845): 1186.

48. See *Legal Protection of Dogs*. Liddell wanted it to be considered in the first offense a misdemeanor, and only in the second offense a matter of seven years' transportation. Graham advised against holding out for transportation, which was a barrier to parliamentary acceptance of the new legislation.

49. Mayhew, *London Labour*, 1968 ed., 57.

50. See, for the later nineteenth century, Logsdon, "London Dog-Stealers."

51. *Illustrated London News*, 27 July 1844, 16.

52. See Armstrong, *Desire and Domestic Fiction*, and Poovey, *Uneven Developments*.

53. Nunokawa, *Afterlife of Property.*

54. For a comparable argument, see Langland, *Nobody's Angels.*

55. Nunokawa, *Afterlife of Property,* 4.

56. *Hansard* 76 (1844): 555. The *Times* (11 November 1844, 5), before it changed its mind on the seriousness of the question, lamented that "nothing is too trivial or too ludicrously absurd to be made the subject of Parliamentary discussion or inquiry." When Sir James Graham regretted the inconvenient summer timing of the session, one wit piped up from the backbenches, to laughter, that he was referring to the "dog days" (*Hansard* 76 [1844]: 556). *Punch* noted, to even less humorous effect, that the report on dog stealing was presented to the House in a terribly dog-eared state: see *Times,* 8 August 1844, 5.

57. *Hansard* 76 (1844): 691; 81 (1845): 385.

58. Thomas, *Man and the Natural World,* 102, notes that the "passion for unnecessary dogs" was a marker of class distinction, but it was also crucially a gendered issue.

59. Note the importance in domestication discourse of the virtue attached to submitting to "man's" dominion, with the dog as the very emblem of servility and subordination, physically malleable and genetically manipulable. This is clearly matched by the gender hierarchies and proprieties of the Victorian age.

60. Anderson, "Walk on the Wild Side."

61. McMullen, "The Day the Dogs Died in London."

62. *Dogs and Cats and How to Manage Them,* 1882, cited by Townshend, *Darwin's Dogs,* 26. See *Illustrated London News,* 8 April 1843, 229, for one such out-of-work dog, and accompanying poem.

63. Philo, "Animals, Geography and the City."

64. *Times,* 26 March 1845, 4.

65. *Times,* 28 March 1845, 5.

66. BPP 1844 (549), 30.

67. Karlin, *Robert Browning and Elizabeth Barrett,* 306. The ethologist Konrad Lorenz, in *Man Meets Dog,* 142, quotes Elizabeth Barrett Browning to this effect: "If thou must love me, let it be for nought / Except for love's sake only."

68. See Surridge, "Dogs'/Bodies, Women's Bodies," on the paralleling of beaten women and beaten dogs, both women and pets being placed under the proprietary ownership of the male head of the household.

69. Squier, *Virginia Woolf and London,* 125.

70. Squier, *Virginia Woolf and London,* 134.

71. Woolf, *Flush,* 110.

72. Woolf, *Flush,* 78.

73. Squier, *Virginia Woolf and London,* 128.

74. Thus, Flint (Introduction, xxi–xii) comments, "We are faced with the fact that if for Elizabeth Barrett, Flush was a love object, a person in his own right[,] . . . for another set of people he was an object of economic exchange:

valuable for his breeding, his pedigree, and because emotional worth could be turned into a site of blackmail."

75. Armstrong, "Briton Riviere," 18.

76. Doorways have a specific function, and specific anxieties. Since bodies should ideally be separated and privacy protected, external space such as doorways became wholly public (Daunton, *House and Home in the Victorian City*, cited by Gilbert, *Citizen's Body*, 89).

77. Drawn from life, Briton Riviere's painting of a dog stealer comes not so much layered as lathered in irony. An animal painter like Riviere needed a dealer to provide canine models, but, as the critic Armstrong notes, such dealers often dabbled in the illicit trade of stealing and ransoming dogs. It is entirely possible, therefore, that a producer of sentimental animal pictures like Riviere, engravings of whose pictures might be found on the walls of many bourgeois homes, would employ dog stealers to provide the very subjects of his pictures; another form of trading in affection, perhaps.

78. Ritvo, *Animal Estate*, 2.

79. Munich, "Domesticity."

80. Tuan, *Dominance and Affection*, 1984. Elizabeth Barrett knew this, for sure—in poems like *Aurora Leigh* she regrets an England whose nature is "tamed/And grown domestic" (1.634–35). And in her poetry, Italy, the refuge from the dog stealers, stood in for a world of wildness and passion; there is a vital critique of the domestic subjection of women here, wholly as powerful and compelling as Virginia Woolf's plea for a room of one's own.

81. DeSalvo, *Virginia Woolf*, 286–87.

3. Finding a Forever Home?

1. *Times*, 18 October 1860, 8.

2. See "Pincher Astray," *All the Year Round*, 30 January 1864, 539–41.

3. Greenwood, *Going to the Dogs*, 3.

4. For the counterargument, see Cobbe, "Rights of Man," 598.

5. Cottesloe, *Battersea Dogs' Home*, 27–31.

6. Hollingshead, "Two Dog Shows," 496.

7. Hollingshead, "Two Dog Shows," 497.

8. Kean, *Animal Rights*, 88. Jenkins, *Home of Their Own*, 22, makes much of this "family" ethos and environment, not least in the title of the book.

9. *Freeman's Journal*, 28 August 1863.

10. *Pall Mall Gazette*, 6 August 1870, 12; *Illustrated London News*, 22 August 1868, 182.

11. Moore, "Beastly Criminals," 210.

12. Jenkins, *Home of Their Own*, 24.

13. *Appeal for the Home for Lost and Starving Dogs*, 4–5.

14. Kidd, "Home for Lost Dogs," 566; this article is extracted in *Veterinarian* 34 (1861): 594–98.

15. *Appeal for the Home*, 14.

16. Johnson, *Temporary Home*, emphasis in original.

17. Cobbe, *Confessions of a Lost Dog*, 1867. It is a quirk of fate that the same term, "restoration," was used by the dog stealers' intermediaries.

18. See also *Graphic*, 22 September 1877, 4.

19. *Appeal for the Home*, 10. Compare "Do not let it be imagined that every or any dirty little cur is indiscriminately to be admitted here, and kept in luxury. No! Morbid sympathy has no place in this establishment" (Kidd, "Home for Lost Dogs," 597).

20. Donald, *Picturing Animals in Britain*, 140.

21. There are several changes here from the 1877 engravings, and the painting is rather more obviously cross-class.

22. Hollingshead, "Two Dog Shows," 496.

23. Hollingshead, *Miscellanies*, 203.

24. Greenwood, *Going to the Dogs*, 5–6.

25. Greenwood, *Going to the Dogs*, 7.

26. Moore, "Beastly Criminals and Criminal Beasts," 211.

27. Koven, *Slumming*, 61.

28. Gilbert, *Citizen's Body*, 46.

29. Koven, *Slumming*, 10.

30. Sala, "Key of the Street," 568.

31. For "becoming-animal," see Deleuze and Guattari, *Thousand Plateaus*, particularly chapter 10.

32. Sala, "Key of the Street," 569.

33. Smith, *Governing Animals*, xxi.

34. Koven, *Slumming*, 225.

35. "'Charlie,' The White Sergeant," *Animal World* 1 (1 January 1870): 69.

36. As Brian Harrison determined long ago, animal philanthropy and the state went hand in hand: see Harrison, "Animals and the State," 787. For "policeman-state," see Gatrell, "Crime, Authority and the Policeman-State."

37. *Times*, 12 March 1866, 8.

38. *Times*, 12 August 1867, 10.

39. *Times*, 13 November 1867, 7.

40. See, for instance, the 1870 *Report of the Commissioner of Police of the Metropolis*, 36.

41. "This duty is a very risky one; many of the Police have been severely bitten in ridding the streets of these useless curs" (BPP 1872 [C.652], *Report of the Commissioner of Police of the Metropolis*, 5, quotation in main text from 49).

42. Jenkins, *Home of Their Own*, 32.

43. *Luton Times and Advertiser,* 13 March 1869, 4.

44. 1871 *Report of the Commissioner of Police of the Metropolis,* 38.

45. "The institution was been adopted by the Metropolitan Police as the depôt to which all stray dogs are consigned:" *Times,* quoted in *Tamworth Herald,* 11 December 1875, 3.

46. *Report from the Select Committee of the House of Lords on Rabies,* 176. Commissioner Warren demurred somewhat by noting that the Home kept the income from the sale of unclaimed animals.

47. Jenkins, *Home of Their Own,* 50.

48. Jenkins, *Home of Their Own,* 55.

49. Gilbert, *Citizen's Body,* 76.

50. W. Fisher, Superintendent T Division, 1878 *Report of the Commissioner of Police of the Metropolis,* 45.

51. Thos. Butt, Superintendent N Division, 1878 *Report of the Commissioner of Police of the Metropolis,* 45.

52. *Times,* 18 October 1860, 8.

53. Johnson, *Temporary Home.*

54. *Times,* 23 June 1883, 12. See subsequent correspondence: 29 June 1883, 11; 16 August 1883, 2.

55. *Times,* 16 August 1883, 2. For a case of a dog taken to the Home, sold, and later claimed by its original owner, who accused the Home's agents of acting like the dog stealers, see *John Bull,* 22 July 1879, 189.

56. Kidd, "Home for Lost Dogs," 566.

57. *Morning Post,* 23 December 1896, 3.

58. Behlmer, *Friends of the Family,* 3.

59. *Times,* 12 March 1866, 8.

60. *John Bull,* 8 August 1863, 505.

61. See also *Bell's Life in London and Sporting Chronicle,* 19 July 1863, 3; *Trewman's Exeter Flying Post,* 12 August 1863.

62. *Leicester Chronicle,* 8 August 1863, 7.

63. *Leicester Chronicle,* 8 August 1863, 7.

64. *John Bull,* 8 August 1863, 505.

65. *John Bull,* 8 August 1863, 505.

66. *Sun,* 2 June 1889, 7.

67. *London Standard,* 8 April 1874, 6.

68. *Times,* 4 November 1886, 3.

69. Dogs' Home Annual Report, cited by the *Morning Post,* 1 April 1890, 2.

70. Reprinted from the *Daily News* in *Animal World* 1 (1 August 1870): 198.

71. *Newcastle Courant,* 5 July 1878, 6.

72. Greenwood, *Going to the Dogs,* 6.

73. Cited in Salt, *Animals' Rights,* 37.

74. Jenkins, *Home of Their Own*, 76, 90.

75. Kalof, *Looking at Animals*, 142.

76. Battersea Dogs and Cats Home has responded to my enquiries over several years noting that the archives are not in a catalogued state and are unable to be accessed by the researcher.

77. *Morning Post*, 23 December 1886, 3.

78. *Sun*, 2 June, 1889, 7. On the eventual fate of the dogs: "they were all sent to a certain market garden, I won't say where, noted for growing cabbage. So perhaps doggy in his vegetable form may make acquaintance with some of his old friends": *Newcastle Courant*, 5 July, 1878, 6.

79. *Illustrated London News*, 22 August 1868, 182.

80. Hollingshead, *Miscellanies*, 205. At the same time, the RSPCA recorded the wishes of a Miss Pennington, who wanted to leave money at her death for "an asylum for dogs where no slaughter of such inmates should be permitted": see RSPCA Minute Book, no. 11, 11 April 1870.

81. *Morning Post*, 23 March 1876, 3.

82. *Morning Post*, 28 April 1876, 6.

83. For derogatory, sometimes deadly, animalization, see Roberts, *Mark of the Beast*; for the violent *institution* of speciesism, see Shukin, *Animal Capital*, 24.

84. *Once a Week*, 21 May 1870, 339–340, 340.

85. "Homeless and Starving," *London Society*, November 1875, 418–20.

86. See Homans, *What's a Dog For?*, 207–25. On the practice of killing, see Animal Studies Group, *Killing Animals*, 4; Weil, *Thinking Animals*, xxii; Wolloch, *Subjugated Animals*, 179. For shelters specifically, see Arluke, "Managing Emotions," and Palmer, "Killing Animals."

87. Srinivasan, "Biopolitics of Animal Being and Welfare," 110, emphasis in original.

88. Marvin, "Wild Killing," 15–18.

89. See Arluke, "Managing Emotions," on the "caring-killing paradox."

90. Haraway, *When Species Meet*, 80. For "bare life," see Agamben, *Homo Sacer*, and his specific discussion of animality in *The Open*. For "hopeless, homeless curs," see *The Man about Town*, 28 November 1885, 1514.

4. The Descent of the Dog

1. Ritvo, *Animal Estate*, 39.

2. Rod Preece has done most to challenge what he calls the "Darwinian Myth": see *Brute Souls*, 331–58. For a powerful recent statement of what are taken to be the lessons of Darwinian evolution for the moral balance between the interests of humans and those of other species, affirming humans' priority, see Petrinovich, *Darwinian Dominion*.

3. Cited by Preece, *Brute Souls*, 414.

4. Salt, *Animals' Rights*, 11.

5. For a nontechnical discussion of the role of animals as agents or actants in the "living laboratory," see Harré, *Pavlov's Dogs*.

6. For all the laboratory animal's complex social, epistemological, ethical, and political relationships, see Birke, Arluke, and Michael, *Sacrifice*.

7. Jones, *Darwin's Island*, 91. On the "analogy," see Richards, "Darwin and the Inefficacy of Artificial Selection," who identifies only *disanalogies*, and the subsequent contributions to debate: Sterrett, "Darwin's Analogy," affirms the fine-grain of the analogical reasoning; Gildenhuys, "Darwin, Herschel," accepts that the argument is neither strictly analogical nor disanalogical, but presses the common principle of selection at work, as a general law of nature; while Gregory, "Artificial Selection," bypasses the historical and philosophical niceties entirely, endorsing the utility of the analogy in modern evolutionary research and education.

8. Darwin, *Origin*, ch. 1, 552.

9. See Alter, "Separated at Birth."

10. Darwin, *Origin*, ch. 1, 564.

11. Darwin, *Origin*, ch. 1, 564.

12. Darwin, *Origin*, ch. 3, 602; *Variation*, ch. 1, 40.

13. See, for instance, Dawkins, *Greatest Show on Earth*, 76.

14. Darwin, *Origin*, ch. 1, 560, 567. I retain here the gendered language.

15. Darwin, *Origin*, ch. 4, 624–25. The question is complicated by *sexual* selection, where there is a further analogy between the "aesthetic whims" of the fancier and the selecting female: see Dawkins, *Blind Watchmaker*, 200.

16. Theunissen, "Darwin and his Pigeons," 206. Feeley-Harnik, "'An Experiment on a Gigantic Scale,'" 159, also notes that Darwin downplayed the artisanship of pigeon breeders, for the argument of unconscious selection, considering that he also downplays the complex social relationships involved in domestication. For an orthodox, appreciative account, see Secord, "Nature's Fancy."

17. Theunissen, "Darwin and His Pigeons," 202; Ritvo, *Animal Estate*, 93–96. Indeed, the world's first recognized dog show took place in Newcastle-upon-Tyne in June 1859, fewer than five months before the publication of *Origin of Species*.

18. See Roth and Kutschera, "Darwin's Hypotheses," 178. On adaptation, Darwin repeatedly downplayed the "conditions of life" by repeated use of the dismissive formula of "Climate, food, &c.," but nevertheless recognizes some degree of influence.

19. Darwin, *Variation*, ch. 1, 33–34.

20. Darwin, *Variation*, ch. 1, 37.

21. Levine, *Darwin and the Novelists*, 61.

22. Darwin, *Origin*, 910. Compare *Descent*, 176: "If man had not been his own

classifier, he would never have thought of founding a separate order for his own reception."

23. Wallen, "Foxhounds, Curs," 134.

24. "Belief in God's once-for-all creation of man became confused with belief in the dog's separateness from its wild congeners, and even belief in the specific status or essentialism of dog breeds" (Donald, *Picturing Animals*, 143).

25. Feller, *Hunter's Gaze*.

26. Feller, *Hunter's Gaze*, 96. See also Rheinberger and McLaughlin, "Darwin's Experimental Natural History," 357.

27. Feller, *Hunter's Gaze*, 1.

28. For hunting, see Marvin, "Wild Killing"; Cartmill, *View to a Death in the Morning*.

29. Wallen, "Foxhounds, Curs," critiques this "techno-aesthetic vision" in which human manipulation of animals through selective breeding (the technological) is subsumed within aesthetic discourses that substitute pastoral coherence and transcendent intentionality for human dominance.

30. Darwin, *Origin*, 6th ed., 1872, cited in Moore, "Persuasive Mr. Darwin," 109.

31. Wilner, "Darwin's Artificial Selection as an Experiment."

32. Levine, *Darwin the Writer*, 22.

33. For instance, Ritvo, *Noble Cows*, 124, 131.

34. Richards, "Darwin, Domestic Breeding and Artificial Selection," 109.

35. Ritvo, "Classification and Continuity," 63.

36. Beer, *Darwin's Plots*, and Levine, *Darwin and the Novelists*; "Domestication" may be seen as another of Levine's "themata."

37. Charles Darwin, 25 September 1861, cited in Levine, *Darwin the Writer*, 16. See also Moore, "Persuasive Mr. Darwin," 109.

38. Levine, *Darwin and the Novelists*, 87.

39. Levine, *Darwin the Writer*, 163; Levine, *Darwin and the Novelists*, 136.

40. Wilner, "Darwin's Artificial Selection," 32.

41. For centers of calculation, see Latour, *Science in Action*, 215–57, and Livingstone, *Putting Science in Its Place*, 171–77.

42. Beer, *Darwin's Plots*, 121.

43. Levine, *Darwin and the Novelists*, 137.

44. Darwin, *Origin*, ch. 3, 587.

45. Beer, *Darwin's Plots*, 56.

46. Townshend, *Darwin's Dogs*, 9. On consolation and the fostering of sympathy, see also Donald, "Mind and a Conscience Akin to Our Own."

47. Darwin, *Descent*, 90, 107, my emphasis. See also Townshend, *Darwin's Dogs*, 98.

48. Levine, *Darwin the Writer*, 20.

49. Darwin, *Descent*, 96.

50. Darwin, *Descent*, 105.
51. Jones, *Darwin's Island*, 89.
52. Darwin, *Expression*, 360.
53. Darwin, *Expression*, 62, emphasis in original.
54. Darwin, *Descent*, 92, 104, 127.
55. Darwin, *Descent*, 151. Note that sometimes Darwin seems to use "lower animals" as an all-encompassing group, much as we would say "nonhuman animals," leaving human beings as the only inhabitants of the "higher" category. This of course reproduces the division between humans and animals that natural selection threatened to dissolve.
56. Darwin, *Descent*, 118.
57. For instance, Himmelfarb, *Darwin and the Darwinian Revolution*, 434.
58. Romanes, *Animal Intelligence*, vii.
59. Romanes, *Animal Intelligence*, 426. For this theme today, see Masson, *Dogs Never Lie about Love*, 23.
60. Romanes, *Animal Intelligence*, 471, 437.
61. Mayer, "Expression of the Emotions," 402.
62. Mayer, "Expression of the Emotions," 402.
63. Darwin loved dogs, as Dawkins (*Greatest Show on Earth*, 27) notes, though the puzzlingly inconsequential rider is added: "Who could not love dogs, they are such good sports?" Preece writes, more ambiguously, that Darwin "cared deeply for animals, at least when he was not engaged in his early pastime of sport hunting" ("Darwinism, Christianity," 411).
64. Desmond and Moore, *Darwin's Sacred Cause*, 8, 12. See also Browne, *Power of Place*, 420–21, 442.
65. See Day, "Godless Savages," 70.
66. See, for instance, Moore and Desmond, introduction, xxvi–xxvii, on "The Humanitarian Squire."
67. See White, "Darwin Wept."
68. Beer, *Darwin's Plots*, 35. See Darwin, *Descent*, 126, 89, and *Expression*, 48–49.
69. Mayer, "Expression of the Emotions," 403.
70. Darwin, *Expression*, 119.
71. Darwin, *Expression*, 52.
72. Townshend's account of *Darwin's Dogs* unfortunately does not give vivisection more than a couple of pages.
73. Feller, *Hunter's Gaze*, 267.
74. White, "Darwin Wept," 211; and also White, "Darwin's Emotions."
75. Darwin, *Descent*, 90.
76. Steiner, *Anthropocentrism*, 196, 197.
77. Preece, *Brute Souls*, 347.
78. Collins, *Heart and Science*, ch. 20, 136.
79. Kean, *Animal Rights*, 98.

80. *Report, Royal Commission on the Practice of Subjecting Live Animals to Experiments*, xxiii. Cited by White, "Sympathy under the Knife," 109.

81. *Report, Royal Commission on the Practice of Subjecting Live Animals to Experiments*, 137.

82. Richards, "Redrawing the Boundaries," 132. See also Hamilton, "Still Lives."

83. See Desmond and Moore, *Darwin*, 615–21, where Henrietta is described as a typically "closeted Victorian matriarch," guilty of projecting her own hypochondriachal sensitivity to pain (615).

84. On the participation of women in the movement, and its gendering, see French, *Antivivisection*, 239–50, and Elston, "Women and Anti-vivisectionism."

85. Richards, "Redrawing the Boundaries," 132.

86. See Ritvo, *Noble Cows*, 13–28.

87. Straley, "Love and Vivisection," 360.

88. See Lansbury, *Old Brown Dog;* Miller, "Necessary Torture?"

89. Grand, *Beth Book*, ch. 46. The vivisected dog, furthermore, is presumed to be a stolen pet.

90. See Harris, "Vivisection," and Bozzetto, "Moreau's Tragi-Farcical Island," 35.

91. As French, *Antivivisectionism*, argues, these were connected phenomena, as antivivisection helped to produce a medical and scientific lobby supporting experimental physiology. In addition to French's still vital study, see Rupke, *Vivisection in Historical Perspective*, and Obenchain, *Victorian Vivisection Debate*.

92. De Chadarevian, "Laboratory Science," 29. Bernstein, "Ape Anxiety," 251–52, considers that Darwin straddles the divide between gentleman and professional scientist, but he is more subject to such criticism than she allows.

93. De Chadarevian, "Laboratory Science," 36.

94. See Levine, *Darwin and the Novelists*, 212–13, following Foucault in seeing the clinical gaze as a "socially sanctioned act of power and aggression." For a useful extension of Foucault's ideas, asserting the emergence of the "veterinary gaze," see Rando, "Cat's Meow."

95. Levine, *Darwin and the Novelists*, 226, 233.

96. Cohen, *Body Worth Defending*, 196.

97. Consider Ritvo, "Animals in Nineteenth-Century Britain," 112, on Pasteur, whose laboratory was portrayed "as a focus of contamination where humans were injected with alien animal material and where, possibly still more disturbing, genteel English people might come into contact with members of other classes and nationalities. . . . The love of dogs merged into the hatred of biomedical research, which was seen as the agent of contamination and decay, and into the hatred of the modern world in general."

98. See Birke, Arluke and Michael, *Sacrifice*. See also Mayer, "Nature of the Experimental Animal," and White, "Laboratory Animal."

99. Miller, "Necessary Torture?," 336.

100. Mayer, "Expression of the Emotions," 402.

101. That said, F. O. Morris could write in 1890 that "there is a very close connection between the monstrous absurdities of Darwinism and the cowardly cruelties of the perpetrators of Experiments on Living Animals" (*Demands of Darwinism*, 61).

102. Both Boddice, "Vivisecting Major," and Feller, "Dog Fight," emphasize the defense of the English gentlemanly character against the calumny of the antivivisectionists.

103. Boddice, "Vivisecting Major," 233.

104. Boddice, "Vivisecting Major," 236.

105. Morgan, *Animal Life and Intelligence*, v.

106. Morgan, *Animal Life and Intelligence*, 196.

107. Homans, *What's a Dog For?*, 103.

108. Homans, *What's a Dog For?*, 204.

109. Jones, *Darwin's Island*, 4.

110. Tosh, *Man's Place;* see also Hatten, *End of Domesticity.*

111. Ritvo, *Noble Cows*, 68, 182.

112. Homans, *What's a Dog For?*, 99.

113. Mason, *Civilized Creatures*, 54.

114. Rorison, *Three Barriers*, 73.

115. Richter, *Literature After Darwin*, drawing on themes essayed by Bernstein, "Ape Anxiety."

116. Beer, *Darwin's Plots*, 10. As a contrast to the home, see Hochadel, "Darwin in the Monkey Cage," exploring the place of the zoo as a medium for the reception, development, and distortion of the discourse of Darwinism.

117. Morris, *Demands of Darwinism*, 38.

118. For the remote, the exotic, and the imperial, see Miller, *Empire and the Animal Body*. Note, however, that Miller considers the practice of bringing the exotic back home, the "domestication of animal otherness" (20).

119. Danahay, "Nature Red in Hoof and Paw," 105.

120. Danahay, "Nature Red in Hoof and Paw," 115.

121. Romanes, *Animal Intelligence*, 439. See also Donald, *Picturing Animals in Britain*, 141.

122. Something similar is at work in Frances Power Cobbe's comment that "the masterless dogs of Constantinople and Cairo are to the English mastiff what a nomad Tartar is to a law-abiding Anglo-Saxon" ("Consciousness of Dogs," 112–13).

123. Levine sees Darwin "bourgeoisified," indeed "domesticated," but rather by social Darwinism and political impressment (*Darwin and the Novelists*, 11–12), once more placing emphasis on malign external influences.

124. Darwin, *Expression*, 244, 302, 309.

125. Richter, *Literature after Darwin*, 188.

126. Esposito, *Third Person*, 7, 32.

127. Danahay, "Wells, Galton and Biopower," 469, 470.

128. Darwin, *Descent*, ch. 5, 159. See Greene, "Darwin as a Social Evolutionist," 11.

129. Beasley, *Victorian Reinvention of Race*, 97–111. For Desmond and Moore's avoidance of the issue of Darwin's racism, see *Darwin's Sacred Cause*, 370, where the disparagement of the "lower" races in the *Descent of Man* is described merely as "impossible to comprehend by twenty-first century standards."

130. Walter Bagehot, "Letters on the French Coup de État of 1851," 1852, cited in Beasley, *Victorian Reinvention of Race*, 75.

131. Darwin, *Descent*, 26–27.

132. See also Huff, "Victorian Exhibitionism," for Galton's eugenic interest in breeding of dogs as a guide to breeding of humans.

5. A Place for the Animal Dead

1. Lord Henry Wotton's words, in Wilde, *Picture of Dorian Gray*, ch. 4, 49.

2. Hamilton, "Reading and the Popular Critique of Science," 76. For Cobbe, see her famous pamphlet *Light in Dark Places*.

3. Huxley to James Knowles, 6 June 1875, cited by White, "Darwin Wept," 211. Compare Birke, Arluke, and Michael, *Sacrifice*, 92, on the strategy practiced by students of dissection, of "rational emotionality," defending the use of animals in research, but also acknowledging emotional responses.

4. Collins, *Heart and Science*; see Straley, "Love and Vivisection," for Collins's conflation of physiology and psychology.

5. See Kean, "'Smooth Cool Men of Science'"; Donovan, "Animal Rights and Feminist Theory," 352.

6. See Gates, *Kindred Nature*, 147–49, and Kete, *Beast in the Boudoir*, 1–21. This argument against modern science and materialism may be compared to the culture of antimodernism in the United States, as discussed by Lears, *No Place of Grace*.

7. Kete, *Beast in the Boudoir*, 11.

8. See Gates, *Kindred Nature*. For critiques of the gendering of science, see also Jordanova, *Sexual Visions*, and Russett, *Sexual Science*.

9. Hatten, *End of Domesticity*, 25.

10. On the study of memorial landscapes and "deathscapes," see Kong, "Cemeteries and Columbaria," and O'Dwyer and Alderman, "Memorial Landscapes."

11. Raber, "From Sheep to Meat," 93.

12. Donald, *Picturing Animals in Britain*, 158.

13. See Kean, *Animal Rights*, 86–88.

14. Morley, *Death and the Victorians*, 201, n. 1.

15. Tosh, *Man's Place*, 4.

16. Gillis, *World of Their Own Making*, 76.

17. Hodgetts, "Cemetery for Dogs," 627.

18. See, for instance, Tague, "Dead Pets."

19. Donald, *Picturing Animals in Britain*, 157.

20. Mangum, "Animal Angst," 18.

21. Mangum, "Animal Angst," 19, 31.

22. Mangum, "Animal Angst," 31. For a striking counterargument, see Kean, "Exploration of the Sculptures," who notes that the Greyfriars Bobby and Old Brown Dog sculptures were not set apart, as was the pet cemetery, but located in places defined by political geographies, narratives, and publics.

23. Gillis, *World of Their Own Making*, 76. For the history and present status of pet cemeteries, see Kean, "Human and Animal Space."

24. Hodgetts, "Cemetery for Dogs," 630.

25. Hodgetts, "Cemetery for Dogs," 629–30.

26. Kean, "Human and Animal Space," 31.

27. Kean, "Human and Animal Space," 34.

28. Hodgetts, "Cemetery for Dogs," 633.

29. See Brooks, *Mortal Remains*; Curl, *Victorian Celebration of Death*; and Ragon, *Space of Death*.

30. See Morley, *Death and the Victorians*, 97.

31. Jalland, *Death in the Victorian Family*, 204.

32. Strange, *Death, Grief and Poverty*, 146–47; Laqueur, "Bodies, Death, and Pauper Funerals." See also Allen, *Cleansing the City*, 127–28, on paupers as "waste."

33. See Richardson, *Death, Dissection and the Destitute*.

34. Although the risk of anatomization had dramatically decreased by the later nineteenth century, vivisection controversies were taking off.

35. Hoppen, *Mid-Victorian Generation*, 501, and Turner, *Reckoning with the Beast*, 247.

36. Lansbury, *Old Brown Dog*, 83–84.

37. Kete, *Beast in the Boudoir*, 17.

38. Kete, *Beast in the Boudoir*, 7.

39. Hodgetts, "Cemetery for Dogs," 625.

40. Marcus, *Apartment Stories*, 130.

41. Famously by White, "Historical Roots of Our Ecological Crisis." However, Thomas, *Man and the Natural World*, 17–25, and Preece, *Brute Souls*, 24–65, remind us that the Western tradition is more various and ambiguous than sometimes imagined.

42. Li, "Union of Christianity."

43. Li, "Union of Christianity," 269.

44. Preece, *Brute Souls*, 357; "Darwinism, Christianity," 419. Note that Al-

fred Russel Wallace, in line with his deep and developing divergence from "Darwinism," regarded vivisection as "brutalizing and immoral" (*World of Life*, 1911, 381).

45. Salt, *Animals' Rights*, 9.

46. Thomas, "Homeless and Starving," 419.

47. Tortorici, "In the Name of the Father," 97.

48. Tortorici, "In the Name of the Father," 102, 112. For the idea of animal immortality "making more headway in England than anywhere else" in the early modern period, see Thomas, *Man and the Natural World*, 137–42.

49. Tague, "Dead Pets," 298–99.

50. Strange, *Death, Grief and Mourning*, 15, 164.

51. For Wood, see Lightman, "'The Voices of Nature,'" 200–203, and Lorimer, "Science and the Secularization of Victorian Images of Race," 218–19.

52. *Pall Mall Gazette*, 9 February 1875, 12.

53. Wood, *Man and Beast*, 27

54. Wood, *Man and Beast*, 169–70.

55. Wood, *Man and Beast*, 116.

56. See Froude, *Letters and Memorials of Jane Welsh Carlyle*, 23–24, and Holme, *Carlyles at Home*, 137–39.

57. Carlyle, *New Letters and Memorials of Jane Welsh Carlyle*, 223–25.

58. Barley, *Dancing on the Grave*, 172–78. Townshend, *Darwin's Dogs*, 136, notes that "from the middle stone age, dogs were buried alongside their owner, a life's companion going out into the hereafter, a protector for the unknown dangers of an unknown journey."

59. Cobbe, "Consciousness of Dogs," 449.

60. For a summary, see Senior, "Souls of Men and Beasts."

61. Butler, *Analogies of Religion*, 1.1.21.

62. Taylor, *Physical Theory of Another Life*, 314–15.

63. Taylor, *Physical Theory of Another Life*, 316–17.

64. Morris, *Curse of Cruelty* and *Records of Animal Sagacity*.

65. Macaulay, *Plea for Mercy*, 30.

66. French, *Antivivisectionism*.

67. Morris, *Curse of Cruelty*, 6. See Huxley, "Hypothesis That Animals Are Automata." This address was first given in 1874.

68. Morris, *Records of Animal Sagacity*, xix.

69. For post-Victorian exemplars, see Archer, *Soul of a Dog*, and Buckner, *Immortality of Animals*.

70. French, *Antivivisectionism*, 375, 377.

71. French, *Antivivisectionism*, 379.

72. See Adams, *Shaggy Muses*, 250.

73. Taylor, *Physical Theory of Another Life*, 24.

74. Branks, *Heaven Our Home*, iv.

75. Gillis, *World of Their Own Making*, 112. See also Tosh, *Man's Place*, 38; Hilton, *Age of Atonement*, 335–36; Jalland, *Death in the Victorian Family*, 265–83; Wheeler, *Death and the Future Life*.

76. Dickens, *Nicholas Nickleby*, ch. 35.

77. Armstrong, *Dickens and the Concept of Home*, 15–16.

78. Branks, *Heaven Our Home*, 274. See Knight, *Nineteenth-Century Church*, 58–59.

79. Jalland, *Death in the Victorian Family*, 271.

80. Jalland, *Death in the Victorian Family*, 2, 276.

81. McDannell and Lang, *Heaven*, 300.

82. Cobbe, "Confessions of a Lost Dog," 36.

83. Shand, *Life of General Sir Edward Bruce Hamley*, 29.

84. Phelps, *Gates Ajar*, ch. 10, 140; see also McDannell and Lang, *Heaven*, 266.

85. Phelps, *Gates Ajar*, ch. 12, 188.

86. Phelps, *Gates Ajar*, ch. 13, 194.

87. Phelps, *Beyond the Gates*, ch. 9, 124–25, cited in McDannell and Lang, *Heaven*, 267.

88. David Gordon White, quoted in Serpell, "From Paragon to Pariah," 245–56, 249, 254.

89. See, for example, Felski, *Gender of Modernity*, 131–36.

90. Thomas, *Man and the Natural World*, 121–36.

91. Note the Weberian argument for demagicification/disenchantment here: the move to separate a disenchanted immanent world and a transcendent, heavenly afterlife.

92. Burt, "John Berger's 'Why Look at Animals,'" 213.

93. See Derrida's commentary and critique of Heidegger's theses, in *Of Spirit* and in *Animal That Therefore I Am*, 141–60. See also Lippit, *Electric Animal*, 57–58, and Weil, "Killing Them Softly," 89–90.

94. Weil, *Thinking Animals*, 113, considering Judith Butler's anthropocentric examination of mourning. Emphasis in original.

95. Clark, "Animal Interface," 49.

96. Mangum, "Animal Angst," 31.

97. Derrida and Dufourmantelle, *Of Hospitality*, 2; Derrida, *Animal That Therefore I Am*; Oliver, *Animal Lessons*, 239.

98. Derrida and Dufourmantelle, *Of Hospitality*. For commentary, see Still, *Derrida and Hospitality*, ch. 6, esp. 220–24. On the uncalculating and unpredictable nature of embodied generosity toward nonhuman animals, see Clark, "Animal Interface." For "zoosphere," see Derrida, *Animal That Therefore I Am*, 37.

99. Lynn, "Animals, Ethics and Geography," 286. See also Desmond, "Animal Deaths," on the challenge to anthropocentric definitions of social worth and public mourning.

100. For contemporary pet cemeteries, see Homans, *What's a Dog For?*, 229–

30. For the recovery of an ethic of care, see Parry, "Sentimentality and the Enemies of Animal Protection."

101. Rollin, "Moral Status of Animals," 15. See also Clark, *Animals and Their Moral Standing.*

6. Assembling the Dog-Walking City

1. By "walking city," I mean not so much the compactness of the eighteenth- and early-nineteenth-century city, to which the term is sometimes attached, but the urban experience and forms of resistance predicated on the rhetoric of walking explored, most famously, by de Certeau, *Practice of Everyday Life,* 91–110.

2. For discipline and governmentality in nineteenth-century Britain, see Joyce, *Rule of Freedom* and *State of Freedom;* and Goodlad, *Victorian Literature and the Victorian State,* 1–31.

3. For the worst kind of colonial and imperial liberalism, see Nally, *Human Encumbrances.* For an example of the dyad of freedom and control, see Beckingham, "Historical Geography of Liberty."

4. Note that Thierman, "Apparatuses of Animality," allows for a far less anthropocentric Foucault.

5. "Assemblage theory," or at least the stress on heterogeneity, impermanence, and process, may be approached from several directions: see, for instance, Marcus and Saka, "Assemblage," for Deleuzian ideas; for Actor-Network Theory, Murdoch, "Towards a Geography of Heterogeneous Associations"; for productive overlaps with Foucauldian thought, see Thierman, "Apparatuses of Animality," and Legg, "Assemblage/Apparatus."

6. See Legg, "Assemblage/Apparatus," for clarification, particularly with regard to Foucault's conception of *dispositif.* See Latour, *Reassembling the Social,* for a discussion from the perspective of actor-network theory.

7. Walton, "Mad Dogs and Englishmen," 226. Also see Keller, *Triumph of Order,* 209–10, for a brief nod to the disciplining of animals in a wider discussion of the nineteenth-century "regulated city."

8. *Times,* 20 April 1897, 7.

9. For "improvement," modernity, and the production and representation of disorderly space, see Dennis, *Cities in Modernity,* and Nead, *Victorian Babylon.*

10. See, for instance, Allen, *Cleansing the City,* 126–28, and Bivona and Henkle, *Imagination of Class,* 12–13.

11. Gilbert, *Citizen's Body,* 40.

12. British National Archives (hereafter BNA) HO 45/3390, 20 September 1850.

13. For discussion of biosecurity and biopolitics, see Hinchliffe and Bingham, "Securing Life." This question entails a biopolitical consideration of animal and human life in states of emergency, a matter of what Eric Santner calls "creaturely life" (*On Creaturely Life*).

14. Kete, *Beast in the Boudoir*, 112.
15. Teigen, "Global History of Rabies," 319.
16. Kete, *Beast in the Boudoir*, 98.
17. See Walton, "Mad Dogs and Englishmen"; Pemberton and Worboys, *Mad Dogs and Englishmen*.
18. Pemberton and Worboys, *Mad Dogs and Englishmen*, 26.
19. BNA HO44/20/236, 2 June 1830.
20. Fleming, *Rabies and Hydrophobia*, ix.
21. BNA HO44/20/195, 24 May 1830, 363; June 1830.
22. See Foucault, *Discipline and Punish*, 198, and *Abnormal*, 44–46.
23. Pemberton and Worboys, *Mad Dogs and Englishmen*, 94.
24. Ritvo *Animal Estate*, 176.
25. Kean, *Animal Rights*, 91.
26. Fleming, *Rabies and Hydrophobia*, 353–54.
27. *Pall Mall Gazette*, 31 December 1877, 10.
28. British Parliamentary Papers (hereafter BPP) 1887 (322), 74.
29. BPP 1887 (322), 190.
30. See BNA HO 45/5303, 29 March 1854.
31. BPP 1887 (322), 179.
32. BPP 1887 (322), 179.
33. BPP 1887 (322), 86.
34. BPP 1887 (322), 64, 86.
35. BPP 1887 (322), 77.
36. See BPP 1886 (268), 3.
37. The Privy Council passed a muzzling order in 1889 for the City of London and the Metropolitan Police districts. This was restated by the Board of Agriculture later in the year, and extended to Cheshire, Lancashire, the West Riding, Essex, Hertford, Kent, London, Middlesex, and Surrey, in effect from 1 January 1890. With the diminution of rabies, from 1 November 1892 all former orders were suspended, and left to local authorities to make regulations as to muzzling and requiring them to seize and dispose of stray dogs. In 1894 the Contagious Diseases (Animals) Acts were consolidated under the Diseases of Animals Act of 1894, and the Board of Agriculture reissued the Rabies Order of 1892 under the title the Rabies Order of 1895.
38. BPP 1897 (C.8320) (C.8378), 7–8.
39. BPP 1887 (322), 60.
40. BNA HO45/9515/19194.
41. *Daily Graphic*, 1 January 1891, 4; 2 January 1891, 5.
42. "A Dog on Muzzling," *Daily Graphic*, 1 January 1891, 4.
43. BNA HO45/9515/19194, 13 December 1877.
44. BPP 1887 (322), 70.
45. BPP 1887 (322), 10.

46. BNA HO45/9515/19194, 10 June 1879.

47. BNA HO45/9515/19194, 9 May 1874, 26 May 1874.

48. "When Are Dogs Under Control?," *Ormskirk Advertiser*, 21 May 1874, in BNA HO45/9515/19194.

49. BNA HO45/9515/19194, correspondence of 25 May 1874.

50. *Times*, 10 August 1886, 3.

51. *Times*, 11 January 1886, 3.

52. *Times*, 21 August 1886, 3; and 28 August 1886, 13.

53. *Times*, 23 August 1886, 13.

54. Walton, "Mad Dogs and Englishmen"; Ritvo, *Animal Estate*, 167–202; Pemberton and Worboys, *Mad Dogs and Englishmen*.

55. Kean, *Animal Rights*, 92.

56. For an overview, see Porter, *Health, Civilization and the State*, 128–46.

57. Ouida, *Dogs*, 110–11.

58. *Times*, 23 August 1886, 13.

59. *Times*, 22 October, 1889, 13, cited in Pemberton and Worboys, *Mad Dogs and Englishmen*, 142.

60. *Ladies Kennel Gazette*, September 1897, 103, cited in Pemberton and Worboys, *Mad Dogs and Englishmen*, 155.

61. Thus, given that fear of Prussianism was endemic in British society, it was impolitic for one "hydrophobist," the Honorary Secretary of the Society for the Prevention of Hydrophobia, to assure readers of the *Times* that it was possible for dogs to be muzzled in the attempt to stamp out rabies, by pointing to the favorable statistics coming from Prussia as to the effects of muzzling (*Times*, 7 October 1889, 13).

62. *Daily Graphic*, 5 January 1891, 4.

63. Kean, *Animal Rights*, 92.

64. Pemberton and Worboys, *Mad Dogs and Englishmen*, 135.

65. Pemberton and Worboys, *Mad Dogs and Englishmen*, 162.

66. BPP 1897 (322), 197.

67. BPP 1897 (322), 198. For a discussion of the "ocular economy" of Victorian London, see Nead, *Victorian Babylon*, 71, and also Otter, *Victorian Eye*.

68. BPP 1887 (322), 81.

69. Ritvo, *Animal Estate*, 192.

70. On the possibilities for considering animals within the rubric of "subjectivation," see Srinivasan, "Biopolitics of Animal Being."

71. *Morning Post*, 1 April 1886, 5.

72. Pemberton and Worboys, *Mad Dogs and Englishmen*, 162.

73. "F.R.S.," *Times*, 15 January 1890, 13.

74. Cited in Walton, "Mad Dogs and Englishmen," 232.

75. *Times*, 3 October 1889, 13.

76. BPP 1887 (322), iv.

77. Colam, in BPP 1887 (322), 182.

78. Joyce, *Rule of Freedom*, 88.

79. Power, "Domestication and the Dog," 371.

80. Joyce, *Rule of Freedom* and *State of Freedom*.

81. Hribal, "Animals, Agency, and Class," 102.

82. Laurier, Maze and Lundin, "Putting the Dog Back in the Park," 19.

83. Pandian, "Pastoral Power," 108, citing Foucault on "permanent provocation" (104).

84. See Shapiro, "Dogs, Domestication, and the Ego," 55.

85. See Sloterdijk, "Rules for the Human Zoo," 25, for a characteristic critique of domestication, following in the wake of Nietzsche: "Humans are self-fencing, self-shepherding creatures. Wherever they live they create parks around themselves. In city parks, national parks, provincial or state parks, eco-parks—everywhere people must create for themselves rules according to which their comportment is to be governed."

86. See Patton, "Language, Power and the Training of Horses," 95.

87. Haraway, *Companion Species Manifesto*, 16.

88. Mason, "Dogs, Detectives," 297.

89. Donaldson and Kymlicka, *Zoopolis*, 114.

90. See Haraway, *Companion Species Manifesto*, and the extended argument in Haraway, *When Species Meet*.

91. Haraway, *Companion Species Manifesto*, 4.

92. For assemblage theory applied to the urban realm, see Amin and Thrift, *Cities*, and Farías and Bender, *Urban Assemblages*. For a comparable discussion of "heterogeneous biosocial collectivities," see Holloway et al., "Biopower."

Conclusion

1. For the notion of the "anthropological machine," creating the human with and against the animal, see Agamben, *Open*, 37.

2. See Kipling, "The Cat That Walked by Himself," in *Just So Stories*, 149–68.

3. Haraway, *Companion Species Manifesto*, 38.

4. Salt, *Animals' Rights*, 55; for a related critique, see Pollock, "Ouida's Rhetoric of Empathy." For the most extreme "indifferentism," and the target of Salt's ire, see Austin, *Our Duty towards Animals*.

5. See Donaldson and Kymlicka, *Zoopolis*, for the most advanced discussion.

6. Calvino, *Marcovaldo*, 101.

7. Donaldson and Kymlicka, *Zoopolis*, 6.

8. Merleau-Ponty (see Oliver, *Animal Lessons*, 208–28) apparently preferred the oxymoronic language of "strange kinship," but the archaic "kith" suggests to me the right balance between close family and complete stranger, anthropomorphism and alterity.

9. Salt, *Animals' Rights*, 34–35.

10. Ouida, *Puck*, 83.

11. See once more the admirable exploration of these themes in Chase and Levenson, *Spectacle of Intimacy.*

12. Donaldson and Kymlicka, *Zoopolis*, 116–22, focus on animals' ability to exercise cooperation, self-regulation, and reciprocity as indices of political participation.

13. Latour, *We Have Never Been Modern*, 29–32.

14. Bennett, *Vibrant Matter*, 100–104.

15. On the limits of an anthropocentric conception of biopolitics, see Srinavasan, "Biopolitics of Animal Being."

16. See Jaquet, *Kennel Club*. For a classic account, see Ritvo, "Evolution of the Victorian Dog Fancy."

17. See Howell, "Dog Fancy at War," for an extended discussion of this theme.

18. Kete, *Beast in the Boudoir*, 53–55.

19. Smith, *Governing Animals*, 58.

20. British Parliamentary Papers (BPP) 1897 [C.8320] [C.8378], 176–77. Apologies here to Scotland and Ireland, which had, and have, separate jurisdictions. In 1871 there was one dog license for every twenty-three people: see Harrison, "Animals and the State," 786. Today that figure is about one for every eight.

21. The *Times* (12 March 1866, 8) estimated perhaps as many as three million dogs in the mid-1860s.

22. Salt, *Animals' Rights.*

23. Passmore, "Treatment of Animals," 212.

24. Miele, "Horse-Sense," 133.

25. On property as the basis for animals' subjection, see Francione, *Introduction to Animal Rights*. Smith's recent *Governing Animals*, 70–98, mounts a notably weak defense of property ownership in animals, warning against interference with human freedoms and taking aim only at the *predominance* of market relations.

26. This argument runs counter to that of Ingrid Tague, "Eighteenth-Century English Debate on a Dog Tax," who argues that the right to keep dogs was acknowledged by earlier taxation.

27. Howell, "Dog Fancy at War."

28. Tenner, "Citizen Canine," 71.

29. For a wonderful discussion of the long journey of dogs (and cats) from wild animal to quasi-citizenship, which was published just as this manuscript was delivered to the press, see Grimm, *Citizen Canine.*

30. Haraway, *Companion Species Manifesto*, 63.

31. Brown, *Homeless Dogs*, 13.

Bibliography

Archival Sources

Blue Cross Archives, Carterton, Oxfordshire.

Dogs Trust, London.

London Metropolitan Archives, London.

Mass Observation Archive, University of Sussex, Falmer, Brighton.

National Archives, Kew, London.

RSPCA Archives, Horsham, West Sussex.

British Parliamentary Papers

BPP 1844 (549), *Report from the Select Committee on Dog Stealing (Metropolis)*.

BPP 1867 (186), *Report from the Select Committee of the House of Lords, on the Traffic Regulation (Metropolis) Bill*.

BPP 1870 [C.150], *Report of the Commissioner of Police of the Metropolis for the Year 1869*.

BPP 1871 [C.358], *Report of the Commissioner of Police of the Metropolis for the Year 1870*.

BPP 1876 [C.1397] [C.1397-I], *Report of the Royal Commission on the Practice of Subjecting Live Animals to Experiments for Scientific Purposes*.

BPP 1878 [C.2129], *Report of the Commissioner of Police of the Metropolis for the year 1877*.

BPP 1886 (268), *Contagious Diseases (Animals)*. *[H.L.] A Bill Intituled an Act to Amend the Contagious Diseases (Animals) Act, 1878*.

BPP 1887 (322), *Report from the Select Committee of the House of Lords on Rabies in Dogs*.

BPP 1897 [C.8320] [C.8378], *Committee on Laws Relating to Dogs. Report of the Departmental Committee Appointed by the Board of Agriculture to Inquire into and Report upon the Working of the Laws Relating to Dogs*.

Primary Sources

An Appeal for the Home for Lost and Starving Dogs. By A Member of the Society. London: Home for Lost and Starving Dogs, 1861.

Archer, F. M. *The Soul of a Dog*. London: Churchman, c. 1930.

Armstrong, W. "Briton Riviere, R. A." *Art Annual* (1891): 1–32.

Ash, E. C. *This Doggie Business*. London: Hutchinson, c. 1934.

Austin, Philip. *Our Duty Towards Animals: A Question Considered in the Light of Christian Philosophy*. London: Kegan Paul, Trench, 1885.

Beeton's Book of Poultry and Domestic Animals: Showing How to Rear and Manage Them in Sickness and in Health. London: Ward, Lock & Tyler, 1871.

Branks, William. *Heaven Our Home.* Edinburgh: William P. Nimmo, 1861.

Brayley Hodgetts, E. A. "A Cemetery for Dogs." *Strand Magazine* 36 (December 1893): 625–33.

Browning, Elizabeth Barrett. *Aurora Leigh.* 1856. Reprint, New York: Norton, 1996.

Buckner, E. D. *The Immortality of Animals and the Relation of Man as Guardian, from a Biblical and Philosophical Hypothesis.* Philadelphia: George W. Jacobs, 1903.

Butler, Joseph. *The Analogy of Religion, Natural and Revealed, to the Constitution and Course of Nature.* 1736. Reprint, Oxford: Oxford University Press, 1907.

Carlyle, Alexander, ed. *New Letters and Memorials of Jane Welsh Carlyle.* Vol. 2. London: John Lane, 1883.

Cassell's Household Guide to Every Department of Practical Life: Being a Complete Encyclopaedia of Domestic and Social Economy. London: Cassell, Petter & Galpin, c. 1877.

"Charles Dickens and Vivisection." *Animal's Defender and Zoophilist* 22 (1903): 94–96.

"'Charlie,' The White Sergeant." *Animal World* 1 (1 January 1870): 69.

Chesterton, G. K. *Charles Dickens.* 1906, as *Charles Dickens: A Critical Study.* Reprint, London: Wordsworth, 2007.

The Children's Household Pets. London: Ward, Lock & Tyler, c. 1868.

Cobbe, Frances Power. *Confessions of a Lost Dog.* London: Griffith & Farran, 1867.

———. "The Consciousness of Dogs." *Quarterly Review* 133 (October 1872): 419–51.

———. *Light in Dark Places.* London: Victoria Street Society for the Protection of Animals from Vivisection, c. 1883.

———. "The Rights of Man and the Claims of Brutes." *Fraser's Magazine for Town and Country* 68 (1863): 586–602.

Collins, Wilkie. *Heart and Science: A Story of the Present Time.* 1883. Reprint, Peterborough, Ontario: Broadview, 1996.

Croker, T. F. Dillon, "A Canine Chapter." *Young Folks Paper: Literary Olympic and Tournament* (21 May 1887): 326.

Darwin, Charles. *The Descent of Man, and Selection in Relation to Sex.* 1871. Reprint, London: Penguin, 2004.

———. *The Expression of the Emotions in Man and Animals.* 1872. Reprint, London: HarperCollins, 1998.

———. *The Origin of Species and The Voyage of the Beagle.* 1859 and 1839. Reprint, London: Vintage, 2009.

———. *The Variation of Animals and Plants under Domestication.* Vol. 1. 1868. Reprint, Cambridge: Cambridge University Press, 2010.

Dickens, Charles. *Barnaby Rudge*. 1841. Reprint, London: Penguin, 2003.

———. *Bleak House*. 1853. Reprint, London: Penguin, 1996.

———. *A Christmas Carol and Other Christmas Books*. 1843–46. Reprint, Oxford: Oxford University Press, 2006.

———. *David Copperfield*. 1850. Reprint, Harmondsworth: Penguin, 1966.

———. *Dombey and Son*. 1848. Reprint, London: Penguin, 1984.

———. *Great Expectations*. 1860. Reprint, Harmondsworth: Penguin, 1965.

———. *Hard Times*. 1854. Reprint, Oxford: Oxford University Press, 2006.

———. *Little Dorrit*. 1857. Reprint, Oxford: Oxford University Press, 1999.

———. *Martin Chuzzlewit*. 1844. Reprint, London: Penguin, 1986.

———. *Memoirs of Joseph Grimaldi, Edited by "Boz."* London: George Routledge & Sons, 1838.

———. *Nicholas Nickleby*. 1839. Reprint, London: Collins, 1953.

———. *The Old Curiosity Shop*. 1841. Reprint, London: Penguin, 2000.

———. *Oliver Twist*. 1838. Reprint, Oxford: Oxford University Press, 2008.

———. *Our Mutual Friend*. 1865. Reprint, Harmondsworth: Penguin, 1971.

———. *Selected Journalism, 1850–1870*. London, Penguin, 1997.

———. *Sketches by Boz*. 1836. Reprint, London: Penguin, 1995.

Dickens, Mamie. *My Father as I Recall Him*. Westminster: Roxburghe Press, 1897.

Dixon, Edmund Saul. "Domestic Pets." *Household Words* 7 (1853): 248–53.

Fields, James T. "Some Memories of Charles Dickens." *Atlantic Magazine*, August 1870, 235–44.

Fitzgerald, Brian Vesey. "Dogs in Britain." *Nature* 162 (October 1948): 553.

Fitzgerald, Percy. "Dickens's Dogs: or, the Landseer of Fiction." *London Society* 4 (1863): 48–61.

———. *Memories of Charles Dickens*. Bristol: J. W. Arrowsmith, 1913.

Fleming, George. *Rabies and Hydrophobia: Their History, Nature, Causes, Symptoms, and Prevention*. London: Chapman & Hall, 1872.

Forster, John. *The Life of Charles Dickens*. Boston: James R. Osgood, 1875.

Froude, James Anthony, ed. *Letters and Memorials of Jane Welsh Carlyle*. Vol. 2. London: Longmans, Green, 1883.

Grand, Sarah. *The Beth Book*. New York: D. Appleton, 1897.

Greenwood, James, *Going to the Dogs*. London: C. Beckett, 1866.

Hamley, E. B. *Our Poor Relations: A Philozooic Essay*. Boston: J. E. Tilton, 1872.

Hand-Book about Our Domestic Pets. London: Cassell, Petter & Galpin, 1862.

Harwood, Dix. *Love for Animals and How It Developed in Great Britain*. 1928. Reprint, Lewiston, NY: Edwin Mellen Press, 2003.

Hollingshead, John. *Miscellanies: Stories and Essays*. London: Tinsley Brothers, 1874.

———. *My Lifetime*. London: Sampson Low, Marston, 1895.

———. "Two Dog Shows." *All the Year Round*, 2 August 1862, 463–67.

Huxley, Thomas H. "On the Hypothesis That Animals Are Automata, and Its History." In *Method and Results: Essays*. London: Macmillan, 1912: 199–250.

"Inhumane Humanity." *All the Year Round*, 17 March 1866, 238–41.

Jaquet, E. W. *The Kennel Club: A History and Record of Its Work*. London: Kennel Gazette, 1905.

Johnson, James. *Temporary Home for Lost and Starving Dogs*, Lower Wandsworth Road, Battersea. London, 1871.

Kidd, W. "The Home for Lost Dogs." *Leisure Hour*, 5 September 1861, 564–66.

Kipling, R. *Just So Stories*. 1902. Reprint, Oxford: Oxford University Press, 1995.

Legal Protection of Dogs from the Increasing Evil of Dog Stealers and Receivers. London, printed for the author, 1845.

Leighton, Robert. *Dogs and All about Them*. London: Cassell, 1910.

Logsdon, Robert. "London Dog-Stealers." *Sporting Times*, 6 March 1880, 5.

Loudon, Jane. *Domestic Pets, Their Habits and Management*. London: Grant & Griffith, 1851.

Macaulay, James. *Plea for Mercy to Animals*. London: S. W. Partridge, c. 1880.

"Magenta." *The Treatment of our Domesticated Dogs*. Edinburgh: William Blackwood & Sons, 1868.

Massey, Gerald. *The Natural Genesis*. Vol. 1. 1883. Reprint, Baltimore: Black Classic Press, 2004.

Mayhew, Henry. *London Labour and the London Poor*. 1850–62. Reprint of selection, New York: Dover, 1968.

———. *London Labour and the London Poor*. 1850–62. Reprint of selection, Oxford: Oxford University Press, 2012.

———. *London's Underworld*. Reprint of selection from *London Labour and the London Poor*, 1850–62. London: Spring Books, 1950.

Morgan, C. Lloyd. *Animal Life and Intelligence*. Boston: Ginn, 1891.

Morris, F. O. *The Curse of Cruelty*. London: Elliot Stock, 1886.

———. *The Demands of Darwinism on Credulity*. London: Partridge, 1890.

———. *Records of Animal Sagacity and Character; With a Preface on the Future Existence of the Animal Creation*. London: Longman, Green, Longman & Roberts, 1861.

Nietzsche, Friedrich. *Thus Spoke Zarathustra*. 1883–85. Translated by Walter Kaufmann. Reprint, New York: Viking, 1966.

Ouida. *Dogs*. London: Simpkin, Marshall, Hamilton, Kent, 1897.

———. *Puck: His Vicissitudes, Adventures, Observations, Conclusions, Friendships, and Philosophies*. London: Chatto & Windus, 1878.

Phelps, Elizabeth Stuart. *Beyond the Gates*. Boston: Houghton, Mifflin, 1883.

———. *The Gates Ajar*. Boston: Fields, Osgood, 1869.

"Pincher Astray." *All the Year Round*, 30 January 1864: 539–41.

Romanes, George J. *Animal Intelligence*. London: Kegan Paul, Trench, 1882.

————. *Mental Evolution in Animals.* London: Kegan Paul, Trench, 1885.

Rorison, Gilbert. *The Three Barriers: Notes on Mr. Darwin's "Origin of Species."* Edinburgh: Blackwood & Sons, 1861.

Sala, George Augustus. "The Key of the Street." *Household Words,* 6 September 1851: 565–72.

Salt, Henry S. *Animals' Rights Considered in Relation to Social Progress.* London: Macmillan, 1892.

Shaler, Nathaniel Southgate. *Domesticated Animals, Their Relation to Man and to His Advancement in Civilization.* New York: Charles Scribner's Sons, 1908.

————. "The Negro Problem." *Atlantic Monthly,* November 1884: 696–709.

Shand, Alexander Innes. *The Life of General Sir Edward Bruce Hamley, K.C.B., K.C.M.G.* William Blackwood & Sons: Edinburgh and London, 1895.

Stephen, J. F. *A History of the Criminal Law of England.* Vol. 3. London: Macmillan, 1883.

Taylor, Isaac. *Physical Theory of Another Life.* London: William Pickering, 1836.

Thomas, Annie. "Homeless and Starving." *London Society,* November 1875: 418–20.

Thompson, J. *Public and Private Lives of Animals.* London: Sampson Low, Marston, Searle & Rivington, 1877. Originally published by P-J. Stahl (P-J. Hetzel) with illustrations by J. J. Grandville, as *Scènes de la vie privée et publique des animaux,* Paris, 1842.

Trollope, Anthony. *The American Senator.* 1877. Reprint, Oxford: Oxford University Press, 1986.

Tytler, Sarah. *Landseer's Dogs and Their Stories.* London: Marcus Ward, 1877.

Wallace, Alfred Russel. *The World of Life: A Manifestation of Creative Power, Directive Mind, and Ultimate Purpose.* London: Chapman & Hall, 1911.

Ward, Adolphus William. *English Men of Letters: Charles Dickens.* New York: Harper & Brothers, 1900.

Wilde, Oscar. *The Picture of Dorian Gray.* 1891. Reprint, New York: Norton, 1988.

Wood, J. G. *Man and Beast: Here and Hereafter.* London: Daldy, Isbister, 1874.

Woolf, Virginia. *Flush: A Biography.* London: Hogarth Press, 1933.

Secondary Sources

Adams, Maureen. *Shaggy Muses: The Dogs Who Inspired Virginia Woolf, Emily Dickinson, Elizabeth Barrett Browning, Edith Wharton, and Emily Brontë.* New York: Ballantyne Books, 2007.

Agamben, Giorgio. *Homo Sacer: Sovereign Power and Bare Life.* Translated by Daniel Heller-Roazen. Stanford, CA: Stanford University Press, 1998.

————. *The Open: Man and Animal.* Translated by Kevin Attell. Stanford, CA: Stanford University Press, 2004.

Allen, Michelle. *Cleansing the City: Sanitary Geographies in Victorian London.* Athens: Ohio University Press, 2008.

Alter, Stephen G. "Separated at Birth: The Interlinked Origins of Darwin's Unconscious Selection Concept and the Application of Sexual Selection to Race." *Journal of the History of Biology* 40, no. 2 (2007): 231–58.

Amin, Ash, and Nigel Thrift. *Cities: Reimagining the Urban.* Cambridge: Polity Press, 2002.

Anderson, Kay. "Animal Domestication in Geographic Perspective." *Society and Animals* 6, no. 2 (1998): 119–35.

———. "Animals, Science, and Spectacle in the City." In *Animal Geographies: Place, Politics and Identity in the Nature-Culture Borderlands,* edited by Jennifer Wolch and Jody Emel, 27–50. London: Verso, 1998.

———. "A Walk on the Wild Side: A Critical Geography of Domestication." *Progress in Human Geography* 21, no. 4 (1997): 463–85.

Animal Studies Group, eds. *Killing Animals.* Urbana: University of Illinois Press, 2006.

Arluke, Arnold. "Managing Emotions in an Animal Shelter." In *Animals and Human Society: Changing Perspectives,* edited by Aubrey Manning and James Serpell, 145–65. London: Routledge, 1994.

Armstrong, Frances. *Dickens and the Concept of Home.* Ann Arbor: UMI Research Press, 1990.

Armstrong, Nancy. *Desire and Domestic Fiction.* Oxford: Oxford University Press, 1987.

Atkins, Peter, ed. *Animal Cities: Beastly Urban Histories.* Farnham: Ashgate, 2012.

Bachelard, Gaston. *The Poetics of Space.* Translated by Maria Jolas. Boston: Beacon Press, 1964.

Baker, J. H., ed. *The Reports of Sir John Spelman.* Vol. 2. London: Selden Society, 1978.

Baker, Steve. *The Postmodern Animal.* London: Reaktion, 2000.

Baratay, Eric, and Elisabeth Hardouin Fugier. *Zoo: A History of Zoological Gardens in the West.* Translated by Oliver Welsh. London: Reaktion, 2003.

Barley, Nigel. *Dancing on the Grave: Encounters with Death.* London: Abacus, 1995.

Baumgarten, Murray. "Fictions of the City." In *The Cambridge Companion to Charles Dickens,* edited by John O. Jordan, 106–19. Cambridge: Cambridge University Press, 2001.

Beasley, Edward. *The Victorian Reinvention of Race: New Racisms and the Problem of Grouping.* Abingdon: Routledge, 2010.

Beckingham, David. "An Historical Geography of Liberty: Lancashire and the Inebriates Acts." *Journal of Historical Geography* 36, no. 4 (2010): 388–401.

Beer, Gillian. *Darwin's Plots: Evolutionary Narrative in Darwin, George Eliot and Nineteenth-Century Fiction.* 2nd ed. Cambridge: Cambridge University Press, 2000.

Behlmer, George K. *Friends of the Family: The English Home and Its Guardians, 1850–1940.* Milton Keynes: Open University Press, 2002.

Bellamy, Liz. "It-Narrators and Circulation: Defining a Sub-Genre." In *The Secret Life of Things: Animals, Objects and It-Narratives in Eighteenth-Century England*, edited by Mark Blackwell, 117–46. Lewisburg, PA: Bucknell University Press, 2007.

Bennett, Jane. *The Enchantment of Modern Life: Attachments, Crossings, and Ethics*. Princeton, NJ: Princeton University Press, 2001.

———. *Vibrant Matter: A Political Ecology of Things*. Durham, NC: Duke University Press, 2010.

Benson, Etienne. "Animal Writes: Historiography, Disciplinarity, and the Animal Trace." In *Making Animal Meaning*, edited by Linda Kalof and Georgina M. Montgomery, 3–16. East Lansing: Michigan State University Press, 2011.

Berger, John. *Pig Earth*. London: Bloomsbury, 1999.

———. *Why Look at Animals?* London: Penguin, 2009.

Bernstein, Susan D. "Ape Anxiety: Sensation Fiction, Evolution and the Genre Question." *Journal of Victorian Culture* 6, no. 2 (2001): 250–71.

Birke, Lynda, Arnold Arluke, and Mike Michael. *The Sacrifice: How Scientific Experiments Transform Animals and People*. West Lafayette, IN: Purdue University Press, 2007.

Bivona, Dan, and Roger B. Henkle. *The Imagination of Class: Masculinity and the Victorian Urban Poor*. Columbus: Ohio State University Press, 2006.

Blunt, Alison, and Ann Varley. "Geographies of Home." *Cultural Geographies* 11, no. 3 (2004): 3–6.

Blunt, Alison, and Robyn Dowling. *Home*. Abingdon: Routledge, 2006.

Boddice, Rob. *A History of Attitudes and Behaviours toward Animals in Eighteenth- and Nineteenth-Century Britain: Anthropocentrism and the Emergence of Animals*. Lewiston, NY: Edward Mellen Press, 2008.

———. "Vivisecting Major: A Victorian Gentleman Scientist Defends Animal Experimentation, 1876–1885." *Isis* 102, no. 2 (2011): 215–37.

Bodenheimer, Rosemarie. *Knowing Dickens*. Ithaca, NY: Cornell University Press, 2007.

Bowen, John. *Other Dickens: Pickwick to Chuzzlewit*. Oxford: Oxford University Press, 2003.

Bozzetto, Roger, "Moreau's Tragi-Farcical Island." *Science Fiction Studies* 20, no. 1 (1993): 34–44.

Brantz, Dorothee, ed. *Beastly Natures: Animals, Humans, and the Study of History*. Charlottesville: University of Virginia Press, 2010.

———. "The Domestication of Empire: Human-Animal Relations at the Intersection of Civilization, Evolution, and Acclimatization in the Nineteenth Century." In *A Cultural History of Animals in the Age of Empire*, edited by Kathleen Kete, 73–93. Oxford: Berg, 2007.

Braverman, Iris. *Zooland: The Institution of Captivity*. Stanford, CA: Stanford University Press, 2013.

Briggs, Asa. *Victorian Things.* London: B. T. Batsford, 1988.

Brooks, Chris. *Mortal Remains: The History and the Present State of the Victorian and Edwardian Cemetery.* Exeter, UK: Wheaton, 1989.

Brown, Laura. *Homeless Dogs and Melancholy Apes: Humans and Other Animals in the Modern Literary Imagination.* Ithaca, NY: Cornell University Press, 2010.

Browne, Janet. *Charles Darwin.* Vol. 2, *The Power of Place.* London: Pimlico, 2003.

Buckmaster, Jonathan. "'A Man of Great Feeling and Sensibility': The Memoirs of Joseph Grimaldi and Tears of a Clown." *19: Interdisciplinary Studies in the Long Nineteenth-Century* 14 (2011).

———. "'We Are All Actors in the Pantomime of Life': Charles Dickens and the Memoirs of Joseph Grimaldi." *Victorian Network* 3, no. 2 (2011): 7–29.

Bulliet, Richard W. *Herders, Hunters, and Hamburgers: The Past and Future of Human-Animal Relationships.* New York: Columbia University Press, 2005.

Burt, Jonathan. "John Berger's 'Why Look at Animals': A Close Reading." *Worldviews* 9 (2005): 203–18.

———. *Rat.* London: Reaktion, 2006.

Butler, Judith. *Frames of War: When Is Life Grievable?* London: Verso, 2010.

Callow, Simon. *Charles Dickens.* London: HarperPress, 2012.

Calvino, Italo. *Marcovaldo, or The Seasons in the City.* Translated by William Weaver. London: Vintage, 2001.

Cartmill, Matt. *A View to a Death in the Morning: Hunting and Nature through History.* Cambridge, MA: Harvard University Press, 1993.

Cassidy, Rebecca. "Introduction: Domestication Reconsidered." In *Where the Wild Things Are Now: Domestication Reconsidered,* edited by Rebecca Cassidy and Molly Mullin, 1–25. Oxford: Berg, 2007.

Chadarevian, Soraya de. "Laboratory Science versus Country-House Experiments: The Controversy between Julius Sachs and Charles Darwin." *British Journal for the History of Science* 29, no. 1 (1996): 17–41.

Chase, Karen, and Michael Levenson. *The Spectacle of Intimacy: A Public Life for the Victorian Family.* Princeton, NJ: Princeton University Press, 2000.

Cheang, Sarah. "Women, Pets, and Imperialism: The British Pekingese Dog and Nostalgia for Old China." *Journal of British Studies* 45, no. 2 (2006): 359–87.

Clark, Nigel. "Animal Interface: The Generosity of Domestication." In *Where the Wild Things Are Now: Domestication Reconsidered,* edited by Rebecca Cassidy and Molly Mullin, 49–70. Oxford: Berg, 2007.

Clark, Stephen R. L. *Animals and Their Moral Standing.* London: Routledge, 1997.

Clark, Timothy. "Dickens through Blanchot: The Nightmare Fascination of a World without Interiority." In *Dickens Refigured: Bodies, Desires and Other Histories,* edited by John Schad, 22–38. Manchester: Manchester University Press, 1996.

Clutton-Brock, Juliet. "The Unnatural World: Behavioural Aspects of Humans and Animals in the Process of Domestication." In *Animals and Human Society:*

Changing Perspectives, edited by Aubrey Manning and James Serpell, 23–35. London: Routledge, 1994.

Coetzee, J. M. *The Lives of Animals*. London: Profile Books, 1999.

Cohen, Ed. *A Body Worth Defending: Immunity, Biopolitics, and the Apotheosis of the Modern Body*. Durham, NC: Duke University Press, 2009.

Cohen, Monica F. *Professional Domesticity in the Victorian Novel: Women, Work, and Home*. Cambridge: Cambridge University Press, 1998.

Cottesloe, Gloria. *The Story of the Battersea Dogs' Home*. Newton Abbott: David & Charles, 1979.

Creaney, Conor. "Paralytic Animation: The Anthropomorphic Taxidermy of Walter Potter." *Victorian Studies* 53, no. 1 (2010): 7–35.

Curl, James Steven. *The Victorian Celebration of Death*. Detroit: Partridge Press, 1972.

Curran, Cynthia. "Pets." In *Encyclopedia of the Victorian Era*, 189–93. Danbury, CT: Scholastic Library Publishing, 2004.

Danahay, Martin A. "Nature Red in Hoof and Paw: Domestic Animals and Violence in Victorian Art." In *Victorian Animal Dreams: Representations of Animals in Victorian Literature and Culture*, edited by Deborah Denenholz Morse and Martin A. Danahay, 97–119. Aldershot: Ashgate, 2007.

———. "Wells, Galton and Biopower: Breeding Human Animals." *Journal of Victorian Culture* 17, no. 4 (2012): 468–79.

Daunton, Martin. *House and Home in the Victorian City: Working-Class Housing, 1850–1914*. London: Edward Arnold, 1983.

Davidoff, Leonore, and Catherine Hall. *Family Fortunes: Men and Women of the English Middle-Class, 1750–1850*. London: Hutchinson, 1987.

Dawkins, Richard. *The Blind Watchmaker*. London: Penguin, 1988.

———. *The Greatest Show on Earth: The Evidence for Evolution*. London: Black Swan, 2010.

Day, Matthew. "Godless Savages and Superstitious Dogs: Charles Darwin, Ethnography, and the Problem of Human Uniqueness." *Journal of the History of Ideas* 69, no. 1 (2008): 49–70.

de Certeau, Michel. *The Practice of Everyday Life*. Translated by Steven F. Rendall. Berkeley: University of California Press, 1984.

Deleuze, Gilles, and Felix Guattari. *A Thousand Plateaus: Capitalism and Schizophrenia*. Translated by Brian Massumi. London: Continuum, 2004.

Dennis, Richard. *Cities in Modernity: Representations and Productions of Metropolitan Space, 1840–1930*. Cambridge: Cambridge University Press, 2008.

Derrida, Jacques. *The Animal That Therefore I Am*. Translated by David Wills. New York: Fordham University Press, 2008.

———. *Of Spirit: Heidegger and the Question*. Translated by Geoffrey Bennington and Rachel Bowlby. Chicago: University of Chicago Press, 1989.

Derrida, Jacques, and Anne Dufourmantelle. *Of Hospitality: Anne Dufourmantelle*

Invites Jacques Derrida to Respond. Translated by Rachel Bowlby. Stanford, CA: Stanford University Press, 2000.

DeSalvo, Louise A. *Virginia Woolf: The Impact of Childhood Sexual Abuse on Her Life and Work.* London: Women's Press, 1989.

Desmond, Adrian, and James Moore. *Darwin.* London: Penguin, 1991.

———. *Darwin's Sacred Cause: Race, Slavery and the Quest for Human Origins.* London: Allen Lane, 2009.

Desmond, Jane. "Animal Deaths and the Written Record of History: The Politics of Pet Obituaries." In *Making Animal Meaning*, edited by Linda Kalof and Georgina M. Montgomery, 99–111. East Lansing: Michigan State University Press, 2011.

Donald, Diana. "'Beastly Sights': The Treatment of Animals as a Moral Theme in Representations of London c. 1820–1850." In *The Metropolis and Its Image: Constructing Identities for London, c. 1750–1950*, edited by Dana Arnold, 48–78. Oxford: Blackwell, 1999.

———. "'A Mind and a Conscience Akin to Our Own': Darwin's Theory of Expression and the Depiction of Animals in Nineteenth-Century Britain." In *Endless Forms: Charles Darwin, Natural Science and the Visual Arts*, edited by Diana Donald and Jane Munro, 195–213. New Haven, CT: Yale University Press, 2009.

———. *Picturing Animals in Britain, 1750–1850.* New Haven, CT: Yale University Press, 2007.

Donald, Moira. "Tranquil Havens? Critiquing the Idea of Home as the Middle-Class Sanctuary." In *Domestic Space: Reading the Nineteenth-Century Interior*, edited by Inga Bryden and Janet Floyd, 103–20. Manchester: Manchester University Press, 1999.

Donaldson, Sue, and Kymlicka, Will. *Zoopolis: A Political Theory of Animal Rights.* Oxford: Oxford University Press, 2011.

Donovan, Josephine. "Animal Rights and Feminist Theory." *Signs* 15, no. 2 (1990): 350–375.

Douglas, Mary. "The Idea of a Home: A Kind of Space." *Social Research* 58, no. 1 (1991): 287–307.

Douglas-Fairhurst, Robert. *Becoming Dickens: The Invention of a Novelist.* Cambridge, MA: Harvard University Press, 2011.

———. Introduction to *London Labour and the London Poor*, by Henry Mayhew, 1850–62. Reprint, Oxford: Oxford University Press, 2012.

Driver, Felix. "Moral Geographies: Social Science and the Urban Environment in Mid-Nineteenth Century England." *Transactions of the Institute of British Geographers* 13, no. 3 (1988): 275–87.

Elias, Norbert. *The Civilizing Process.* Oxford: Blackwell, 1994.

Elston, Mary Ann. "Women and Anti-vivisection in Victorian England, 1870–

1900." In *Vivisection in Historical Perspective*, edited by Nicolaas A. Rupke, 259–94. London: Croom Helm, 1987.

Emel, Jody, and Jennifer Wolch. "Witnessing the Animal Moment." In *Animal Geographies: Place, Politics, and Identity in the Nature-Culture Borderlands*, edited by Jennifer Wolch and Jody Emel, 1–24. London: Verso, 1998.

Enkvist, Nils Erik. "Charles Dickens in the Witness Box." *Dickensian* 47, no. 4 (1951): 201.

Esposito, Roberto. *Third Person: Politics of Life and Philosophy of the Impersonal*. Translated by Zakiya Hanafi. Cambridge: Polity Press, 2012.

Fairholme, Edward G., and Wellesley Pain. *A Century of Work for Animals: The History of the R.S.P.C.A., 1824–1934*. 2nd ed. London: John Murray, 1934.

Farías, Ignacio, and Thomas Bender. *Urban Assemblages: How Actor-Network Theory Changes Urban Studies*. London: Routledge, 2010.

Feeley-Harnik, Gillian. "'An Experiment on a Gigantic Scale': Darwin and the Domestication of Pigeons." In *Where the Wild Things Are Now: Domestication Reconsidered*, edited by Rebecca Cassidy and Molly Mullin, 147–82. Oxford: Berg, 2007.

Feller, David Allan. "Dog Fight: Darwin as Animal Advocate in the Vivisection Controversy of 1875." *Studies in History and Philosophy of Science Part C: Studies in History and Philosophy of Biological and Biomedical Sciences* 40, no. 4 (2009): 265–71.

———. "The Hunter's Gaze: Charles Darwin and the Role of Dogs and Sport in Nineteenth Century Natural History." PhD dissertation, University of Cambridge, 2010.

Felski, Rita. *The Gender of Modernity*. Cambridge, MA: Harvard University Press, 1995.

Fenton, Edward. "Portrait of a Victorian Painter, with Dogs." *Metropolitan Museum of Art Bulletin* 10, no. 5 (1952): 154–64.

Flanders, Judith. *The Victorian City: Everyday Life in Dickens' London*. London: Atlantic Books, 2012.

———. *The Victorian House: Domestic Life from Childbirth to Deathbed*. London: HarperCollins, 2003.

Flint, Kate. Introduction to *Flush*, by Virginia Woolf. 1933. Reprint, Oxford: Oxford University Press, 1998.

———. "Origins, Species and Great Expectations." In *Charles Darwin's "The Origin of Species": New Interdisciplinary Essays*, edited by David Amigoni and Jeff Wallace, 152–73. Manchester: Manchester University Press, 1995.

Foucault, Michel. *Abnormal: Lectures at the Collège de France 1974–1975*. Translated by Graham Burchell. London: Verso, 2003.

———. *Discipline and Punish: The Birth of the Prison*. Translated by Alan Sheridan. London, Penguin, 1991.

————. "The Force of Flight." Translated by Gerald Moore. In *Space, Knowledge and Power: Foucault and Geography,* edited by Jeremy W. Crampton and Stuart Elden, 169–72. Aldershot: Ashgate, 2007.

Francione, Gary L. *Introduction to Animal Rights: Your Child or the Dog?* Philadelphia: Temple University Press, 2007.

Franklin, Adrian. *Animals and Modern Cultures: A Sociology of Human-Animal Relations in Modernity.* London: Sage, 1999.

French, Richard D. *Antivivisectionism and Medical Science in Victorian Society.* Princeton, NJ: Princeton University Press, 1975.

Fudge, Erica. *Animal.* London: Reaktion, 2002.

————. *Brutal Reasoning: Animals, Rationality, and Humanity in Early Modern England.* Ithaca, NY: Cornell University Press, 2006.

————. "A Left-Handed Blow: Writing the History of Animals." In *Representing Animals,* edited by Nigel Rothfels, 3–18. Bloomington: Indiana University Press, 2002.

————. *Perceiving Animals: Humans and Beasts in Early Modern English Culture.* Basingstoke: Macmillan, 2000.

————. *Pets.* Stocksfield, UK: Acumen, 2008.

Garner, Robert. *A Theory of Justice for Animals: Animal Rights in a Nonideal World.* Oxford: Oxford University Press, 2013.

Gates, Barbara T. *Kindred Nature: Victorian and Edwardian Women Embrace the Living World.* Chicago: University of Chicago Press, 1999.

Gatrell, V. A. C. "Crime, Authority, and the Policeman-State." In *The Cambridge Social History of Britain, 1750–1950,* vol. 3, *Social Agencies and Institutions,* edited by F. M. L. Thompson, 243–310. Cambridge: Cambridge University Press, 1990.

Gilbert, Pamela K. *The Citizen's Body: Desire, Health, and the Social in Victorian England.* Columbus: Ohio State University Press, 2007.

Gildenhuys, Peter. "Darwin, Herschel, and the Role of Analogy in Darwin's *Origin.*" *Studies in History and Philosophy of Science Part C: Studies in History and Philosophy of Biological and Biomedical Sciences* 35, no. 4 (2004): 593–611.

Gillis, John R. *A World of Their Own Making: Myth, Ritual, and the Quest for Family Values.* New York: Basic Books, 1996.

Gleadle, Kathryn. *Borderline Citizens: Women, Gender, and Political Culture in Britain, 1815–1867.* Oxford: Oxford University Press, 2009.

————. "Revisiting Family Fortunes: Reflections on the Twentieth Anniversary of the Publication of L. Davidoff & C. Hall (1987) *Family Fortunes: Men and Women of the English Middle Class, 1780–1850* (London: Hutchinson)." In *Women's History Review* 16, no. 5 (2007): 773–82.

Goodlad, Lauren. *Victorian Literature and the Victorian State: Character and Governance in a Liberal Society.* Baltimore, MD: Johns Hopkins University Press, 2003.

Gray, Beryl. "Dickens and Dogs: 'No Thoroughfare' and the Landseer Connection." *Dickensian* 100 (2004): 5–22.

———. Review of *A Home of Their Own*, by Garry Jenkins. *Dickensian* 107, no. 2 (2011): 151–53.

Greene, John C. "Darwin as a Social Evolutionist." *Journal of the History of Biology* 10, no. 1 (1977): 1–27.

Gregory, T. Ryan. "Artificial Selection and Domestication: Modern Lessons from Darwin's Enduring Analogy." *Evolution: Education and Outreach* 2, no. 1 (2009): 5–27.

Grier, Kathleen C. "Childhood Socialization and Companion Animals: United States, 1820–1870." *Society and Animals* 7, no. 2 (1999): 95–120.

Griffin, Carl J. "Animal Maiming, Intimacy, and the Politics of Shared Life: The Bestial and the Beastly in Eighteenth- and Early Nineteenth-Century England." *Transactions of the Institute of British Geographers* 37, no. 2 (2012): 301–16.

Grimm, David. *Citizen Canine: Our Evolving Relationship with Cats and Dogs.* New York: PublicAffairs, 2014.

Ham, Jennifer, and Matthew Senior, eds. *Animal Acts: Configuring the Human in Western History.* London: Routledge, 1997.

Hamilton, Susan. "Reading and the Popular Critique of Science in the Victorian Anti-vivisection Press: Frances Power Cobbe's Writing for the Victoria Street Society." *Victorian Review* 36, no. 2 (2010): 66–79.

———. "Still Lives: Gender and the Literature of the Victorian Vivisection Controversy." *Victorian Review* 17, no. 2 (1991): 21–34.

Hancock, David. "In Cavalier Style." *Dogs Monthly* 16, no. 9 (1998): 10–13.

Haraway, Donna. *The Companion Species Manifesto: Dogs, People and Significant Otherness.* Chicago: Prickly Paradigm Press, 2003.

———. *When Species Meet.* Minneapolis: University of Minnesota Press, 2008.

Hardy, Anne. "Pioneers in the Victorian Provinces: Veterinarians, Public Health, and the Urban Animal Economy." *Urban History* 29, no. 3 (2002): 372–87.

Harré, Rom. *Pavlov's Dogs and Schrödinger's Cat: Scenes from the Living Laboratory.* Oxford: Oxford University Press, 2009.

Harris, Mason. "Vivisection, the Culture of Science, and Intellectual Uncertainty in *The Island of Doctor Moreau*." *Gothic Studies* 4, no. 2 (2002): 99–115.

Harrison, Brian. "Animals and the State in Nineteenth-Century England." *English Historical Review* 88, no. 349 (1973): 786–820.

Hartley, Jenny. *Charles Dickens and the House of Fallen Women.* London, Methuen, 2008.

Hatten, Charles. *The End of Domesticity: Alienation from the Family in Dickens, Eliot, and James.* Newark: University of Delaware Press, 2010.

Hilton, Boyd. *The Age of Atonement: The Influence of Evangelicalism on Social and Economic Thought, 1785–1865.* Oxford: Oxford University Press, 1988.

Himmelfarb, Gertrude. *Darwin and the Darwinian Revolution*. New York: Anchor, 1962.

Hinchliffe, Steve. *Geographies of Nature: Environments, Societies, Ecologies*. London: Sage, 2007.

Hinchliffe, Steve, and Nick Bingham. "Securing Life: The Emerging Practices of Biosecurity." *Environment and Planning A* 40, no. 7 (2008): 1534–51.

Hitchings, Russell. "At Home with Someone Nonhuman." *Home Cultures* 1, no. 2 (2004): 169–86.

Hochadel, Oliver. "Darwin in the Monkey Cage: The Zoological Garden as a Medium of Evolutionary Theory." In *Beastly Natures: Animals, Humans, and the Study of History*, edited by Dorothee Brantz, 81–107. Charlottesville: University of Virginia Press, 2010.

———. "Watching Exotic Animals Next Door: 'Scientific' Observations at the Zoo (ca. 1870–1910)." In Science in Context 24, no. 2 (2011): 183–214.

Hodder, Ian. *Entangled: An Archaeology of the Relationships between Humans and Things*. Oxford: Wiley-Blackwell, 2012.

Holloway, Lewis, Carol Morris, Ben Gilna, and David Gibbs. "Biopower, Genetics and Livestock Breeding: (Re)Constituting Animal Populations and Heterogeneous Biosocial Collectivities." *Transactions of the Institute of British Geographers* 34, no. 3 (2009): 394–407.

Holme, Thea. *The Carlyles at Home*. Oxford: Oxford University Press, 1965.

Homans, John. *What's a Dog For? The Surprising History, Science, Philosophy and Politics of Man's Best Friend*. London: Penguin, 2012.

Hoppen, K. Theodore. *The Mid-Victorian Generation, 1846–1886*. Oxford: Oxford University Press, 1998.

House, Madeline, and Graham Storey. *The Letters of Charles Dickens*. Vol. 1, *1820–1839*. Oxford: Oxford University Press, 1965.

Howell, Philip. "The Dog Fancy at War: Breeds, Breeding, and Britishness, 1914–1918." *Society and Animals* 21, no. 6 (2013): 546–67.

Hribal, Jason C. "Animals, Agency, and Class: Writing the History of Animals from Below." *Human Ecology Forum* 14, no. 1 (2007): 101–12.

Huff, Cynthia. "Victorian Exhibitionism and Eugenics: The Case of Francis Galton and the 1899 Crystal Palace Dog Show." *Victorian Review* 28, no. 2 (2002): 1–20.

Jalland, Pat. *Death in the Victorian Family*. Oxford: Oxford University Press, 1996.

Jenkins, Garry. *A Home of Their Own: The Heart-Warming 150-Year History of Battersea Dogs and Cats Home*. London: Bantam Press, 2010.

Jerolmack, Colin. "How Pigeons Became Rats: The Cultural-Spatial Logic of Problem Animals." *Social Problems* 55, no. 1 (2008): 72–94.

John, Juliet. *Dickens's Villains: Melodrama, Character, Popular Culture*. Oxford: Oxford University Press, 2001.

Jones, Robert W. "'The Sight of Creatures Strange to Our Clime': London Zoo and the Consumption of the Exotic." *Journal of Victorian Culture* 2, no. 1 (1997): 1–26.

Jones, Steve. *Darwin's Island: The Galapagos in the Garden of England.* London: Abacus, 2010.

Jordanova, Ludmilla. *Sexual Visions: Images of Gender in Science and Medicine between the Eighteenth and Twentieth Centuries.* Madison: University of Wisconsin Press, 1989.

Joyce, Patrick. *The Rule of Freedom: Liberalism and the Modern City.* London: Verso, 2003.

———. *The State of Freedom: A Social History of the British State since 1800.* Cambridge: Cambridge University Press, 2013.

Kalof, Linda. *Looking at Animals in Human History.* London: Reaktion, 2007.

Kalof, Linda, and Amy Fitzgerald, eds. *The Animals Reader: The Essential Classic and Contemporary Writings.* Oxford: Berg, 2007.

Kalof, Linda, and Brigitte Resl. *A Cultural History of Animals.* 6 vols. Oxford: Berg, 2007.

Karlin, Daniel, ed. *Robert Browning and Elizabeth Barrett: The Complete Correspondence.* Oxford: Oxford University Press, 1989.

Kean, Hilda. *Animal Rights: Political and Social Change in Britain since 1800.* London: Reaktion, 1998.

———. "An Exploration of the Sculptures of Greyfriars Bobby, Edinburgh, Scotland, and the Brown Dog, Battersea, London, England." *Society and Animals* 11, no. 4 (2003): 353–73.

———. "Human and Animal Space in Historic 'Pet' Cemeteries in London, New York and Paris." In *Animal Death*, edited by Jay Johnston and Fiona Probyn Rapsey, 21–42. Sydney: Sydney University Press, 2013.

———. "The 'Smooth Cool Men of Science:' The Feminist and Socialist Response to Vivisection." *History Workshop Journal* 40 (Autumn 1995): 16–38.

Keller, Lisa. *Triumph of Order: Democracy and Public Space in New York and London.* New York: Columbia University Press, 2009.

Kete, Kathleen. *The Beast in the Boudoir: Petkeeping in Nineteenth-Century Paris.* Berkeley: University of California Press, 1994.

———. "La Rage and the Bourgeoisie: The Cultural Context of Rabies in the French Nineteenth Century." *Representations* 22 (1988): 89–107.

King, James. *Virginia Woolf.* Harmondsworth, UK: Penguin, 1994.

Knight, Frances. *The Nineteenth-Century Church and English Society.* Cambridge: Cambridge University Press, 1998.

Kong, Lily. "Cemeteries and Columbaria: Memorials and Mausoleums: Narrative and Interpretation in the Study of Deathscapes in Geography." *Australian Geographical Studies* 37, no. 1 (1999): 1–10.

Koven, Seth. *Slumming: Sexual and Social Politics in Victorian London.* Princeton, NJ: Princeton University Press, 2004.

Kreilkamp, Ivan. "Dying like a Dog in Great Expectations." In *Victorian Animal Dreams: Representations of Animals in Victorian Literature and Culture*, edited by Deborah Denenholz Morse and Martin A. Danahay, 81–94. Aldershot: Ashgate, 2007.

Kristeva, Julia. *Powers of Horror: An Essay on Abjection*. Translated by Leon S. Roudiez. New York: Columbia University Press, 1982.

Langland, Elizabeth. *Nobody's Angels: Middle-Class Women and Domestic Ideology in Victorian Culture*. Ithaca, NY: Cornell University Press, 1995.

Lansbury, Coral. *The Old Brown Dog: Women, Workers, and Vivisection in Edwardian England*. Madison: University of Wisconsin Press, 1985.

Laqueur, Thomas. "Bodies, Death, and Pauper Funerals." *Representations* 1, no. 1 (1983): 109–31.

Latour, Bruno. *Reassembling the Social: An Introduction to Actor-Network-Theory*. Oxford: Oxford University Press, 2005.

———. *Science in Action: How to Follow Scientists and Engineers through Society*. Cambridge, MA: Harvard University Press, 1987.

———. *We Have Never Been Modern*. Translated by Catherine Porter. Cambridge, MA: Harvard University Press, 1993.

Laurier, Eric, Ramia Maze, and Johan Lundin. "Putting the Dog Back in the Park: Animal and Human Mind-in-Action." *Mind, Culture and Activity* 13, no. 1 (2006): 2–24.

Leach, Edmund. "Anthropological Aspects of Language: Animal Categories and Verbal Abuse." In *New Directions in the Study of Language*, edited by E. H. Lenneberg, 23–63. Cambridge, MA: Harvard University Press, 1964.

Lears, T. J. Jackson. *No Place of Grace: Antimodernism and the Transformation of American Culture*. Chicago: University of Chicago Press, 1981.

Lee, Hermione. *Virginia Woolf*. London: Chatto & Windus, 1996.

Legg, Stephen. "Assemblage/Apparatus: Using Deleuze and Foucault." *Area* 43, no. 2 (2011): 128–33.

Levine, George. *Darwin and the Novelists: Patterns of Science in Victorian Fiction*. Cambridge, MA: Harvard University Press, 1988.

———. *Darwin the Writer*. Oxford: Oxford University Press, 2011.

Li, Chien-hui. "Mobilizing Literature in the Animal Defense Movement in Britain, 1870–1918." *Concentric: Literature and Cultural Studies* 32 (2006): 27–55.

———. "A Union of Christianity, Humanity and Philanthropy: The Christian Tradition and the Prevention of Cruelty to Animals in Nineteenth-Century England." *Society and Animals* 8, no. 3 (2000): 265–85.

Lightman, Bernard. "'The Voices of Nature': Popularizing Victorian Science." In *Victorian Science in Context*, edited by Bernard Lightman, 187–211. Chicago: University of Chicago Press, 1997.

Linzey, Andrew, and Priscilla N. Cohn. "Terms of Discourse." *Journal of Animal Ethics* 1, no. 1 (2011): vii–ix.

Lippit, Akira Mizuta. *Electric Animal: Towards a Rhetoric of Wildlife.* Minneapolis: University of Minnesota Press, 2008.

Livingstone, David N. *Putting Science in Its Place: Geographies of Scientific Knowledge.* Chicago: University of Chicago Press, 2003.

Lorenz, Konrad. *Man Meets Dog.* London: Methuen, 1954.

Lorimer, Douglas A. "Science and the Secularization of Victorian Images of Race." In *Victorian Science in Context,* edited by Bernard Lightman, 212–35. Chicago: University of Chicago Press, 1997.

Lynn, William S. "Animals, Ethics and Geography." In *Animal Geographies: Place, Politics and Identity in the Nature-Culture Borderlands,* edited by Jennifer Wolch and Jody Emel, 280–97. London: Verso, 1998.

Macdonald, Tara. "'Red-Headed Animal': Race, Sexuality and Dickens's Uriah Heep." *Critical Survey* 17 (2005): 48–62.

MacGregor, Arthur. *Animal Encounters: Human and Animal Interaction in Britain from the Norman Conquest to World War One.* London: Reaktion, 2012.

Majumdar, Robin, and McLaurin, Allen, eds. *Virginia Woolf: The Critical Heritage.* London: Routledge, 1997.

Malamud, Randy. *Reading Zoos: Representations of Animals and Captivity.* New York: New York University Press, 1998.

Mangum, Teresa. "Animal Angst: Victorians Memorialize Their Pets." In *Victorian Animal Dreams: Representations of Animals in Victorian Literature and Culture,* edited by Deborah Denenholz Morse and Martin A. Danahay, 15–34. Aldershot: Ashgate, 2007.

———. "Dog Years, Human Fears." In *Representing Animals,* edited by Nigel Rothfels, 35–47. Bloomington: Indiana University Press, 2002.

Marcus, George E., and Erkan Saka. "Assemblage." *Theory, Culture and Society* 23, nos. 2–3 (2006): 101–9.

Marcus, Sharon. *Apartment Stories: City and Home in Nineteenth-Century Paris and London.* Berkeley: University of California Press, 1999.

Markus, Julia. *Dared and Done: The Marriage of Elizabeth Barrett and Robert Browning.* London: Bloomsbury, 1997.

Marvin, Garry. "Wild Killing: Contesting the Animal in Hunting." In *Killing Animals,* edited by the Animal Studies Group, 10–29. Urbana: University of Illinois, 2006.

Mason, Emma. "Dogs, Detectives and the Famous Sherlock Holmes." *International Journal of Cultural Studies* 11, no. 3 (2008): 289–300.

Mason, Jennifer. *Civilized Creatures: Urban Animals, Sentimental Culture, and American Literature, 1850–1900.* Baltimore, MD: Johns Hopkins University Press, 2005.

Masson, Jeffrey. *Dogs Never Lie about Love.* London: Jonathan Cape, 1997.

Mayer, Jed. "The Expression of the Emotions in Man and Laboratory Animals." *Victorian Studies* 50, no. 3 (2008): 399–417.

————. "The Nature of the Experimental Animal: Evolution, Vivisection, and the Victorian Environment." In *Considering Animals: Contemporary Studies in Human-Animal Relations*, edited by Carol Freeman, Elizabeth Leane, and Yvette Watt, 93–104. Farnham: Ashgate, 2011.

McDannell, Colleen, and Bernhard Lang. *Heaven: A History*. New Haven, CT: Yale University Press, 1988.

McKechnie, Claire Charlotte, and John Miller. "Victorian Animals." *Journal of Victorian Culture* 17, no. 4 (2012): 436–41.

McKenzie, Kirsten. "Dogs and the Public Sphere: The Ordering of Social Space in Early Nineteenth-Century Cape Town." *South African Historical Journal* 48, no. 1 (2003): 235–51.

McMullen, M. B. "The Day the Dogs Died in London." *London Journal* 23, no. 1 (1998): 32–40.

McShane, Clay, and Joel A. Tarr. *The Horse in the City: Living Machines in the Nineteenth Century*. Baltimore, MD: Johns Hopkins University Press, 2007.

Mee, Jon, ed. *The Cambridge Introduction to Charles Dickens*. Cambridge: Cambridge University Press, 2010.

————. "Dickens, Gender, and Domesticity: 'Be It . . . Ever So Ghastly . . . There's No Place Like It.'" In *The Cambridge Introduction to Charles Dickens*, edited by Jon Mee, 64–83. Cambridge: Cambridge University Press, 2010.

Miele, Kathryn. "Horse-Sense: Understanding the Working Horse in Victorian London." *Victorian Literature and Culture* 37, no. 1 (2009): 129–40.

Miller, Daniel. "Why Some Things Matter." In *Material Cultures: Why Some Things Matter*, edited by Daniel Miller, 3–21. Chicago: University of Chicago Press, 1998.

Miller, D. A. *The Novel and the Police*. Cambridge, MA: Harvard University Press, 1988.

Miller, Ian. "Necessary Torture? Vivisection, Suffragette Force-Feeding, and Responses to Scientific Medicine in Britain c. 1870–1920." *Journal of the History of Medicine and Allied Sciences* 64, no. 3 (2009): 333–72.

Miller, John. *Empire and the Animal Body: Violence, Identity and Ecology in Victorian Adventure Fiction*. London: Anthem Press, 2012.

Milsom, S. F. C. *Historical Foundations of the Common Law*, 2nd ed. London: Butterworths, 1981.

Moody, Jane. *Illegitimate Theatre in London, 1770–1840*. Cambridge: Cambridge University Press, 2007.

Moore, Grace. "Beastly Criminals and Criminal Beasts: Stray Women and Stray Dogs in Oliver Twist." In *Victorian Animal Dreams: Representations of Animals in Victorian Literature and Culture*, edited by Deborah Denenholz Morse and Martin A. Danahay, 201–14. Aldershot: Ashgate, 2007.

Moore, James, and Adrian Desmond. Introduction to *The Descent of Man, and Selection in Relation to Sex*, by Charles Darwin, xi–lviii. London: Penguin, 2004.

Moore, Randy. "The Persuasive Mr. Darwin." *Bioscience* 47, no. 2 (1997): 107–14.

Morey, Darcy F. *Dogs, Domestication and the Development of a Social Bond.* Cambridge: Cambridge University Press, 2010.

Morley, John. *Death and the Victorians.* London: Studio Vista, 1971.

Morrison, Kevin A. "Elizabeth Barrett Browning's Dog Days." *Tulsa Studies in Women's Literature* 30, no. 1 (2011): 93–115.

Munich, Adrienne. *Queen Victoria's Secrets.* New York: Columbia University Press, 1996.

Murdoch, Jonathan. "Towards a Geography of Heterogeneous Associations." *Progress in Human Geography* 21, no. 3 (1997): 321–27.

Nally, David. *Human Encumbrances: Political Violence and the Great Irish Famine.* Notre Dame, IN: University of Notre Dame Press, 2010.

Nash, Roderick. *The Rights of Nature: A History of Environmental Ethics.* Madison: University of Wisconsin Press, 1989.

Nast, Heidi. "Critical Pet Studies." *Antipode* 38 (2006): 894–906.

Nead, Lynda. *Victorian Babylon: People, Streets and Images in Nineteenth-Century London.* New Haven, CT: Yale University Press, 2000.

Nunokawa, Jeff. *The Afterlife of Property: Domestic Security and the Victorian Novel.* Princeton, NJ: Princeton University Press, 1994.

Obenchain, Theodore G. *The Victorian Vivisection Debate: Frances Power Cobbe, Experimental Science and the "Claims of Brutes."* Jefferson, NC: McFarland, 2012.

O'Dwyer, Owen J., and Derek H. Alderman. "Memorial Landscapes: Analytic Questions and Metaphors." *Geojournal* 73, no. 3 (2008): 165–78.

Oliver, Kelly. *Animal Lessons: How They Teach Us to Be Human.* New York: Columbia University Press, 2009.

Otter, Chris. *The Victorian Eye: A Political History of Light and Vision in Britain, 1800–1910.* Chicago: University of Chicago Press, 2008.

Palmer, Clare. "Killing Animals in Animal Shelters." In *Killing Animals,* edited by the Animal Studies Group, 170–87. Urbana: University of Illinois Press, 2006.

———. "Placing Animals in Urban Environmental Ethics." *Journal of Social Philosophy* 34, no. 1 (2003): 64–78.

Pandian, Anand. "Pastoral Power in the Postcolony: On the Biopolitics of the Criminal Animal in South India." *Cultural Anthropology* 23, no. 1 (2008): 85–117.

Parry, José. "Sentimentality and the Enemies of Animal Protection." *Anthrozoös* 24 (2011): 117–33.

Pascoe, David, ed. *Charles Dickens: Selected Journalism, 1850–1870.* London: Penguin, 1997.

Passmore, John. "The Treatment of Animals." *Journal of the History of Ideas* 36, no. 2 (1975): 195–218.

Patton, Paul. "Language, Power and the Training of Horses." In *Zoontologies: The*

Question of the Animal, edited by Cary Wolfe, 83–99. Minneapolis: University of Minnesota Press, 2003.

Pearson, Susan J. *The Rights of the Defenseless: Protecting Animals and Children in Gilded Age America.* Chicago: University of Chicago Press, 2011.

Pearson, Susan J., and Mary Weismantel. "Does 'The Animal' Exist? Towards a Theory of Social Life with Animals." In *Beastly Natures: Animals, Humans, and the Study of History,* edited by Dorothee Brantz, 17–37. Charlottesville: University of Virginia Press, 2010.

Peggs, Kay. *Animals and Sociology.* London: Palgrave Macmillan, 2012.

Pemberton, Neil, and Michael Worboys. *Mad Dogs and Englishmen: Rabies in Britain, 1830–2000.* London: Palgrave, 2007.

Petrinovich, Lewis. *Darwinian Dominion: Animal Welfare and Human Interests.* Cambridge, MA: MIT Press, 1999.

Philo, Chris. "Animals, Geography, and the City: Notes on Inclusions and Exclusions." In *Animal Geographies: Place, Politics and Identity in the Nature-Culture Borderlands,* edited by Jennifer Wolch and Jody Emel, 51–71. London: Verso, 1998.

Philo, Chris, and Chris Wilbert, eds. *Animal Spaces, Beastly Places: New Geographies of Human-Animal Relations.* London: Routledge, 2000.

Plotkin, David. "Home-Made Savages: Cultivating English Children in 'Bleak House.'" *Pacific Coast Philology* 32, no. 1 (1997): 17–31.

Pollock, Mary Sanders. "Ouida's Rhetoric of Empathy: A Case Study in Victorian Anti-vivisection Narrative." In *Figuring Animals: Essays on Animal Images in Art, Literature, Philosophy, and Popular Culture,* edited by Mary Sanders Pollock and Catherine Rainwater, 135–59. New York: Palgrave Macmillan, 2005.

Poovey, Mary. *Uneven Developments: The Ideological Work of Gender in Mid-Victorian England.* Chicago: University of Chicago Press, 1988.

Porter, Dorothy. *Health, Civilization and the State: A History of Public Health from Ancient to Modern Times.* London: Routledge, 1999.

Power, Emma. "Domestication and the Dog: Embodying Home." *Area* 44, no. 3 (2012): 371–78.

———. "Furry Families: Making a Human-Dog Family through Home." *Social & Cultural Geography* 9, no. 5 (2008): 535–55.

Preece, Rod. *Brute Souls, Happy Beasts, and Evolution: The Historical Status of Animals.* Vancouver: UBC Press, 2005.

———. "Darwinism, Christianity, and the Great Vivisection Debate." *Journal of the History of Ideas* 64, no. 3 (2003): 399–419.

Raber, Karen. "From Sheep to Meat, from Pets to People: Animal Domestication, 1600–1800." In *A Cultural History of Animals in the Age of Enlightenment,* edited by Matthew Senior, 73–99. Oxford: Berg, 2007.

Ragon, Michel. *The Space of Death: A Study of Funerary Architecture, Decoration, and Urbanism.* Charlottesville: University of Virginia Press, 1983.

Rando, David. "The Cat's Meow: Ulysses, Animals, and the Veterinary Gaze." *James Joyce Quarterly* 46, no. 3 (2009): 529–43.

Rheinberger, Jörg, and Peter McLaughlin. "Darwin's Experimental Natural History." *Journal of the History of Biology* 17, no. 3 (1984): 345–68.

Richards, Evelleen. "Redrawing the Boundaries: Darwinian Science and Victorian Women Intellectuals." In *Victorian Science in Context*, edited by Bernard Lightman, 119–42. Chicago: University of Chicago Press, 1997.

Richards, Richard A. "Darwin and the Inefficacy of Artificial Selection." *Studies in History and Philosophy of Science* 28, no. 1 (1997): 75–97.

———. "Darwin, Domestic Breeding and Artificial Selection." *Endeavour* 22, no. 3 (1998): 106–9.

Richardson, Ruth. *Death, Dissection and the Destitute*. London: Routledge, 1987.

———. *Dickens and the Workhouse: Oliver Twist and the London Poor*. Oxford: Oxford University Press, 2012.

Richter, Virginia. *Literature after Darwin: Human Beasts in Western Fiction, 1859–1939*. Basingstoke: Palgrave Macmillan, 2011.

Ritvo, Harriet. *The Animal Estate: The English and Other Creatures in the Victorian Age*. London: Penguin, 1990.

———. "Animals in Nineteenth-Century Britain: Complicated Attitudes and Competing Categories." In *Animals and Human Society: Changing Perspectives*, edited by Aubrey Manning and James Serpell, 106–26. London: Routledge, 1994.

———. "Classification and Continuity." In *Charles Darwin's "The Origin of Species": New Interdisciplinary Essays*, edited by David Amigoni and Jeff Wallace, 47–67. Manchester: Manchester University Press, 1995.

———. *The Dawn of Green: Manchester, Thirlmere, and Modern Environmentalism*. Chicago: University of Chicago Press, 2009.

———. "The Evolution of the Victorian Dog Fancy." *Victorian Studies* 29, no. 2 (1986): 227–53.

———. *Noble Cows and Hybrid Zebras: Essays on Animals and History*. Charlottesville: University of Virginia Press, 2010.

———. *The Platypus and the Mermaid, and Other Figments of the Classifying Imagination*. Cambridge, MA: Harvard University Press, 1998.

Roberts, Mark. *The Mark of the Beast: Animality and Human Oppression*. West Lafayette, IN: Purdue University Press, 2008.

Rollin, Bernard E. "The Moral Status of Animals." In *Pet Loss and Human Bereavement*, edited by William J. Kay, Herbert A. Nieburg, Austin H. Kutscher, Ross M. Grey, and Carole E. Fudin, 3–15. Ames: Iowa State University Press, 1984.

Rose, Natalie. "Flogging and Fascination: Dickens and the Fragile Will." *Victorian Studies* 47, no. 4 (2005): 505–33.

Roth, Tina, and Ulrich Kutschera. "Darwin's Hypotheses on the Origins of Domestic Animals and the History of German Shepherd Dogs." *Annals of the History and Philosophy of Biology* 13 (2008): 175–87.

Rubin, James H. *Impressionist Cats and Dogs: Pets in the Painting of Modern Life.* New Haven, CT: Yale University Press, 2003.

Rupke, Nicolaas A., ed. *Vivisection in Historical Perspective.* London: Croom Helm, 1987.

Russett, Cynthia Eagle. *Sexual Science: The Victorian Construction of Womanhood.* Cambridge, MA: Harvard University Press, 1989.

Rybczynski, Witold. *Home: A Short History of an Idea.* London: Heinemann, 1988.

Ryder, Richard. *Animal Revolution: Changing Attitudes towards Speciesism.* Oxford: Berg, 2000.

Sadrin, Anny. *Parentage and Inheritance in the Novels of Charles Dickens.* Cambridge: Cambridge University Press, 1994.

Santner, Eric L. *On Creaturely Life: Rilke, Benjamin, Sebald.* Chicago: University of Chicago Press, 2006.

Sasaki, Toru. Introduction to *Charles Dickens,* by G. K. Chesterton, vii–xii. London: Wordsworth, 2007.

Sax, Boria. *Animals in the Third Reich.* New York: Continuum, 2000.

Schlicke, Paul. *Dickens and Popular Entertainment.* London: Allen & Unwin, 1985.

Scholtmeijer, Marian. *Animal Victims in Modern Fiction: From Sanctity to Sacrifice.* Toronto: University of Toronto Press, 1993.

Schwarzbach, F. S. *Dickens and the City.* London: Athlone Press, 1979.

Secord, James A. "Nature's Fancy: Charles Darwin and the Breeding of Pigeons." *Isis* 72, no. 2 (1981): 162–86.

Seipp, David J. "The Concept of Property in the Early Common Law." *Law and History Review* 12, no. 1 (1994): 29–91.

Senior, Matthew. "The Souls of Men and Beasts, 1630–1764." In *A Cultural History of Animals in the Age of Enlightenment,* edited by Matthew Senior, 23–45. Oxford: Berg, 2007.

Serpell, James. "From Paragon to Pariah: Some Reflections on Human Attitudes to Dogs." In *The Domestic Dog: Its Evolution, Behaviour, and Interactions with People,* edited by James Serpell, 245–56. Cambridge: Cambridge University Press, 1995.

Shapiro, Gary. "Dogs, Domestication, and the Ego." In *A Nietzschean Bestiary: Becoming Animal beyond Docile and Brutal,* edited by Christa Davis Acampora and Ralph R. Acampora, 53–60. Lanham, MD: Rowman & Littlefield, 2004.

Shell, Marc. "The Family Pet." *Representations* 15 (1986): 121–53.

Shipstone, Samuel. "Becoming-Rat: An Examination of the Politics of Vermin." Master's thesis, Durham University, 2007.

Shukin, Nicole. *Animal Capital: Rendering Life in Biopolitical Times.* Minneapolis: University of Minnesota Press, 2009.

Simons, John. *Animal Rights and the Politics of Literary Representation*. Basingstoke: Palgrave, 2002.

———. *Rossetti's Wombat: Pre-Raphaelites and Australian Animals in Victorian London*. London: Middlesex University Press, 2008.

———. *The Tiger That Swallowed the Boy: Exotic Animals in Victorian England*. Faringdon: Libri, 2012.

Slater, Michael. *Charles Dickens*. New Haven, CT: Yale University Press, 2009.

Sloterdijk, Peter. "Rules for the Human Zoo: A Response to the Letter on Humanism." *Environment and Planning D: Society and Space* 27, no. 1 (2009): 12–28.

Smiley, Jane. *Charles Dickens*. Harmondsworth: Penguin, 2002.

Smith, Kimberly K. *Governing Animals: Animal Welfare and the Liberal State*. Oxford: Oxford University Press, 2012.

Snaith, Anna. "Of Fanciers, Footnotes, and Fascism: Virginia Woolf's *Flush*." *Modern Fiction Studies* 48, no. 3 (2002): 614–36.

Squier, Susan Merrill. *Virginia Woolf and London: The Sexual Politics of the City*. Chapel Hill: University of North Carolina Press, 1985.

Srinivasan, Krithika. "The Biopolitics of Animal Being and Welfare: Dog Control and Care in the UK and India." *Transactions of the Institute of British Geographers* 38, no. 1 (2013): 106–19.

Steinbach, Susie. "Can We Still Use 'Separate Spheres'? British History 25 Years after *Family Fortunes*." *History Compass* 10, no. 11 (2012): 826–37.

Steiner, Gary. *Anthropocentrism and Its Discontents: The Moral Status of Animals in the History of Western Philosophy*. Pittsburgh, PA: University of Pittsburgh Press, 2005.

Sterrett, Susan G. "Darwin's Analogy between Artificial and Natural Selection: How Does It Go?" *Studies in History and Philosophy of Science Part C: Studies in History and Philosophy of Biological and Biomedical Sciences* 33, no. 1 (2002): 151–68.

Still, Judith. *Derrida and Hospitality: Theory and Practice*. Edinburgh: Edinburgh University Press, 2010.

Storey, Graham. *The Letters of Charles Dickens*. Vol. 11, *1865–67*. Oxford: Oxford University Press, 1999.

Stott, Andrew McConnell. *The Pantomime Life of Joseph Grimaldi*. Edinburgh: Canongate, 2009.

Straley, Jessica. "Love and Vivisection: Wilkie Collins's Experiment in *Heart and Science*." *Nineteenth-Century Literature* 65, no. 3 (2010): 348–73.

Strange, Julie-Marie. *Death, Grief and Poverty in Britain, 1870–1914*. Cambridge: Cambridge University Press, 2005.

Surridge, Lisa. "Dogs'/Bodies, Women's Bodies: Wives as Pets in Mid-Nineteenth-Century Narratives of Domestic Violence." *Victorian Review* 20, no. 1 (1994): 1–34.

Szladits, Lola L. "The Life, Character and Opinions of Flush the Spaniel." *Bulletin of the New York Public Library* 74 (1970): 211–18.

Tague, Ingrid H. "Dead Pets: Satire and Sentiment in British Elegies and Epitaphs for Animals." *Eighteenth-Century Studies* 41, no. 3 (2008): 289–306.

———. "Eighteenth-Century English Debate on a Dog Tax." *Historical Journal* 51, no. 4 (2008): 901–20.

Tambling, Jeremy. *Going Astray: Dickens and London*. Harlow: Pearson, 2009.

Tange, Andrea Kaston. *Architectural Identities: Domesticity, Literature, and the Victorian Middle Classes*. Toronto: University of Toronto Press, 2010.

Teigen, Philip M. "The Global History of Rabies and the Historian's Gaze: An Essay Review." *Journal of the History of Medicine and Allied Sciences* 67, no. 2 (2012): 327.

Tenner, Edward. "Citizen Canine." *Wilson Quarterly* 22, no. 3 (1998): 71–79.

Theunissen, Bert. "Darwin and His Pigeons: The Analogy between Artificial and Natural Selection Revisited." *Journal of the History of Biology* 45, no. 2 (2012): 179–212.

Thierman, Stephen. "Apparatuses of Animality: Foucault Goes to a Slaughterhouse." *Foucault Studies* 9 (2010): 89–110.

Thomas, Keith. *Man and the Natural World: Changing Attitudes in England, 1500–1800*. Harmondsworth: Penguin, 1984.

Thrift, Nigel. *Knowing Capitalism*. London: Sage, 2005.

Tomlinson, Niles. "Animal Crossings: Contagion and Immunologic in Gothic American Literature." PhD dissertation, Columbian College of Arts and Sciences, George Washington University, 2008.

Tortorici, Zeb. "'In the Name of the Father and the Mother of All Dogs': Canine Baptisms, Weddings and Funerals, in Bourbon Mexico." In *Centering Animals in Latin American History*, edited by Martha Few and Zeb Tortorici, 93–119. Durham, NC: Duke University Press, 2013.

Tosh, John. *A Man's Place: Masculinity and the Middle-Class Home in Victorian England*. New Haven, CT: Yale University Press, 1999.

Townshend, Emma. *Darwin's Dogs: How Darwin's Pets Helped Form a World-Changing Theory of Evolution*. London: Frances Lincoln, 2009.

Trotter, David. *Cooking with Mud: The Idea of Mess in Nineteenth-Century Art and Fiction*. Oxford: Oxford University Press, 2000.

Tuan, Yi-Fu. *Dominance and Affection: The Making of Pets*. New Haven, CT: Yale University Press, 1984.

Turner, James. *Reckoning with the Beast: Animals, Pain and Humanity in the Victorian Mind*. Baltimore, MD: Johns Hopkins University Press, 1980.

Urbanik, Julie. *Placing Animals: An Introduction to the Geography of Human-Animal Relations*. Lanham, MD: Rowman & Littlefield, 2012.

Van Sittert, Lance, "Class and Canicide in Little Bess: The 1893 Port Elizabeth Rabies Epidemic." *South African Historical Journal* 48, no. 1 (2003): 207–34.

Van Sittert, Lance, and Sandra Swart, "*Canis Familiaris:* A Dog History of South Africa." *South African Historical Journal* 48, no. 1 (2003): 138–73.

Veyne, Paul. *Foucault: His Thought, His Character.* Translated by Janet Lloyd. Cambridge: Polity Press, 2010.

Vickery, Amanda. "Golden Age to Separate Spheres? A Review of the Categories and Chronology of English Women's History." *Historical Journal* 36, no. 2 (1993): 383–414.

Walder, Dennis. Introduction to *Sketches by Boz,* by Charles Dickens. London: Penguin, 1995.

Wallen, Martin. "Foxhounds, Curs, and the Dawn of Breeding: The Discourse of Modern Human-Canine Relations." *Cultural Critique* 79 (Fall 2011): 125–51.

Walton, John K. "Mad Dogs and Englishmen: The Conflict over Rabies in Late Victorian England." *Journal of Social History* 13, no. 2 (1979): 219–39.

Waters, Catherine. *Dickens and the Politics of the Family.* Cambridge: Cambridge University Press, 1997.

Watts, Michael. "Afterword: Enclosure." In *Animal Spaces, Beastly Places: New Geographies of Human-Animal Relations,* edited by Chris Philo and Chris Wilbert, 291–304. London: Routledge, 2000.

Weil, Kari. "Killing Them Softly: Animal Death, Linguistic Disability, and the Struggle for Ethics." *Configurations* 14, nos. 1–2 (2006): 87–96.

———. *Thinking Animals: Why Animal Studies Now?* New York: Columbia University Press, 2012.

Whatmore, Sarah. *Hybrid Geographies: Natures, Cultures, Spaces.* London: Sage, 2002.

Wheeler, Michael. *Death and the Future Life in Victorian Literature and Theology.* Cambridge: Cambridge University Press, 1990.

White, Lynn Townsend. "The Historical Roots of Our Ecologic Crisis." *Science* 155, no. 3767 (1967): 1203–7.

White, Paul. "Darwin's Emotions: The Scientific Self and the Sentiment of Objectivity." *Isis* 100, no. 4 (2009): 811–26.

———. "Darwin Wept: Science and the Sentimental Subject." *Journal of Victorian Culture* 16, no. 2 (2011): 195–213.

———. "The Experimental Animal in Victorian Britain." In *Thinking with Animals: New Perspectives on Anthropomorphism,* edited by Lorraine Daston and Gregg Mitman, 59–81. New York: Columbia University Press, 2005.

———. "Sympathy under the Knife." In *Medicine, Emotion and Disease, 1700–1950,* edited by Fay Bound Alberti, 100–124. London: Palgrave, 2006.

Wilner, Eduardo. "Darwin's Artificial Selection as an Experiment." *Studies in History and Philosophy of Science Part C: Studies in History and Philosophy of Biological and Biomedical Sciences* 37, no. 1 (2006): 26–40.

Winter, James. *Secure from Rash Assault: Sustaining the Victorian Environment.* Berkeley: University of California Press, 1999.

Wolch, Jennifer. "Anima Urbis." *Progress in Human Geography* 26, no. 6 (2002): 721–42.

Wolch, Jennifer, and Jody Emel, eds. *Animal Geographies: Place, Politics, and Identity in the Nature-Culture Borderlands.* London: Verso, 1998.

———. "Bringing the Animals Back In." *Environment and Planning D: Society and Space* 13, no. 6 (1995): 632–36.

Wolfe, Cary. *Before the Law: Humans and Other Animals in a Biopolitical Frame.* Chicago: University of Chicago Press, 2013.

Wolloch, Nathaniel. *Subjugated Animals: Animals and Anthropocentrism in Early Modern European Culture.* New York: Humanity Books, 2006.

Wylie, Lynne. "Caught between Two Spheres: The Relationship of Charles Dickens' Street People to the Victorian Concept of Home." Master's thesis, Oregon State University, 1999.

Index

Page numbers in italics refer to figures.